EXTRA TIME

Kevin Sampson lives and writes on Merseyside. His acclaimed first novel, *Awaydays*, is about football violence and Joy Division. His second, *Powder*, about sex, drugs and insanity in the music business, will be published by Jonathan Cape in 1999. *Extra Time* is his first non-fiction book.

Extra Time

KEVIN SAMPSON

YELLOW JERSEY PRESS
LONDON

Published by Yellow Jersey Press 1998

2 4 6 8 10 9 7 5 3 1

First published in Great Britain in 1998 by
Yellow Jersey Press
Random House, 20 Vauxhall Bridge Road,
London SW1V 2SA

Random House Australia (Pty) Limited
20 Alfred Street, Milsons Point, Sydney,
New South Wales 2061, Australia

Random House New Zealand Limited
18 Poland Road, Glenfield,
Auckland 10, New Zealand

Random House South Africa (Pty) Limited
Endulini, 5A Jubilee Road, Parktown 2193, South Africa

Random House UK Limited Reg. No. 954009

A CIP catalogue record for this book
is available from the British Library

ISBN 0 224 05289 6

Papers used by Random House UK Limited are natural,
recyclable products made from wood grown in sustainable forests.
The manufacturing processes conform to the environmental
regulations of the country of origin

Printed and bound in Great Britain by
Mackays of Chatham plc

For my father Les,
for my Red blood.

Dramatis Personae (my mates)

Agent Johnson   AKA Peter Johnson, Everton's
                     Chairman and Liverpool's finest fan.
                     Invested millions of his own money in
                     order to bring once-middling Everton
                     F.C. to its knees.
Anna   Author's daughter and apple of his eye.
Ally   Long-standing ex-Road End pal of
                     Jegsy and Fat Eddie. Came to Man. U
                     with us.
Banner   AKA Frank. One of The Betty Ford
                     Clinic, a group of hard-living
                     Liverpool fans. Often to be seen with
                     Terry Miles.
Bard from Norway   Good drinker. On the committee of
                     the Scandinavian Supporters Club.
                     Stronger Scouse accent than author.
Boffins   Boffin 1 and Boffin 2 have sat next to
                     Roy Boulter and me in the Upper
                     Centenary for three seasons. We don't
                     know their names, but suspect, as they
                     are young and bald, that they work in
                     computers. Nice lads.
Bon Viveur   A fat chap who sits on the end of our
                     row. Always places huge bets and, to
                     look at him, eats huge meals. Gets
                     along famously with . . .
Boulter   Roy Boulter. Author's mate. Sits next
                     to me, puts up with my constant,
                     constantly wrong analysis of matches

vii

and players – and eats a great deal.

Brittles, Jeff	AKA Lovely Jeff. Robert Mitchum lookalike, uncomplaining driver of John (Prima) Garner and sundry Chains (residents of Halewood). Always happy. Watches a lot of porn.
Bucko	AKA Bucko from Bootle. Friend of everyone, fine fan. Was allowed to be Leader in Paris last year, and unfortunately broke leg as result. Consequently, v. poor footballer.
Clowy	Marty Clow. One of Jegsy's mates from Moreton. Quiet, funny, enormous Adam's apple.
Colonel, The	AKA Colonel Hogan. Anthony Hogan, been going for years, famous Liverpudlian. One of our finest.
Cross, Tommy	Roy's pal from schooldays. Contender with Roy White for Funniest Man in the World. Mad things happen to him.
Danny	Danny Giles, the Singing Brickie, King of the Swallee. Officially, the Fourth Drunkest Irishman in Birkenhead. Waiting for his own Nessie Shankly.
Davey	Davey Hurst from Halewood, postman, Bunnymen fan and owner of Liverpool's last flat-top.
De Asha, Tony	Drunk at Crewe. My esteemed brother-in-law.
Dixon, Mike	AKA Paul Byatt. *Brookside* stalwart. Top geezer.
Dr David Marsh	Former Toffees Chairman and potential Saviour yet?
Dool, The	AKA Dave Dooley, Double D, Proprietor of Dooley's, the greatest

café in GB (Greater Birkenhead). Regular pre-match haunt of the author.

Donny, Keith from	Keith Johnson, formerly of Doncaster, now resident of Liverpool – the better to pursue his obsessive love of the city and its football club. Used to write strange letters to *The End*.
Eddie, Fat	AKA Fat Eddie. Along with Jegsy, Mick Potter, Ally, Hogan etc. has been to more away games than you can shake a stick at.
Eggeye	Worked on Conway Park station with Danny. Came to Bolton. Went to Australia.
Evertonians	An endangered species. Surviving examples include Chopadopalis, Gary Hart, Markoosh, Micky Musker, John Potter, Tom Russell, Tony Sage, Andrew, Liam and Willie Streuth and TC – gentlemen to whom our sympathies should be extended.
Fiona	Very beautiful woman who travels on Liverpool Away Supporters Club coaches. Doesn't look much like Nessie Shankly, but would make a great Keegan to Danny's Toshack.
Flowers, Jimmy	Chairman of Liverpool Away Supporters Club. Runs coaches everywhere. If Liverpool are opening an Academy of Excellence in Chad, he'll run a coach there. Great man.
Gag	AKA Señor Gag. Glen. Patron Saint of Fun. Paul Scholes lookalike from Formby. Given to taking clothes off

when he's had a pint.

Gaghan, John — One of the main Chains (resident of Halewood). Always grinning. Seemed to enjoy the ruck at Old Trafford much more than me.

Garner, John — AKA Prima Garner. King of The Kop. If there was ever any doubt, his AGENT JOHNSON banner confirmed his position as The Kop's most creative attacking force. Always making up songs. Always, too, nudging you with his elbows and arguing about nothing.

Geordie, John the — Roy's cynical, thieving pal from Newcastle. Always after my ticket.

Graham, Bobby — My first Liverpool F.C. hero, later discredited by my dad as a 'one game in three' player.

Gram — Another of the Halewood Chains, who include Mono, Garner, Spen, Davey, Lovely Jeff, Gaghan, Jam and some fat lad.

Head, Tin — AKA Phil Olivier. *Brookside* baddie. Also top geezer.

Holt, Nicky — Nicky and brother Gary from Kirkby go everywhere. Often see Nicky with Banner.

Hooton, Peter — My old pal. Used to be the singer in The Farm and co-editor of *The End*, football's best ever fanzine. Peter, Mick, Potter, Jegsy, Roy, Gag and Danny are the nucleus of my mob. It was Peter's decision to leave Mick Potter in a Glasgow jail.

Hope, Mr — The man who made my year by

	lending me a pair of Predator boots.
Jane, The Lovely	Wife of author. Far from being long suffering, greets each and every game with unbridled joy on grounds of spouse absence.
Jegsy	Jegsy Dodd, AKA Birkenhead Bard, Urban Dub Poet, Jegs. Bad Moreton poet in crap trainies. Unbelievable lass-lassoo. Enjoys what can only be termed the Life of Riley. My mate.
Jimmy the Jock	AKA James Gardiner, Liverpool's biggest fan.
Joe	My fine, strapping boy.
Jonesy	AKA Colin Jones. Another home-and-away diehard. Knows everyone.
Liddell, Billy	Legendary Liverpool goalscorer.
Mallett, Timmy	1980s children's television presenter who pioneered the use of slime, poured from large, suspended vat held above quiz contestants' heads as a deterrent for getting questions wrong.
McLelland, Tony	AKA Jagger, Mick Jagger. Good pal and one of the founding fathers of *The End* magazine. Looks nothing like Mick Jagger.
Miles, Terry	Legendary Liverpool character.
Mono	AKA Steven Monaghan. The Peter Pan of Halewood. Looks 23, is in fact 47. Uses his diminutive stature (5 feet tall) to secure all the best seats at aways – i.e. half-price children's tickets. Has not been child since 1967.
Mum	Little Tracey's ma.
Murphy, Paul	AKA Murphy. Big, funny Birkenhead buck. Hands as big as the European

	Cup. Arch tormentor of Danny Giles. Good footballer. Has son called Little Murphy – even better footballer.
Neil	My fine, strapping brother.
Nuisance, Upper Centenary	A joy to be around. See book.
Philly	Puffa's mate. Came to see The Farm in L.A. Now involved in paper recycling business.
Potter, Mick	Scotland Road's finest. Former brawler, famous drinker, wit, humorist and raconteur. Telescopic chin. I love this man.
Puffa	Very amusing man, cultured midfielder, looks a bit like Keith Allen. Philly's paper recycling partner.
Sampson, Les	My dad. Great fan. R.I.P.
Scotsman, Nice	Sits behind Roy at Anfield. Wears 1995 green L.F.C. jacket. Is (a) Scottish, (b) nice.
Smash, Chas	A member of the popular musical combination The Madness.
Smith, Tommy	The Anfield Iron. Former Liverpool F.C. hardman, famous for nobbling fancy-dans and scoring with head in Rome. Now famous for provocative letters columns in local newspaper the *Echo*. Author writes to him many times per season – always under a pseudonym.
Spen	Yet another fine fellow from Halewood. Like others is small, witty and has a nickname.
Spencer, Paul	Jegsy's mate who lives in Orange

County, Los Angeles. Once presented
Steve McManaman with Man of the
Match Award after blagging way into
Carlsberg lounge claiming to be Head
of Marketing (California).

Suggs   The singer in aforementioned singing
troubadors The Madness. Chelsea
supporter.

Sully   One of Liverpool's very greatest
supporters. It's between him, Wilcox
and Lenny Woods. And Agent
Johnson.

Tracey, Little   Liverpool's No. 1 fan in Harpenden.
Goes to every game with mum. Is not
little.

Vialli, Tommy   The Spirit of Football.

White, Roy   Only known resident of Speke.
Funniest Man in the World. Still has
author's hat. Once returned, will be
relegated to more realistic sixth
Funniest Man in the World.

Wilcox, Bobby   Legendary Liverpool supporter. Knows
songs which only people over 50 can
possibly know. Has the laziest shuffle
in Christendom.

Woods, Lenny   Bobby's friend, enemy and rival. The
competition to be recognised as
Liverpool's Greatest Fan is intense.
There are many contenders. But,
leaving the best until the last, L.
Woods gets the author's vote. Decision
has nothing to do with L. Woods still
owing author £2 for end of season
party ticket.

FRIDAY, 23 MAY 1997

The Holiday Inn, Liverpool

'I mean it. If we sign Ravanelli, that's the end. I'm not going any more.'

Roy laughed.

'He's an Italian international striker! A proven goalscorer. He might be brilliant for us . . .'

'No way. He's exactly the sort of player we should never be interested in. He should play for Chelsea. If we sign him . . . I'm not renewing my season-ticket.'

'Don't talk soft. You'll be there if we sign Carlton Palmer, never mind Ravanelli!'

Exchanges like this, unheard of in the past, had been becoming more and more prevalent among Liverpool fans. Renewing your season-ticket, should you be so fortunate to have one, was not optional. It was something you'd do in your sleep on the first possible day after the end of the previous season, just in case your membership lapsed or someone on the 40,000-long waiting list nipped in ahead of you. But we're different, now – the club and the fans. We never used to sit for hours debating all that was wrong with the club, where and when it started to go wrong and how we could put it right again. We do now. There's a thriving Merseyside forum for disaffected fans who need to get it all off their chests via phone-ins to the three local radio stations, letters to Tommy Smith's page in the *Football Echo* and now the new midweek sound-off – Smithy's Midweek Match column. Here, all the would-be managers and amateur psychologists indulge them-selves with fantasies (about unattainable players) and doggerel (about 4–4–2, bite in the midfield, passion and those cursed white Armani suits at Wembley).

The reality is more simple. We're panicking. Nobody really knows what's up, how it happened or how to get things back to normal, but we are flapping. And it's not just because Liverpool haven't won the League (we still call it the League) for seven years. What's worse is that during that barren spell, Manchester United have buried their own baleful record and won every domestic trophy going. They even did the double Double, something which seemed inevitable for Liverpool in the late '80s, but never quite came to be. We got into a frame of mind where, banned from Europe, it was a barren season if we didn't win the Double. Wimbledon stopped us in '88, Arsenal with the last kick of '89 and Crystal Palace in 1990. As long as Man. U continue to keep their noses in front – without playing particularly well – Liverpool Football Club will have the feel of a mighty monument, toppling. And while this persists, everything is under the constant scrutiny and questioning of the fans. Everything from the players' wage packets to their social habits to their motives and motivation. The fans are paranoid. Quite simply, we need to win the League again.

I went to my first Liverpool match, home against West Ham, when I was four. I was mad about Liverpool, obsessive even for a kid, something I inherited from my dad, Les, who started supporting The Reds in 1948. I went pretty well everywhere with him and he knew everything. It was he who first told me that Millwall had the maddest fans, he who told me that Bobby Graham, my hero, was a 'one-game-in-three' performer. It's my most abiding regret that he didn't live to see us win the European Cup – he died on 30 September 1976. I inherited his season-ticket as well as his all-consuming passion. Rather than counting sheep, which is dull, I can still rock myself off to sleep at night with images of Roy Evans turning to the new, unknown, 36-year-old shock-signing he spotted playing in Birkenhead Park two days ago. We're at Old

Trafford. It's 1–1 on aggregate in the European Cup semi-final. They have the away goal. Roy turns to me and tells me to strip off:

'It's down to you, now, Kev,' he says, his voice a mix of fear and confidence.

I allow such nonsense to run through my mind more often than might be considered reasonable for a boy of my age.

These days I sit in the Upper Centenary Stand next to my chum Roy Boulter. Tonight, we're sitting in the bar of the Liverpool Moathouse Hotel, observing a whole procession of Liverpool Legends make their way through to the function room. Alec Lindsay, tipsy already, hobbles by with Tommy Smith himself. Phil Neal walks in with David Fairclough. Ray Clemence is there as is, contrary to local rumour of a Smithy-inspired fatwa, Emlyn Hughes. The run-up to this evening's event has been intensified by a hilarious sideshow between Anfield Iron, Smith, and unpopular Tory, Hughes, both denying that they bear each other any grudge and both insisting that 'The Event' and 'The Club' take precedence over any personal issues. Everyone knows they hate each other's guts and the congregation is bristling in anticipation of, at the very least, a fist-fight. Sadly, they make good their promise and put The Event first.

'The Event' is the *Liverpool Echo*-sponsored *Boys Of 77 Red & White Cabaret Dinner*, featuring live music from Schooner and a '70s disco. This is to be the start of a weekend of events commemorating that night in Rome which Les missed out on, the first of Liverpool's four European Cup victories, 25 May 1977. It seems a long 20 years ago. The news in tonight's *Echo* is that, in a desperate-seeming bid to recapture those glory, glory years, Liverpool have been linked with Fabrizio Ravanelli, a player I personally would hate to see at Anfield. Given that we've just got shot of Stan 'The Man' Collymore, why does Roy now want to bring in another of that brooding, isolationist type? I just hope it all falls through.

3

Nobody really expects Kevin Keegan to turn up tonight but then, suddenly, there he is, right there within touching distance in all his puckish, greyish, diminutive Keegan-ness. Once the shock has subsided, groups of men in their thirties and forties mill sheepishly around him, proffering old match-day programmes and other mementoes for signature. There's so much to say to him, so much to ask that I clam up in the presence of my first real Liverpool hero. Bobby Graham? Pah! Bloody one-in-three-er, and Alun Evans just wasn't around long enough to change your life. Keegan did. He walked on water. And he was called Kevin. My first ever attempts at concocting my own signature were based upon the treasured Kevin Keegan autograph on the Kevin Keegan T-shirt which was bought for me in 1972 and was still too big when he left for Hamburg in 1977. If Bryan Ferry was The Man, and David Bowie was The Duke, there's no doubt that Keegan was God to me. I worshipped him. Later, much later, he will be chaired around the Moathouse bar. For now, it's just a miracle that he's here, four feet away, chatting amiably with the punters. David Fairclough is in slightly less great demand. There are wicked stories circulating that Supersub, now Super Financial Services Consultant, has a briefcase full of insurance policies hidden behind reception, ready to foist upon unwary victims as they ask him to re-live The St Etienne Goal.

Inevitably, the night progresses to drunken buffoonery, with Alec Lindsay having to be escorted from the premises by security. He is given a standing ovation. The 1977 anthem *We're On Our Way To Roma* (set to the tune of *Arrivederci Roma*) is sung again and again and again. Our table – Roy and me, Jegsy, Gag, Paul Murphy and Danny – is particularly exuberant. At one point we berate a table of businessmen for failing to applaud Nessie Shankly into the room. Berating businessmen at football matches is a common failing of mine, and one I aim to improve upon during the coming season. Just because they're in suits, come from Weymouth and appear to know nothing about Liverpool F.C. doesn't give me the right to strangle them. Must do better.

We dance to Schooner. There is a ratio of one woman (trouser-suits and very blonde hair, all of them) to every 16 men. It doesn't matter. I'm dancing with Danny Giles, the singing brickie. We're trying to do that *Tiger Feet* dance, simplicity itself when practised by the sensational Mud, but for Danny and me it's way too complex and we're way too pie-eyed. We end up in a heap on the floor and decide to repair to the bar. Passing through, we overhear dozens of Liverpool fans answering their own questions to the likes of Davey Johnson, Phil Neal and King Kev himself:

'Who d'you reckon we need, Davey. You're a striker. We need a Bergkamp, don't we, to complement Robbie . . . The midfield's got no teeth. We need Draper or that little snarler from Leicester . . . Lennon, that's him. How come we never got Draper from Villa when we sold Stan? . . . What d'you reckon to the defence, Phil? We should play 4–4–2, shouldn't we? We should have that Ferdinand. How come we never got him when our youth team beat West Ham when he was the captain? Right here in front of the manager's eyes . . . can't he recognise class when it's brought into his own back yard . . .'

'Er . . . I'm at Peterborough now. I don't really have a say in Liverpool's transfer policy.'

The night drifts on in similar vein. The players put up with it, even seem to enjoy it, most of them. Keegan is one of the last to leave. He says it's a privilege to be able to sit among the people and just talk. He says he'll sit there till Sunday if people still have things they want to ask him. And he says that if Liverpool manage to persuade Paul Ince to come back from Inter, then Liverpool will win the League. We still call it the League.

10 JULY 1997

North Wales Mountain Zoo

The tally so far:

Everton 2
Blackburn 3
Tranmere 3
Man. City 5
Man. United 23
Liverpool 27

I'm not sure whether this is good or bad. Colwyn Bay, surely, should be a hotbed of insincere support for Manchester United PLC. I know that Evertonians would take perverse pleasure in their team shirt having the lowest representation of everyone bar Wrexham and Crewe (one each) amongst day-trippers at this popular Welsh resort. You don't really want to be the most popular team in Colwyn Bay, do you? But then, listening to the accents, most of them are Merseysiders, anyway. My own two, Joe and Anna, are wearing their shirts, but even without those two we're still ahead. Yes, we'll take the win, thank you very much. Bigger than Man. United. Much bigger.

A young Man. U fan in the blue away kit, maybe 12 years old, wanders by, lost in his ice-cream. He looks up, actually scratches his head and turns back to me:

'You don't know where falconry display is, do you?'

'FOUR EUROPEAN CUPS, 18 LEAGUE CHAMPIONSHIPS, THAT'S WHAT YOU CALL THE GREATEST EVER – YOU'LL NEVER GET ANYWHERE NEAR US!!'

He scratches his head again. I wipe the spittle from my chin and clear my throat.

'Er, that's it, just there. Should be starting in about ten minutes.'

4 AUGUST 1997

Crewe, away

Crewe Alexandra, away. Our last warm-up match before the big kick-off at Wimbledon on Saturday. We didn't sign Ravanelli. Hallelujah! Better still, he's going to Everton. Lord, be praised!! Roy Evans has spent very prudently, bringing in Oyvind Leonhardsen, Danny Murphy and, after a summer-long pursuit, Paul Ince. A new government and a new midfield. Hurrah!! To cap it all, two-goal European Cup Final hero Karlheinz Riedle has just signed for a very modest £1.6 million. Collymore has gone and Robbie Fowler has suffered a knock during the annual summer fixture in Norway, so to get Riedle, at that price, is great news. Excellent business, Roy Evans. Well done. This, surely, looks like a squad capable of taking on anybody. Wenger and Gullit have spent extravagantly on yet more exotic French and Italian talent. Evans' squad looks better equipped to withstand the vagaries of the English season. With Paul Ince, in particular, we can win the League.

The main problem Paul Ince brings with him is a difficult name to set to song. There are certain traditions at Liverpool. We don't set songs to the tune of *Go West*, for example. That's for silly, spotter-type fans who phone David Mellor and say:

'Hello. D'you remember me from not last season but the season before?'

Blokes who have matching, pink-faced girlfriends in football shirts who thought *Here We Go* was a good thing to chant.

7

They like nothing more than to stand up, grinning, and belt out:

'Stand up!! If you hate Man. U!!'

They think it's all great fun and expect everyone else to join in. But Liverpool don't do that. We don't join in.

Jegsy and I drive to Crewe in his car. It's only 45 minutes and, on arrival, we note that Liverpool's wool-contingent is not growing any smaller with failure. Everywhere, those horrid new yellow away shirts are bobbing around with bags of chips to hand and sad trainies on their feet. (About 'sad', by the way. It's a Liverpool term dating back to the '70s, meaning 'embarrassing' or 'dire', not a new invention of David Baddiel meaning 'friendless'. These things matter.)

As does the getting of a good song for our new captain. Mono and John Garner from Halewood are standing outside the ground. Mono hasn't got a ticket. This is someone who hasn't missed a game, anywhere, for 27 seasons. When Old Trafford was being rebuilt and they gave Liverpool 45 tickets, Mono got in, so Gresty Road should present him with no problems. Of more concern is the Ince song. Garner, one of the main songmeisters on The Kop, inventor of some great anthems – including the McManaman song to the tune of *The Boxer* – is worried. He jerks his thumb at a couple of teds in brand new away shirts.

'You know what these'll be like.'

He imitates what can only be described as a 'girl'.

'One Paul Ince! There's only one Paul Ince!!'

He shakes his head in exasperation.

'Every time we get a new player! "One Karlheinz Riedle . . . one Michael Owen" . . . I bet you!'

He pauses, his face a picture of disgust.

'Talentless twats!!'

This takes a second to sink in then we're all laughing. Garner takes his work seriously. Mono tells us his Michael Owen song, to the tune of *Michael Rowed the Boat Ashore*. It started out as 'Michael Owen's gonna score' and has evolved into 'Michael Owen scores the goals'. Owen scored a beauty at Wimbledon at the end of last season and nearly forced the winner at Sheffield Wednesday that would've got us into the Champions League. He's an amazing prospect, whippet swift and utterly dead-eye in front of goal – but he has time on his side. We'll probably continue to bring him on gradually.

The game's a nonentity. A couple of the Crewe midfielders try to make a name for themselves against Paul Ince, but he and Michael Thomas quickly sort the men from the boys. A feeble chant of 'One Paul Ince' goes up, but it isn't taken any further. We score. They score. I see Tony, my brother-in-law, at half time. He is inexplicably drunk, considering the low profile of the occasion. Drunk at Crewe, pre-season. What an excellent fellow! There's a stomach convention by the tea-bar, with Jimmy the Jock explaining himself to a group of junior beerbellies. Jimmy is a great fan, in every sense. He's a 25-stone mammoth from Edinburgh who's been following Liverpool since 1965. He made the mistake of admitting, on the TV show *Reds In Europe*, that some Liverpool fans should accept some of the blame for the Heysel Stadium disaster. Some Liverpool fans didn't like that, and he had to take out an ad in the *Liverpool Echo*'s personal columns to apologise for his remarks. It looks like being a long season for Jimmy, which is a shame. He's one of the good 'uns.

The second half is quite a good laugh. Stig Inge Bjornebye gets some mild flack from the crowd for the amount of time he wants on the ball before getting his cross in. He seems to be losing the advantage time and again by taking an extra touch, killing the moving ball, allowing the defender he's already beaten to snap back at him and make him play his cross under unnecessary pressure.

'First time, Stig!!', shout those nearest to that flank. Bjornebye hammers his cross way beyond the box. Not even the spring-heeled Riedle can reach that. A sigh of dismay goes

9

up. A female copper and a steward turn to face the Liverpool fans, as though Stig's lousy cross is going to provoke a pitch invasion. A lad in the front row leans over to the lady cop. She tenses herself. He twists up his face and shouts:

'Hey! Missus! Will you tell Stig first time!!'

Laughter all round. Some drunks behind try to start a chant of 'Watch out, Riedle's about', to the tune of the iconic Jeremy Beadle's popular show *Beadle's About*. The song is, quite correctly, ignored. The game is so exciting that I drift into thinking about that *Sunday Mirror* story a few years ago, where Mrs Beadle describes Jeremy as the most vigorous and imaginative lover she has ever experienced. Jeremy Beadle! The unlikely stallion! I don't quite get to imagining Jeremy Beadle in the nack but . . . actually I do. I do. I sit there for a whole minute allowing a slowly developing mental polaroid of a wild-eyed Jeremy Beadle giving his wife one from behind, grinning conspiratorally as he beckons us all into the bedroom while her head's buried in the pillow. These are the things you think about during those rare let-ups in the frenzy of a pre-season at Crewe.

By the end, we've run out comfortable 3–1 winners without stretching ourselves. Fowler was rested again as a precaution for Saturday, but Riedle looks great. He's *quality*. That's the word the ever-growing army of pundits have been launching pre-season. Quality. Glenn Hoddle says he's looking for that extra bit of quality. Venables says England should stick with Gazza because he can give you quality on the night. Quality, it would seem, is not a judicious concept of merit. It's a thing. We don't know what, yet, but professional football people do. There was quality in evidence right throughout Liverpool's side tonight, even if it was only Crewe. Owen is, obviously, even at this stage, a world phenomenon about to happen. Forget bringing him on slowly – he's superb. McManaman made a few of those hallmark runs of his, those big, dramatic dribbles where he leaves everyone in his wake, on their arse.

He was doing it at will up to about Christmas '96. He was obviously playing with some sort of a knock after New Year '97 and it might have made sense to have had it looked at as long ago as the time Chelsea came back to beat us 4–2 in the Cup. (I'll always hate Dan Petrescu for the way he held up four fingers on one hand and two on the other and stuck them in McAteer's face.) McManaman, though, looks like his summer's recuperation has done the trick. He's fallen out with Glenn Hoddle over Le Tournoi, but he's rejuvenated. He's fit. He's back. Things are looking good. A Crewe mascot, a giant red fluffy rabbit, makes its way around the perimeter track, waving to departing supporters. Two Scousers beckon him over to shake hands and ask him something. As the giant rabbit bends over the hoarding, the two ne'er-do-wells grab him around the neck and pull his enormous head off, parading it in triumph as they leave the ground. Roll on Saturday.

9 AUGUST 1997

Wimbledon, away

This has been a farce to organise, mainly due to our own complacency. None of the £17.50 Shuttle tickets is available. All the cheap Apex seats have been snapped up for every train out of Lime Street. Even trains from Chester are booked up. The only available fare, Liverpool to Thornton Heath, is £49.50. Murphy, Gag and Jegsy drop out. Roy makes a half-hearted offer to drive me and Danny, but we book on the 08.45. It's pathetic how excited we are.

Even at 8.00 a.m. it's uncomfortably hot. I'm in Dooley's Café on Argyle Street, reading every inch of every newspaper's back few pages, waiting for Danny. Dave Dooley's Breakfast

Special is famed throughout Merseyside. Nobody makes a fry-up like The Dool, which is why his café has been packed for 13 years. I'll be quite happy for Danny to be another five or ten minutes late so that I can finish the *Mirror* and my remaining three slices of toast without having to offer him one.

Roy's there at Lime Street. I complain about his shorts and he complains about me having my shirt tucked in. It's definitely loose-fitting weather, but you can't go around looking like a Geordie. There's no excuse for shirts outside of waistbands this close to the end of the century. I'm wearing a very sensible, almost-pink Mulberry shirt which features one slim, button-down breast pocket. This is essential for ticket-storing. The shirt is tucked into a pair of Paul Smith jeans which have, frankly, seen better days. Paul Smith seems to pride himself on classic durables, but the Paul Smith jeans range has always disappointed me. Buttons come off the flies, seams split – not very impressive. I'm going back to Levis in future. With no socks and a battered pair of Bass I imagine myself to be the last word in understated cool, but Boulter puts me right on that one. I look like a Parisian homosexual, it seems. The train's full of hyperactive Liverpudlians and leaves on time.

We speculate about team formations. We each write out our best team from the squad available. There's not much variation. What is striking, though, is that each of us, John Barnes devotees all, omits JB from our line-up. There's been a schism among the fans for over a season, now, about whether Barnes is the creative maestro, the visionary who makes everything happen, or whether he's become so slow that he's cranking the rest of the team down to his own calm pace. I love Barnes. In my adult lifetime, the time I've been able to properly appreciate true genius on the ball, there has only been Kenny Dalglish to touch him for God-given, instinctive brilliance. Those two would be the first names on my list of any All Time Liverpool Greats XI. And now I've left him out against Wimbledon.

It's clear from all of our selections that we're looking for a new Liverpool. One that inspires you with confidence again. Not so long ago, you'd watch your team line up against anyone, defending The Kop, and you'd *know* you were going to win. If Dalglish wasn't on song there was Souness and McDermott to provide guile and steel. Even if they decided to have a collective off-day, standing 50 yards to my left were the impregnable defensive stallions, Hansen and Lawrenson. And even if everyone in the team had a stinker, Ian Rush could not walk onto a football pitch without scoring at least two. I can't remember a match when Rush didn't score. It was automatic. Go to match. Watch convincing Liverpool win. Sing praises of I. Rush, goalscorer. Drink many pints of low-grade lager in Liverpool pubs. I idled away whole decades doing that.

Perhaps, inevitably, you start to take it for granted. Certainly it's time it started over again. We're here to win Doubles and European Cups. That's what Liverpool do. The '95–6 team could have become one of the great sides, but they blew it. So maybe we need to think again. John Barnes, we salute you – but you're not in the team today. Here are the sides we choose.

Danny (4–4–2)

James

McAteer   Kvarme   Wright   Bjornebye

McManaman   Ince   Leonhardsen   Berger

Riedle   Fowler

13

Roy (3–5–2)

James

Kvarme   Wright   Matteo

Jones   Bjornebye

McManaman   Ince   Leonhardsen

Riedle   Fowler

Me (4–1–3–2)

James

McAteer   Wright   Babb   Jones

Matteo

Leonhardsen   Ince   McManaman

Riedle   Fowler

We all agree that it's crazy leaving Owen out, but with Riedle and Fowler available, what do you do? Berger, too, would be an instant choice, if not for the superhuman, all-action, running, tackling and scoring figure of Oyvind Leonhardsen. Danny Murphy and Jamie Carragher will soon be mainstays of the midfield and with Jamie Redknapp returning from injury in the New Year it's a formidable squad that we have. The only real arguments are over the ideal team formation, and whether Rob Jones or Jason McAteer is best suited to the right-side defensive role. I argue that in '95–6, a season in which we played some of the best football I've ever seen from a Liverpool team, Rob Jones played most of the season at left wing-back. We agree to differ.

Danny, routinely thirstier than Rab C. Nesbitt, is jockeying for us to start the rounds off as we pass through Stafford. First game of the new season notwithstanding, I can't face a drink at ten in the morning. Danny gets a tea for me, a tea, a sandwich and a cake for Roy and a miniature Bells and a Stella chaser for himself. This is the end product from months of sweat and toil, placing bricks alongside and on top of each other, day after day, all over the world. Liverpool and the gargle. Danny spends his loot on strong liquor and Liverpool F.C. He's looked 43 since he was 19, with his ruthless short back-and-sides and his boozer's burst capillaries giving his face a permanent ruddy beam. He's 35, so his age is catching up with his body. When asked when he's going to 'settle down', Danny tells us it'll be the day he meets a woman with the looks of Nessie Shankly who can name the 1974 Cup-winning team. He never did marry.

It feels like months of sweat and toil on the crammed Epsom train. It must be close to 90 degrees today. Everyone's slick with perspiration, packed tightly together, dying for a drink. The stench of damp armpits is unbearable. The train trundles and stops, trundles and stops. Eventually, mercifully, it spews us out, faint and blinking into a white-hot South London summer's afternoon, and we set about locating pints of cold lager beer.

The streets of Thornton Heath are alive with Liverpool shirts. Liverpool's nationwide and international appeal is everywhere to be seen, with young and old and indeterminate of every shade of skin, every accent and every unthinkable hairstyle thronging the routes to the ground, grinning, chattering, excited to be part of this great mass of culture. On another day this would drive me mad, the New Fan syndrome, but today it all adds to the spectacle and drama of the first day of the season.

My beef about Liverpool's latest intake of followers is not geographic. You can find good fans from far-flung places who know how to support the team and who go to every game – Bard from Norway springs to mind, as does Keith from Doncaster and countless more, besides. Good Reds. I do believe that people in Perth should support St Johnstone, but you can understand them preferring one of the Old Firm, or one of the big teams in England. It's not unreasonable that people from unfashionable places should choose a glamorous club to support. You can understand folk wanting to buy into the instant status and swagger Liverpool gives you. But it's the 'buying into' bit that seems to confuse so many of the recent recruits, especially since Anfield became all-seated. They think that it's like any other purchase. They think that the customer has rights. Specifically, they think they have the right to complain if things don't turn out like they do on the videos, where Liverpool end every season running around Anfield with a sparkling new trophy or two. So many of Liverpool's new fans believe they have bought a package deal, and part of that deal is a promise of success. If they don't get their money's worth, if the team doesn't do the *business*, they vent their disapproval. They pick on the team. They victimise individuals. They boo. This is not the way of Liverpool fans, and if the new fans don't learn to respect this then many more of them will be getting told off before the season's out. At the Man. U home game last season, in particular, when we saw our illusions turn to delusions in 90 painful minutes, many of the booing fraternity were told in heartfelt terms that their support was not wanted or needed.

We see Jimmy Flowers, another splendid fan, chairman of the Liverpool Away Supporters Club and organiser of trips to places as diverse as Paris and Glenbuck, Ayrshire (birthplace of Shankly) last season. Jimmy's outside a corner pub, shirt off, already turning a fetching shade of scarlet. He'll be sore tomorrow. He's perched on a roadside railing like the Pope, greeting every passing coach and belting out some of his 18-versers.

It's mayhem inside the pub. Our shirts are, in actual fact, soaked through with sweat. The temptation to untuck is almost too much, but the threat of a gloating Boulter is worse. The shirt remains tucked into the troos. Sweat trickles down our brows, our ribcages, the backs of our knees, everywhere. Friendly doormen hand us plastic pint pots as we go in. The air is hot and putrid. I can't contemplate coming back in here again. Instead I contemplate the uncontemplatable – a Boro-style round of nine pints between the three of us, which I carry outside on a Boro-style tray. We're thirsty anyway and with the added embarrassment of all those pints standing next to us on the pavement we set about them with alacrity. The first one is heaven, the second is slightly chemical nectar, the last is hard work. Roy keeps tampering with himself. The shorts must itch. We set off, belching and full of anticipation. This is it. The start of the season where Liverpool bring the League Championship back home again.

Inside the ground we stake bravado-laden bets. Our team selections on the train are way out. Leonhardsen has had to succumb to a nagging injury – he's gutted – and Fowler's Norway Knock is much worse than initially feared. He might be out another month. I've got a tenner on Michael Owen to score first goal – Roy has a fiver at 25–1 on Michael Thomas.

The lavatories would instil claustrophobia in a frotteur, let alone anybody who witnessed the Hillsborough crush at close quarters. I'm dying for a leak but I have to get out of there. It's a catastrophe waiting to happen. A single steep flight of steps leads in and out of the stinking piss-cell. People are pushing against each other to get up and down that one set of steps. What happens on a rainy day, a wet floor, people slipping and tumbling over each other? It doesn't bear thinking about. I push my way up and out then, keeping my head down, go straight into the ladies, lock myself in a cubicle and before anyone can say 'Hang on a mo', sir, you've got a tail' I'm all done and out again in record time. Roy wants to queue for pies but I want nothing more than to get out there and sing loudly and slightly off-keyishly about the glorious glories of Liverpool.

Those notoriously sneaky devils, the Selhurst Park grounds-men, have left the grass long. It's a Number 5 crop, where most Premiership pitches are a Number 1 or 2. But what use is a slow pitch when you've got no support in your own stadium for the first game of the season? The entire ground is red and white. There must be 20,000 Liverpool fans there. We're supposed to be away! The roar that hits the players as they come out stuns Karlheinz Riedle enough to make him to turn round and take it all in. Riedle and Owen turn, jink and kick-in, grinning and stopping to natter to each other, but they must be terrified.

The heat, even in the comparative shade of the stands, is horrific. We later learn from *Match of the Day* that it's touching 100 degrees out on the pitch. My almost-pink Parisian homosexual shirt is now dark maroon and very, very wet. Roy looks smug, if ridiculous, in enormous Californian Modern Rock Pest shorts. A couple in their lateish thirties come and occupy the two vacant seats next to us. The woman stands on her tiptoes and does a funny little jump, clapping along to *We*

Shall Not Be Moved. Everyone sits down. We're about ready to embark upon a season of unfettered glory. The woman turns to me, keen to strike up a conversation at this tension-filled moment, the moment I'm about to produce a guttural 'kick-off' roar which consists of no words, just a massive release of hope and noise.

'Who's the Number 13?' she asks.

'His name's Karlheinz Riedle,' I smile.

The first half brings chances for Michael Owen, who shoots when Riedle is better placed, and cheers for every boneshaking Ince tackle. This is fine, but he's so enthusiastic, so eager to win, that he's over-tackling, knocking the ball away from himself so that he has to go sliding in a second time to recover it. He's bound to get booked any minute. Ruddock goes off after twenty minutes or so, limping heavily. Harkness, replacing him, seems taken aback by the pace of the game. Ince gets booked. Half time, o–o, but we're all over them.

So it's quite a shock when Wimbledon take the lead from a Marcus Gayle free-kick. It's in a good position for a left-footer, but still – he makes a lovely job of it, cutting it into the angle of bar and post. There's some dismay about David James' positioning. He's maybe a yard off his line when the kick is taken but, really, the shot was perfectly placed. Nobody could have got to it.

The Reds redouble their efforts. McManaman is through one-on-one but stubs his shot. We're pouring forward, which is good. Last season, going a goal down meant the match was over for Liverpool. We seldom had the heart to fight our way back into matches like this. But for all our pressure, openings are few. Wimbledon are holding strong. It looks grim. Then, from an unpromising move down the right, Riedle twists and tumbles under a tackle from good old Vinnie Jones, who's already tried to hug Paul Ince with his thighs. It's a penalty! Got to be! And, knock me down with a fevver, the ref's giving it! Elation turns to confusion as we wonder who's going to step up and slot the vital kick. Fowler, the regular penalty-taker, is out. John Barnes, another cool operator from the spot, is on the bench. Ruddock has been known to slam the odd spot-kick home, but he's off, injured. Surely it has to be Riedle, the most experienced striker on the pitch? Riedle, or Michael Thomas perhaps. A strange scene is unfolding. Danny Murphy and young Owen are squabbling over who takes the kick. It's great to see the two England Under-21 colleagues so fearless, so passionate, so ready to take responsibility. Owen has the ball and as possession is a jolly big slice of the law, it's he who's going to register Liverpool's, and his, first goal of the season. There's no doubt that he'll score. Never has body language betrayed the future so faithfully. He will score. He steps back. Three or four paces. No messing about. Runs in. SCORES!!

There follow more of those throat-burning guttural noises which go hand in hand with such an enormous relief of tension. The woman next to me is hugged fervently, while I make a contorted face over her shoulder at her concerned-looking partner.

'I see,' says Roy. 'Hugging the tubby fellow's not good enough for you, now??' In the elated aftermath of our first goal of the season I should now reveal that Roy is ... bulky. Certainly not fat. No, no, no – not by any means. But a Big Lad. Very fond of his tuck.

There's about 12 minutes left. A long ball out of defence puts Danny Murphy through. Sullivan, Wimbledon's keeper, is straight out, no second thought, trying to put him off. Murphy tries to lift the ball over the advancing Sullivan but doesn't quite get enough on it, toe-poking it into his chest. That's the last clear-cut chance of the game. Still, 1–1, can't complain. We played pretty well and Wimbledon's a place where a point has come to resemble a result for Liverpool. We applaud them off the pitch and jostle our way out to face that stupendous heat again.

It's not so bad outside. The heat has burnt itself out into a balmy evening haze. We decide to loaf around Selhurst Park, have a drink and let the crowds drift away. Everybody outside that ground is a Liverpool supporter. There are open-topped Cabriolets with thumping sound-systems carrying away jubilant black boys in team shirts. Gangs of young urchins in striped T-shirts and tracksuit bottoms eye up girls in full Liverpool away kits, shorts and all. Husbands and wives in their sixties labour under Reebok duvet jackets. I wonder whose decision that was:

'The forecast says more sunshine, dear . . .'

'The forecast! When's the forecast ever been right! Get the Roy Evans coats out . . .'

I feel strangely proud of each and every one of them. They've all come down here to take communion. We all want the same thing. For today, at least, we're brothers and sisters.

The journey back is a hoot. I've lost Roy and Danny somewhere en route to Thornton Heath. There are still thousands of Liverpool fans around enjoying the now-mellow sunshine, so the trains to Victoria and Euston are slow, hot and rammed tight full. Euston is in chaos. Some outward-bound services are subject to severe delay. It's no surprise. The London to Liverpool train never leaves on time. You can walk up to that display screen in the utterly safe knowledge that the Manchester, Birmingham and Glasgow services will be ready to board, with a nice, welcoming platform number to help weary travellers on their way. The Liverpool information will be blank. If we ever leave within half an hour of the advertised time, it's a bonus. I kill an hour in The Royal George in Eversholt Street, where I'm told that Everton have lost at home to Crystal Palace. Hail Mary! That'll do for me!

I wander back to Euston to see if things are easing up and am overjoyed to spot that the first train out is going to be the Holyhead, which calls at Chester, which will do just fine. I can get a train to Birkenhead from Chester – they could almost be said to be regular. Smashing. It leaves in two minutes. I'm on it.

So, too, are a big, happy band of Huyton vagabonds. They've got crates of lager (warm) and fist-sized lumps of pot (strong). They have family railcards and one dubious child-candidate. They're amazed that I paid £49.50 and make me promise to purchase a family railcard the very moment I get off the train. Out of sympathy they ply me with intoxicants, which have the strange effect of making me recall my grandmother's phone number in Huyton. It started with the prefix STO for Stoneycroft.

'Whatever happened to Stoneycroft?' I slur.

'What?'

'Stoneycroft. It's not there any more.'

They exchange glances which have the same unambiguous meaning all over the world:

'Who's the tithead?'

Then comes the inevitable ribaldry with the ticket inspector over the family railcards. The inspector, a nice man approaching retirement age if his white furze tells it true, is trying to elicit more funds from the Huyton crew, who react in time-honoured fashion. They play dumb. They stare at their train tickets and at the family railcard as if by doing so they're going to make the figures £14.50 disappear and replace them with different numbers. £49.50, say. One of them speaks up in backslang. Whatever he said, nobody's meant to understand it. Everybody starts giggling. It's sly on the inspector, but he's not helping his cause. He rounds on the backslanger.

'YOU ARE IN VIOLATION OF YOUR CONTRACT WITH BRITISH RAIL!!' he shrieks. The gales of laughter nearly take out the window panes.

'Ah, that's what it is, see, auld 'un. This is Virgin. I think you're on the wrong train. That's where you're getting mixed up.'

The others, sensing the kill, join in.

'You're a little bit confused, aren't you lad?'

'You're getting all mixed up, mate.'

'You need a 'oliday.'

The inspector hurls his machine down. 'That's it!! I'm calling the Transport Police. They'll be on at Rugby and you can sort this out with them! You'll laugh the other side of your faces, then . . .'

He storms off. At Rugby, no Transport Police arrive. We see his white head bobbing away down the platform, red pate alight with vexation as he seeks a southbound train. Bobby Wilcox, another legendary fan, plods down the carriage wearing a vest and flip-flops. He finds Lenny Woods, one of the few who remembers Billy Liddell and a rival inventor of songs. They're bickering over who's come up with the best song for Paul Ince. Heroically pissed, now, and not giving a fuck I pipe up, to the tune of *Needles and Pins*, a bad chant which rhymes Riedle and Ince with, erm, needles and, indeed, pins. They waft away imaginary smells and give me the *Fifteen To One* WRONG klaxon noise, WRRRICK-ORR.

The Huyton gang get off at Crewe, urging the handful who're staying on to come into town with them. I'm done for with the cannabis and the cans. It's curtains for me. A point at Wimbledon. Not bad.

13 AUGUST 1997

Leicester, home

I hate Nick Hancock. Not because he's the latest media figurehead for Fashionable Football. He isn't. He's supported Stoke City all his life. You could describe that as 'mad' or 'deviant', but it is most certainly not 'fashionable'. I don't hate him for that smug grin he does in recognition of each and every one of his own pert witticisms. He's very funny. If I was a fraction as funny as him I'd be basking in a veritable nirvana of self-regard. And I don't loathe, despise and detest Nick Hancock for the fact that he's a fat chap with grey hair who's married to a pulchritudinous deity half his age. This only goes to show that losers can be winners, which has to be a good thing.

The reason I wish to strangle Nick Hancock to death or, at least, to a chronic state of laryngitis is his voice. He has the same accent, exactly, as Upper Centenary Nuisance – a resentful, rhetorical Burslem drone that's leaden with life-ain't-fair inflections. This is a voice which for two whole seasons has been making my life hell. So today, although I'm full of anticipation about our first home game of the season, it's an eagerness tempered with the forlorn hope that UCN has taken his business elsewhere.

Roy and me moved to the Upper Centenary Stand in the first place to escape from Scouse Humour, a silver-haired, pock-faced, thick-necked ex-bouncer who was, frankly, a disgusting old bigot. He'd forgive any misdemeanour by one of his blue-eyed boys – Neil Ruddock was a particular Scouse Humour favourite – but if Mark Walters scored anything less than a hat-trick and 100 per cent pass accuracy, he was dead. It seems laughable, now, that Walters was keeping Steve McManaman out of the team. Let's be straight – Walters was never good enough to play for Liverpool and Souness should never have contemplated bringing him down from Rangers, let alone trying to fob him off on us as the new John Barnes. The existing one was still doing very nicely, thank you. But Walters, when he played, always gave everything. When he scored the goal that deprived Man. U of the League for a 26th year in succession (only as recently as 1992, pop-pickers) he ran to the corner flag in front of the old Boys Pen and wept for joy. He knew what it meant to the fans to keep United down.

But Walters was a confidence player. If his tricks failed to come off, which was often as he had only two tricks and defenders quickly sussed them out, the crowd would get on his back and his spunk would visibly drain away. It's hard to understand why fans motivate their players by flaying them in public and none would lash Mark Walters more gleefully than Scouse Humour. You would find yourself recoiling against the onslaught to come when Walters was sent to warm up on the touchline with Liverpool trailing miserably and only eight minutes of the game left. What was he *supposed* to do? Scouse Humour and his band of Kemlyn Road sycophants would almost be beside themselves as Walters, a truly uninspiring sight, shitting himself, trotted onto the football pitch.

'Here he comes! Our saviour!' rasped Scouse Humour. 'The Black Pearl!'

He turned to his adoring public for the punch-line.

'More like the black fucken pudden!'

Oh! Pass the elastoplast while I fix up these splitting sides! That was Scouse at his mildest and most hysterically funny. Requests for him to get off the player's back would be greeted with a puffed-out chest and the assertion that he used to work on the docks. For many, many, many years. More years than you could possibly warrant.

'Don't try and tell me about commitment, lad – I used to werkonderdocks!!'

He could probably justify nun mutilation by telling us he used to work on the docks. Further questioning of his right to vilify honest footballers would result in him telling me how much he paid for his season-ticket, which I already knew because I sat just in front of him and mine cost exactly the same. He was a twat, we hated sitting by him and, painful though it was to give up such a good spec, Roy and I jumped at the chance of a move to the new, swanky seats upstairs when it came.

Unfortunately, they didn't warn us we'd be sitting by Upper Centenary Nuisance. His voice, that defensive, sullen, innately complaining Potteries whine, was clearly audible from our very first game as Upper Centenary new boys, Stan Collymore's debut against Sheffield Wednesday. UCN sits about three rows behind me, a bit to the right. Exactly 30 seconds into the new season, with John Barnes' first touch of the ball, he was onto him, as though he'd been waiting all summer for his opportunity to roast this most extravagant of talents.

'Oh very good, Barnes, very clever.' (Claps his hands) 'Let's all go backwards, shall we?'

It was an improvement on the hideous invective of Scouse Humour, but in other ways he's even more annoying. He tries to be sarcastic. The worst you'll get from him is:

'Ow fookinill, Barnes!! Fookin' brilliant!'

But after the trauma of the Walters Years, you'd still find yourself hunching your shoulders reflexively against the bile from behind whenever Barnes'd turn back towards goal to start everything up from scratch. I hope passionately that, after the disgrace of Paris Saint Germain last season and the meek handing over to Man. United of a title we had only to reach out and take, UCN will have decided that enough is enough. Please let him not be there tonight. Let me be surrounded by good fans who appreciate good football and who don't heap scorn upon the team when things don't always go right. These are my thoughts as I hasten towards The White Star pub in Matthew Street, home of fine Staropremen lager, to meet Danny, Jegsy, Gag and Bard from Norway.

Bard from Norway is an excellent fellow. Like Jan Molby, he is very tall, from Scandinavia, and talks with a thick Liverpool accent. He works for the Scandinavian Liverpool Supporters Club which has 22,000 fully accredited members. Bard organises regular trips to Liverpool games and is involved in the annual pre-season Norway v. Liverpool friendly – the one in which this year Robbie Fowler nearly had his leg broken in two just below the knee.

Talk in The White Star is split between the shock of John

Barnes' transfer request and the prospect of some of the boys making a CD of old Liverpool songs. As a commercial venture this is not a bad idea. An accompanying booklet containing the words to songs like *Liver Bird Upon My Chest* and *Fields of Anfield Road* would, no doubt, be most welcome to many of the new recruits. The only songs the newies know are the tricky *Liverpool, Liverpool, Liverpool* (to the tune of *Here We Go*) and the chorus of *You'll Never Walk Alone* – even then, at Tottenham last season, I found myself next to a splendid character who lustily sung:

> *Walk on, through the wind*
> *Walk on, through the rain*
> *For you're nearly close to home*

So a CD might be just the ticket. Of more immediate concern is the imminent move of John Barnes. I'm racked with guilt, now, at leaving him out of my team for Wimbledon. Somebody obviously told him. It must've been the last straw. He was widely quoted on the Saturday morning as wanting to stay, at least until the end of the year, and fight for his place. If he wasn't getting a regular place, he'd look at it again in January. But after the Wimbledon game he'd been to see Roy Evans who had granted his request for a free transfer. West Ham have already emerged as strong favourites to sign him and he's down in London looking at schools for his four nippers.

Jegsy, almost embarrassed and only after much badgering from me, reveals his latest escapade. Jegsy is 39 and fast approaching 40. Most young men of 36, let alone 39, accept that their roistering days are behind them. We might look longingly at the parades of bare-midriffed lovelies making their way out on a Saturday night as we totter back home after the match, but nobody with any sense of propriety would try to talk to any woman under the age of 30. Jegsy has no such taboos. This is a man who is loved by women. They love him,

27

and they have always loved him. The older he gets, it seems, and the more craggy becomes his face, the more the young come a-knockin' for him. They actually do that, by the way – teenage girls call round to his flat at three, four in the morning, desirous of his company. It's easy to squeeze a confession out of him. All you have to do is pressure him, call his bluff, claim you just happened to be out jogging at 1.30 last night and the latest confession comes tumbling from his lips. All right. I'll tell you. But you've got to PROMISE not to spill the beans. It's widely accepted that I'm a faithful keeper of secrets, so he knows he's safe in telling me all about Mary Wow, a teenage beauty who called for him in midweek. I guarantee him that I'll say nothing to no one. Danny comes in.

'Danny! Ask Richard Asquith who he met in the launderette on Wednesday!'

Jegsy blushes and shakes his head. Mono comes in to meet Bard from Norway. Mono, Peter, Garner – everyone except me and Roy – sit together on The Kop. We get a bit of stick from the diehards for flirting with the toffs in the comely padded seats of the Upper Centenary, but in truth I've never been a Koppite. I've had spells in the Boys Pen – which doesn't count – but most of my time at Anfield has been spent on the Kemlyn Road side of the ground. I could never see from The Kop. I watched the famous St Etienne game from there, having bunked off school and queued with my brother, Neil and our pal Brian Bentley from midday – but I remember the night more for the crush, the heat and the backs of men's donkey jackets than for Davey Fairclough's winner.

The diehards have taken Bard into the fold, amazed by his willingness to travel from a small town near Oslo to even the most insignificant friendly – and impressed by his scouse-butty Jan Molby accent. Bard has also taken conscientiously to the ancient and revered tradition of round-buying.

Everyone agrees that a point at Wimbledon was not a bad start. We should've won the game but, having gone a goal down it was gratifying that the team showed the grit to step it up again, even in that unspeakable heat, and dig something out of the game. Other teams will go there this season and get nothing. We're quite pleased with them. A good win tonight against a Leicester team who are no pushovers for anyone will make for an excellent start to the season. Jegsy, ever the optimist, pipes up – as he always does when everyone's had a couple of drinks and starts talking about championships:

'I wouldn't put it past these to come here tonight and beat us.'

His bonce is resolutely thwacked with rolled-up *Echo*s.

I meet Roy in the Paisley Lounge for a pint and more silly bets. I go for Owen again, at 6–1. Roy won't consider anything under 12–1, and selects Paul Ince at 16s. We head up for the match expecting a good win. In all the hurly-burly of speculation and gambling, we have forgotten about Upper Centenary Nuisance. We even forget to check whether he's there when we take our seats. We sing *Walk On*. We cheer the team onto the pitch. We settle down for kick-off, genuinely expecting a confident, stylish performance from Liverpool and three points on the board. Thomas receives the ball from Ince, turns and plays it back to Bjornebye. Then we hear him:

'Fookinell Thomas! I thought we'd got rid of Barnes!'

My neck perspires in anger, but I'm not getting into a row in the first minute of the new season. Fuck. Another season of that whingeing nincompoop. Let's pray that it's a different story on the pitch – maybe a run of good results'll shut the bastard up.

Liverpool are messing about in defence. Kvarme's the problem. He does not like receiving the ball. His tackling and jockeying are superb, but give him the ball in or around his own goal mouth and it's like pass-the-parcel – his instant reaction is to give it straight back. What's worse is that he does this with a tortured look of concentration, as though his cowardly return to sender is some Beckenbaueresque flourish.

He's like a crab, going sideways and backwards, and all he achieves is to invite nippy opposing forwards to close him down. This is what happens tonight. Kvarme, dithering, is pressurised by Heskey who almost robs him. Kvarme concedes a free-kick. Walsh swings over a hopeful ball from the left and, amazingly – scandalously after the way we conceded goals from set-pieces last season – Elliott strolls through a watchful defence and prods home. 1–0 to Leicester after two minutes. At least there's the whole game to turn this around. But we don't. It's Leicester who show all the bite and endeavour, chasing down and harrying, denying Liverpool time on the ball and creating quite a few more openings themselves. It's desperately disappointing stuff, but Roy and I are left shaking our heads in disbelief as booing cascades from the stands when the team trudges off at half time. Booing at half time! In the first home game of the season!

We have a cup of tea and try to put our finger on the possible reasons for this dispirited, raggedy showing. Obviously it's not Roy Evans' first-choice team we're seeing out there. Fowler, Redknapp and Leonhardsen are all injured but it's a selection that Martin O'Neill would love to call his first-team, any day of the week. My theory is that the defence doesn't know what it's supposed to be doing – we've just switched from 3–5–2 to 4–4–2 and they're still acclimatising to that particular discipline. It will come right, but in the meantime the midfield are wary of being too cavalier, knowing that any loss of possession can quickly be converted into goals. In short, far from pulverising the opposition with our confident, swaggering, offensive football, we're playing fearfully. We're playing with a tentative, defensive edge, which is frustrating the crowd, which is becoming too easily impatient, which is making the team more tense, more prone to mistakes.

Second half is better, as Ince drives the team on from midfield. The more we push forward, though, the more space Leicester are given down the flanks. It's no surprise when, with five minutes left, Heskey breaks away down the left and fires in a useful but not unstoppable cross-shot. James gets down to it well, but can only divert the ball into the path of the totally unmarked and totally average Graham Fenton, a journeyman already at the age of 24. Beaten 2–0 by Leicester. Sobering stuff. People start to leave in their droves, throwing match programmes into the air in disgust. Ince won't have it. Snarling and bellowing at his players he sorties forward and, finding no one in a better position, drives in a rasping daisy-cutter from outside the box. It's in! 2–1! Four minutes to go! We throw everyone forward and in injury time Michael Owen executes one of those weaving, high-speed, humanly-impossible runs for which he will soon become world-famous, manoeuvring in a microscopic scrap of space past three lunging tackles. He's in on goal. It's a tight angle but if anyone can do it . . . he scuds the ball hard and low right across the goalkeeper and, agonisingly, one mere inch past the far post. Any in-rushing striker would have enjoyed the easiest of prods home. Fowler would have put it in in his sleep but nobody in the box reacts quickly enough. That's just about the last action of the game. Leicester have won 2–1.

A draw would have been harsh on Leicester, who are applauded off the pitch, but it's a crushing disappointment for us to lose so early in the season. Another of the truisms about the English League Champions is that they can, generally, afford no more than five defeats over the whole season and they should prolong the taste of their first beating until well into the autumn. Real Championship contenders can be identified by their ability to put together useful unbeaten runs – three wins on the trot, a draw, a couple more wins, two undeserved draws at difficult grounds followed by two more thumping wins. Title winners prefer the trees to be nude of leaves by the time their first defeat is suffered. And they want to get to the New Year with no more than two defeats in the snap bag. They don't always play well – far from it – but they

Birkenhead. He transformed the Friday afternoon game. Instead of ten or twelve mates playing amongst and against each other, it was now Us against Them – and pretty serious, too.

Us was, loosely, a team of ex-, or almost, or mates of musicians. Plus a few who are still at it. We had Hooton, Mullin, Boulter (The Farm), Blackie from Half Man Half Biscuit, Kennedy from The Iliad, Jegsy Dodd, Charlie from Little Prince Records, Mel from The Co-Optimists and his twinkle-toed manager Pete Naylor. Head of Security Mick Potter, Ian Prowse from Pele, Super Accountant to the Arts Community Dickie Wood, caterer to the stars Dave Dooley plus myself and my brother Neil. Them consisted of: Treeman, an eco-warrior who just turned up out of nowhere one day – possibly out of a tree he'd been defending – plus Adam, Cliffy, Ricey, Swordy, Wally, Graham, Robbie, Damien, Terry, Jonah, Jamie, Jason, Rab, Kieron and the inimitable Tommy Vialli.

It's unfair to suggest that any one player is notably worse than another, so rather than suggest it I'll state it in bold. Tommy Vialli was far and away the worst player ever to grace an already poor standard of amateur football at Birkenhead Park on a Friday afternoon. Team-mates'd try and encourage him, forlornly hoping that some gentle persuasion would cure him of his fatal fascination with the defensive dribble. On a weekly basis, several times per game, little carrot-top Tommy would hear the Voices. Those voices would tell him that he was, not Tommy Vialli of Higher Tranmere but Young Alan Hansen, and his Calling was to receive the ball from the keeper, glide past three or four invisible challenges as he penetrated the opposing half of the field, then slide the most graceful of through-passes into the path of grateful goalscoring team-mates, team-mates almost too embarrassed to apply the workmanlike final touch on Tommy's elegant, eloquent, footballing mural. Sadly, it was only Tommy who heard these

Voices. He was one of those players who, when he had the ball, inspired the most talentless, out of condition, battle-weary of opponents to find the extra strength to sprint the length of the pitch to close him down. He gave the other side confidence. While Tommy was playing, there was always a chance. There was always a chance, because he was shite. But he had a great kit. What made Tommy one of the indispensables – tough boys with tattoos would sob without restraint when Tommy failed to show – was his too-big Juventus kit. The too-big kit was a wonderful sight to behold in any event, but what made it beautiful was the enormous shirt, Tommy's freckled hands just about making it out the other end of the sleeves, complete with the word VIALLI emblazoned on the back. The crap lad with the boss kit – that's what football's all about, isn't it?

Over the years the young tinkers have stopped coming, selfishly preferring to get jobs and 'go steady' – things which have always augured badly for football-related fun. The nucleus is still there, two o'clock, every Friday, but the games have now taken on a Liverpool v. Birkenhead slant. Puffa, the fan-friendly ticket conjurist, has started bringing a carload of men with enormous thighs – good footballers and hardy opponents. We can usually muster eight or nine a side, more if Puffa puts his mind to it, and the games are avidly competed.

On Friday, 13 June 1997 I went into a challenge with the avidly competitive Mick Duffy of Liverpool and came away in agony. The first X-ray revealed nothing, but the pain in my side – breathing was murderously painful – got worse. My local quack dug his thumbs into my ribcage and announced that at least two ribs were fractured. He couldn't give me any quick fix for it, only a slow one. Four to six weeks of doing nothing, he recommended. For the remainder of June and the whole of July I did nothing but watch from the sidelines – perhaps more agonising than the injury itself. Only from the side of the pitch do you get a real take on how gloriously, lamentably, hilariously bad is the standard of our game. We're shit – and I know we are, now.

I couldn't even drink with them afterwards. Drinking in itself was painful enough, but laughing at their descriptions of their own Platini-style contributions to the game was torture. Roy has often said that he starts dreaming about next Friday's game on the Friday night, in the bath, feeling every bruise and every aching (rather tubby) limb from that afternoon's game. I've been like that for two months, now. Boy, am I going to come back a new and improved player! No more shouting and shrieking at my own team-mates. I'm going to be affable, sportsmanlike and generous. It's a gift, this Friday football. It is Freedom. I couldn't wait to get back out there with them.

So today . . . today is one of those great days. Enough of a breeze to make the sunshine bearable. Hardly any trace of pain – just a vague pinprick, a little snagging when I go from jog to sprint – but nothing, really. This is great. All we need's a good turnout. I decide to miss out on traditional pre-match cuppas at Dooley's and get down to the park for one o'clock, for a good warm-up.

Titanic nerves as we kick-off. Straight away I'm through, if only Jegsy'd control the fucking thing and look up.

'JEGSY!! FIRST TIME!! FIRST TIME!! FUCKINELL, AY!!'

Mr Fair Play's back, then. Puffa has brought two cars-full of serious amateur players who shout proper footballer things like 'jockey' and 'still have'. Worse, whenever I go in for a challenge against any one of them, a voice shouts out: 'You've won that!' They shout it five whole seconds before we go in on each other, the implication being that Boy A (skinny, blinking, wan-looking, Wirral puff) has no chance, ever, of winning the ball from Boy B (steroid-head, steely-eyed, swarthy, hirsute, and, crucially, from Liverpool). Fuck the broken ribs, the ball's mine. I slide in, completely miss the ball and lie there stranded as Liverpool storm down the other end to equalise. Again.

It's a close game, but we win 12–7. Modesty prevents me from describing the turning point of the game other than to say that it was 7–5 to us, extremely close, with three marauding Liverpool strikers (this is their problem: they're all strikers) bearing down on me – our left-back – and Treeman, our goalie. With exquisite timing I steal the ball off Jimmy Fowler's toe (he looks like Robbie, comes from Tocky and he scores lots of goals) and look up. The instant left-footed pass dissects what there is of the Liverpool midfield. Charlie has one defender and their goalie, 60-year-old Maldini-ish sweeper Joe, to beat. I race down the left wing. Charlie, very right-footed, goes outside the last defender. I'm screaming:

'Chazchazchazchazchazchaz . . .'

He looks up and curls the ball in. It's starting its outswing when I meet it. All along I've been thinking of this as a volley, but as I get within twatting distance of the ball it starts to rise. I shift my weight and, just as it's about to arc past my shoulder, I spin and launch myself at it. It's only a little stab of the head but the ball shoots down to the base of the post, clips it and it's in. 8–5!! The world's second worst header of the ball scores a cracker to open up a decisive lead! He starts and finishes the move! But modesty prevents me from going into any more detail than is strictly necessary. Thankfully Roy Evans caught the whole movement from his position on the touchline. I expect that phone call any day now.

23 AUGUST 1997

Blackburn, away

Eight o'clock, Dooley's café, bacon, egg and tomato sandwich – delicious. The *Mirror* and the *Daily Post* are still full of John Barnes' move to Newcastle – West Ham are gutted – and Steve McManaman's abortive move to Barcelona. McManaman is denying that he ever sought a move – he says he only agreed to fly out and talk to the Catalans after Liverpool agreed a price for him. Liverpool, for their part, are saying that McManaman is stalling over a new deal which will keep him at Anfield for another five years. They say that, rather than risk letting him walk away as a free agent in 18 months' time and receiving no compensation, it's only prudent to listen to offers for a player who may envisage his future elsewhere. A side issue, completely irrelevant but which is not helping McManaman's case, is the fact that he's represented by Simon Fuller whose other clients include the Spice Girls. Simon Fuller is said to be an affable, scrupulous, conscientious, thoroughly decent, utterly professional man – instantly setting himself against the grain of many footballers' agents. But one has to question McManaman's wisdom in choosing this person as his representative, given the harmful and negative Spice Boy press he continues to receive. McManaman cares not, and more power to his bony elbow for selecting his agent on purely business criteria. Me, I think he should've given someone with less profile the job, but now his decision's made I hope to see Mr Fuller negotiating a humungous new contract for his client – with Liverpool.

Danny turns up wearing only a shirt. That is, he has jeans and shoes, too, but no pullover, no jerkin. It's still August, but it's windy and them Lancashire milltowns can be mighty inhospitable places. We have a choice – a train that'll get us into Blackburn just after two, or a really early one. Neither's ideal, but Danny argues convincingly for hitting the swallee trail there, rather than here. We change trains at Preston. By the time we alight at Mill Hill, the stop before Blackburn, it's raining gently but persistently, and I feel extra smug in my chubby Nigel Cabourn puffa jacket.

Even at this time, not long after eleven, there's a smattering of police barking updates into their walkie-talkies. We know for sure that it's updates they're barking because they clear their throats and bark:

'Update! Approximately sixty, six-oh Liverpool supporters just off the 10.37. Twenty or thirty still on the train heading to you . . .'

The police seem to want to advise us to walk in the opposite direction to the ground. Some take their advice. Danny and I weave our way through the drizzly sidestreets, heading roughly for the canal where there's a good bar we were in last season. It's called The Canal or The Towpath or something vaguely waterwayesque. We keep going, up then left, up then left, starting to get a little out of breath without realising how much of a hill we've been traipsing up, when we see the long, reclaimed brick outbuilding of The Waterside. That's it! The Waterside! We walk sideways in a low gear down the slope and over a little footbridge to the pub. Two bouncers on the door, one male one female, frisk us and ask if we're home or away supporters.

'Liverpool,' says Danny at the exact moment that I say 'Rorrvers' in a very unconvincing Jane Horrocks accent. The bouncers grin and let us in.

I wish they hadn't. It's half-eleven, the place is packed with Blackburn skins and the atmosphere is putrid. No one's going to give you any hassle at half-eleven on a Saturday morning, but you want to be able to enjoy your drink. I don't feel too weird about going up to the bar even though all the Blackburn lads seem to know I'm not one of their own. I wait to get served. There's about three or four people who've already been waiting when I step up and, while queue-jumping is an inevitable facet of jungle-law, I always *try* to take my turn. Honest. I let the others get served then start up the ritual of cocking my head back, trying to make eye-contact with the barman, gearing myself up to bang my order in *the moment* he takes the money from the lad next to me. I start to ask for two pints of Guinness when a loud, local voice issues up from behind me and the barman's eyeline is readjusted up and past my shoulders. I'm left talking to thin air. In embarrassment, I start to hum. No particular tune, I just need to do something with my voice to make it clear that I wasn't really expecting to get served that time, I'm just warming up for my next opportunity, when I *will* get served in this nice, friendly Blackburn pub. So I hum and wait for the barman to turn around again. This time I'm going to shout in my order before he's even finished serving the last fella. Not too soon, though. I'll time it right and smile at the same time. I'll do that embarrassed crinkle that people do when they hold the door open for someone, or they're semi-acknowledging someone they don't know. You keep your mouth tight closed and lift your cheek muscles, keeping a suitably apologetic look in your eyes. It's a late twenty-first century substitute for the played-out use of 'Sorry' and 'Thanks', all rolled into one, all-purpose, don't-hit-me-I'm-harmless grimace. My heart is beating fast, now. This is it. He's at the till. I should make my play . . . now! The barman turns, I crinkle and ask him for two pints of Guinness. He makes the most fleeting eye-contact then looks past me again.

'What's yours, Shally?'

I find myself wondering what Shally is short for or whether it is, in fact, a stupid Lancashire inbred's first name. Shallingworth Boscrop, the spindle-mender, perchance? Or Zachary Shallowbottom, the last of the great Darwen dab-flatterers.

'Caught much today, Shally?'

'Couple o' dozen dab.'

'Flatter 'em?'

'Aye.'

I hate it here. If he doesn't serve me next I'm going to lob this ashtray at his spirit display and leg it. My heart is really thumping now. The humming has been replaced by whistling and is now accompanied by the rhythmic beat of my two forefingers, drumming impatiently on the bar. Just about everyone has been served. He's got to do me now, the bastard. He gives me a slight nod.

'Two pints of Guinness, please, mate,' I say, jaunty as you like, as though I completely don't know that he's been taking the piss.

'Two pints of what?'

He's a complete whopper, this big woolly. He must own the bar. No mere barhand would have that amount of antagonistic front.

'*Four* pints of Guinness,' I say, half wise-guy, half pragmatist.

'Four pints of Business?'

His mates at the bar chuckle half-heartedly, not that interested in the little sideshow he's putting on for them.

'Yes.'

He gives me a bit of a look then just turns around and pours them. Quite nice they are, too. It comes back to me that there was supposedly trouble in this place after the game last season. Maybe something nasty happened. Who knows? It doesn't give him licence to abuse his customers. And Shally is one *twat* of a nickname.

We slurp our Business. More Blackburn roughs arrive. Something is obviously afoot. They're not the most worrying mob you'll ever run into but there are now well over a hundred of them, they're starting to get drunk and we're the only Liverpool fans in here. We've had enough of it, we don't want to give Friend of Shally another penny so it's time to amble out of there. We crinkle at the cuddly bouncers and walk all of ten yards to a converted warehouse complex next door. There, we find this social club sort of place which is, verily, sociable and is undeniably a club. We carry on drinking Business until ten to three, and Danny's back on the Jameson's chasers, too.

The first half's a blur of Blackburn attacks and the ref getting in the way. I've never noticed this happening so much in previous seasons, but in the games I've been at so far and the ones I've seen on television since the Charity Shield the referee seems to stray into the path of play at a crucial point at least once per half. This time we're the beneficiaries as he tries to vault over a neat through-ball from McKinlay and kills it stone dead with his heel. We're lucky to go in still 0–0 at half time. We descend into the groaning bogs of Ewood Park for much-needed bowel evacuations and bump into Gag and John Garner, both very down about the first half performance. Danny and I are full of drunken bravado, but I do genuinely feel that we'll come back out and swarm all over them. I tell Garner to go back upstairs and enjoy the second half in the knowledge that we're going to win 2–0. Some of the young urchins Danny knows tell him there's been trouble in town before the game – and in that pub by the canal.

Second half. Michael Owen times his run to perfection to beat Blackburn's offside trap. His pace is shocking – he leaves everyone, players and crowd, gasping as he bears in on goal and slots the ball through Blackburn's reserve goalie's legs. 1–0! Blackburn redouble their efforts and throw everything at Liverpool, but they don't truly threaten. A more likely outcome, the more space they leave at the back, is that Owen or McManaman will add to Liverpool's score. With 12 minutes left McManaman springs their defence and is right through on goal. It's one of those horrible slow-motion moments. If anything, he's got too much time, too many options. Should he go round the keeper? Should he slot it either side of him? After a century of indecision, McManaman cleverly commits the keeper to a dive and digs the ball over his sprawling body. Somehow, unbelievably, this Filan, only a reserve to Tim Flowers after all, throws up a despairing arm and, with his actual fingernails, scratches the ball down and falls on it. McManaman can't believe it. He did everything right. It's a wonderful piece of goalkeeping, but we could have had the match tucked up by now.

McManaman takes a bit of stick, partly a result of the predictable resentment still washing around post-Barcelona but partly, too, because he missed a lot of good chances one-on-one last season and it looks like nothing's changed. His goals might have won us the League last year and he's already muffed great openings against Wimbledon and now here at Blackburn. After Euro 96, no less a hero than Pele rated Steve McManaman one of the greatest players in the world. The World. One of our boys. I think McManaman's a fantastic player – a fantasy player – but he can't finish the page he's reading. Roy Evans always says Macca's goals in training are unbelievable, and that's about right. We don't believe him. Sorry, Mr Pele, McManaman's a gem – but he's never going to set the world alight with his goalscoring.

It's still 1–0 and Blackburn are flinging everyone into attack. James makes a great diving save to tip a rasping shot around the post for a corner, but we don't clear it properly. Martin Dahlin is given a generous amount of space to turn and he hooks the ball in from 12 yards. 1–1. Both teams have half-chances to win it in the last five minutes, but, so close to that first victory of the new campaign, this can only go down as a bad result. The fans aren't happy. In the space of a few weeks our rampant optimism has been reduced to nervous introspection. Three games, no wins, two points, a solitary goal in each game. It's a shit start to the season.

On the way out, as the crowd spills out into a sunny, rainy, rainbow-striped Lancashire evening, Danny stops and points. I can't see who he's pointing at.

'Now *that* – is what I call a woman.'

There are lots of men of all shapes, ages and sizes but only one woman, looking round, lost. She could charitably be called pretty, though that's not the thing which slaps you in the face about her. Before you got round to her pleasant-enough face, you'd have taken in her well-sprayed bubble perm and her amazing, enormous snorkel parka, covered in plate-sized badges of Patrik Berger and Jamie Redknapp. If she'd written her own Woman Seeking advert, it might say:

'Cuddly, experienced blonde, teen-acting, bubbly, football daft, seeks dominant Liverpool-supporting male. Must be able to name 1974 Cup Final side.'

A less romantic but more faithful description might be:

'Fat, middle-aged, Liverpool fanatic (F) seeks similar male, any age. Own voluminous parka. You? All letters answered.'

Danny stares at the blinking woman a moment longer, shaking his head.

'What a cracker!'

I take a moment to marvel at the many and various splendours of humankind, note in passing that wonders never cease and usher Danny off past the McDonalds' tardis and up the hill. We get lost. Figuring that, if we stick close to the canal towpath, we can't go wrong, we plod along in the mud for ten minutes or so. There's a little humpy bridge up ahead and an old stone pub next to it, so we wander in. It's full of the sort of people who like nothing better than a chat about darts. The only person in there who is (a) under 50 and (b) not a man is a terrifying redhead perched at the bar. As we approach, she hops off her stool and back round behind the bar.

'Yes lads?'

It's hard to know where to look, for the sake of politeness, as one eye is listing madly to the left and the other, solid as a steel ballbearing, is staring straight ahead. Dwarves I've known have told me they prefer people to gawp in horror at them than stare past as though they're not there. Grasping the nettle by the stalk I beam directly into her face.

'Two pints of Guinness, please.'

'Coming up.'

This is a doddle. No problem at all. If she doesn't have a problem with it, why should anyone else?

'You're the best-looking lad I've had in here for dogsdays.'

Oh, crikey.

Danny comes back from the bogs.

'Your mate looks hard. Does he want an arm wrestle?'

We say we'll think about it while we sup our pints. The locals grin over. The lively barmaid comes back round and climbs onto her stool again. She fixes the stiff eye on Danny.

'Roog-beh.'

Rugby.

'That's what you call a real sport.'

We both flick our eyes over her Blackburn Rovers shirt.

'So. D'you enjoy the match today then?'

'Blackbunn Rorrvurrs? Ah *ert* um!!'

We both nod and slurp, nod and slurp. Blackburn just isn't working out for us. It's time to go. We bid her a cheery farewell. She tells us that 'this lot' only stay until seven on match days and then she's got the place to herself. She puts her hands on her hips like Calamity Jane, thighs astride, giving us a challenging leer. It's the weirdest thing I've seen in dogsdays. As we leave she gives a little snort of derision, head back slightly, staring north and west simultaneously.

'Wiggin!!' she shouts after us.

I feign slumber all the way home to get out of the rabid debates of the Evans-out lynch mobs on board. It's ten o'clock when I get back to the house. The Lovely Jane offers me coffee and cheese on toast, but I'm too knackered even to stay up for *Match of the Day*. Besides, I want to fall asleep dreaming of my perfectly executed chip over Blackburn's flailing reserve goalkeeper, a goal which I celebrate in the arms of a sight-deficient but muscular barmaid.

26 AUGUST 1997

Leeds, away

It's 3.30 p.m. Present at Dooley's are Jegsy Dodd, Urban Dub Poet; Danny Giles, King of the Swallee; Dave Dooley, the affable proprietor himself; and me. We're munching poached eggs on toast and trying to persuade Jegs to drive to Leeds. This'd suit Danny and me down to the ground as we can be transported to Elland Road and imbibe without restriction. It's slightly less handy for Jegs as he will have to drive – and he doesn't have a ticket for this sold-out, all-ticket game. But these are minor considerations. There's a rumour that Leeds will be opening one cash turnstile for away fans to take account of a bundle of tickets which they forgot to send out to Liverpool, but we're all far too long in the tooth to fall for stories like that. Amazingly, Jegs decides he wants to go. We have a good four hours to get there, but we could do with setting off. We phone Roy and Peter Hooton to see if either fancies it. Peter does. Roy's not in. We pick up Peter in Crosby, fill up the car and we're off.

The journey takes no time at all. We're on the outskirts of Leeds by five o'clock so we pull off the motorway and look for a pub. The first one we find is so outrageously quaint that we feel like inner-city till snatchers the moment we walk in there. The smattering of green-wellied customers do nothing to make us feel uncomfortable, but places like this make you acutely aware of the way Liverpudlians are perceived around the country. We just want a drink, but we've got *that* accent, a couple of us have very short hair, we're wearing hoods and training-shoes and we think that they think that we're going to have them off. They probably think nothing of the sort but we're over-compensating with pleases, thank-yous and crinkles at strangers at the bar. We only stay for one.

The next place is a proper hotel in the middle of a traffic

island in the middle of outer Leeds. A few youths are playing pool. We sit down to gigantic platefuls of roast beef and Yorkshire pudding. I'll never say a thing about Yorkshire cuisine ever again. Once, years ago, in a chippie in Bradford, a little scamp came in Kes-stylee with mad, sticking-up hair and odd socks and asked for a pint of sausages. No joke. The woman behind the counter didn't blink. She fished out a pint pot and scooped it through a vat of hot-dog sausages, patting them firm to make room for one more which she slipped into a gap down the side. For years afterwards we've been scared to eat in Yorkshire – the Lost Continent. But this £4.95 roast dinner special is tremendous. We're too full for another drink afterwards, so we head for the ground. It's still early but Peter and Jegs need to get tickets.

We park up next to The Peacock, reminiscing none-too-fondly that, not long ago, this whole pre-match scenario would've been unthinkable. Leeds were fanatical hooligans, they always seemed to have thousands skulking round before the game and for Liverpool it was very much a case of sticking together – especially if you'd come on the train. It's a long, long walk from the city centre out to Elland Road and it's not a walk which is planted with boulevards and inviting hostelries – it's one barren industrial estate after another, the better for aggro-crazy Leeds zealots to ambush you. The last thing you'd have on your mind is an idle half-hour on the wall outside The Peacock while your pals get their tickets organised. But that's how it's been for a few seasons, now. There are so many fans dawdling around in replica shirts, eating chips and pints of sausages that the old menace of cruel Elland Road has vanished into the ether. We can't agree upon whether this is a good or a bad thing and just to keep us on our toes a moody little firm of ten or twelve boys, two of whom look like mini Brian Deanes, come jostling through, bumping into red-shirted fanclub members.

Like all good fanclub members, these guys have impressive

sideburns. They all look like outsized Robbie Williamses. They have grown-out Oasis suedes or young-but-bald crops. They wear Liverpool shirts, sloppy jeans, bad training-shoes and James Dean-style zip-up blouson jackets. They have *very* impressive sideburns.

We make a pathetic attempt at bluffing our way into the hospitality lounge as guests of Burtons but, having got past the difficult bit we have to give our names to a frightening old man with a clipboard. Once I've dragged my eyes away from his remarkable, liverish, almost o-shaped nose – it actually takes its leave from his face and arcs up and over on itself, joining his kite again just above his top lip – I tell him I'm James Brown, the raffish editor of the *Gentleman's Quarterly*.

'Lak chuff you are!' spits the old boy. 'Ah knorr Jems Brown!'

We leave gracefully. We spot Puffa. If he doesn't know the latest ticket situation, nobody will. He points out a patient gathering of 70 or 80 and tells us there's definitely going to be a pay gate. They don't know how many'll be let in, but it won't be many. Peter and Jegs go off to queue, shaking their heads at the miracle of a rumour steeped in truth. For decades we've turned up at places, assured that there's some local bye-law which stipulates 100 peasants have to be let in free; or a pay-gate must be in operation for 30 minutes on a Sunday; or that any person presenting themselves at 13 minutes past one with a brace of hare has to be allowed into the ground. Of course none of these rumours is ever true. As Peter and Jegs get closer and closer to the turnstile, you can see them tensing up, ready for a steward to jump out and shout:

'Sorry! Full up! That's your lot!'

Danny and I have a pint inside the ground, chatting to Nicky Holt, Terry Miles and a couple of lads who were on our plane to the PSG game. We're laughing at the latest news that Oyvind Leonhardsen, who has never been injured in his entire professional career, might now be out until New Year, having aggravated his thigh in training. The road is not rising with us, just now.

We've got excellent seats. We're right behind the goal, in the middle, on Row 1 of the Upper Tier. Couldn't be better. Liverpool warm up. McManaman applauds the crowd and gets a good hand back. A good few start up his song, to the Muppets tune. No player on God's earth has more songs about him than Steve McManaman. There's Garner's song, a rousing tearjerker set to the chorus of *The Boxer*:

> *Mac-mah-nah-man*
> *Nar-nanarnarnar-nanar*
> *Mac-mah-nah-man . . .*

and so on. And then there's the one, launched on the eve of the 1996 Cup Final, set to the *Addams Family*:

> *He's skinny and he's nippy*
> *He looks just like a hippy*
> *The runs he makes are tricky*
> *He's Steve McManaman –*
> *Mac-manaman (click-click)*
> *Mac-manaman (click-click)*

and so on, too. Clapping is acceptable in place of clicking for the two beats.

None of these has really caught on inside the ground, though. They're drunk-in-the-Albert songs, so it's good to see this Muppet one starting to get going properly, because it's been bubbling around for years. The game kicks off. Wouldantcha just know it – there's two empty seats next to Danny and me. It would've been good to have Hooto and Jegsy next to us, but 15 minutes into the game the seats are taken up by a woman of about 20 and a man who may or may not be her dad.

The girl is wearing the yellow away shirt which we haven't actually had a chance to wear yet. We're in red again tonight. She has an orange-ish tan, but on top of this tan, on her face, she has applied generous quantities of Oriflame-type foundation. Her hair is orange. She is a smouldering orange fireball of a fan and she makes up for lost time as soon as Michael Owen nips in on goal.

'Go on Mikey! Go on babe! Good babe, Mikey! Good babe! Oh you big bald fuckin bastard Molenaar! Ref! He fetched him ovver! He fetched him fuckin ovver!'

She continues like this relentlessly until that piss-poor marksman Steve McManaman drags a shot which was never on right across Nigel Martyn and just inside his net at the far post from a ridiculous angle. It doesn't look spectacular, but it's a wonder goal. 1–0 to us! Let's see if we can hang on this time.

Leeds don't really put us under, but nerves keep the debauched utterances of Ms Orange to a minimum in the second half. Jimmy Floyd Hasselbaink manages to turn on a spoon and stab a shot goalwards, but somehow David James gets down to it and keeps it out. He's the best shot-stopper in the world, James. If he could just learn when to come for the ball and when to leave it to his defence he'd be up there with Schmeichel. There again, it can't be too confidence-building for the bloke who has to keep goal behind those domineering centre-backs of ours, renowned for their tight marking and incisive tackling. Small wonder he sometimes feels the need to rush out and do their job, too.

From that save we push upfield. Karlheinz Riedle runs with the ball. The Leeds defence keep backing off and backing off. Riedle drops his shoulder and darts at the angle of the box, cuts back inside and draws Martyn off his line. With a lazy, dismissive clip he lifts the ball over Martyn. For a second it looks as though it will clear the crossbar, too, but he's put a lovely topspin on it and it drops into the net right in front of us. Danny, the orange girl, her dad and me are all hugging each other, dancing round in a little circle. We break for air, but I feel I have more hugs in me, yet, and I set about hugging a large man behind me who has been encouraging the team throughout – a patient and shrewd observer, who is now rewarded with an overpowering bearhug from a chap he's never met before.

For the remaining eight minutes or so, our whole end keeps up a chorus of Riedle's name to the old Alun Evans tune, *Kiss Him Goodbye*:

> *Na-na-na-na*
> *Hey-hey!*
> *Karlheinz Riedle . . .*

I believe the supergroup Bananarama might have released a cover version of the song at some point. We keep the Riedle chorus going until full-time. A 2–0 win at Leeds! Jolly good show. The season hath commenced. We clap the lads off and dash out to the car, hoping the other two are there. They're not long. We nudge our way out of the car-park, through the congestion onto the M62 and we're away while Radio 5 are still going on about Riedle's wonder-strike. I thought McManaman's was better, or more difficult, at least – but who gives a toss.

We're approaching Saddleworth Moor and it's after 10.30. This could be our last chance of a drink, so we pull off and follow a winding dirt-track over the bleak moorland. There's no sign of a pub anywhere. Jegs says he can't turn around, he'll have to carry on until we find a side road or something. The road takes a mad, sudden dip and as it flattens out there's a dark, game-poachers' inn nestling before us in an asphalt car-park. Is it an inn? Is it open? There don't appear to be any lights on. Are dark happenings taking place inside?

Not half. The lighting is subdued and mellow while a scrum of merry diners complete their meals. In the pub part, empty fireplaces remind us it's still August. There's a snug which announces itself as the Ghost Story Parlour. Two very intelligent-looking, very beautiful women sit on the Yorkstone bunks by the hearth, drinking pints. One of them has a totally unnecessary piece of purple cheesecloth tied around her throat. I have half an impulse to be chirpy with them but they're deep in conversation. Why should they want to start up a conversation with a total stranger at 10.48 p.m? Back in my apologetic-for-being-a-football-fan frame of mind I ask them if they mind if the large table becomes occupied by men with extremely short hair.

'It usually is,' smiles one of the women.

We talk football. The women sup up and leave. We talk sex. Jegs is pressurised into recounting yet more of his implausible romantic scenarios. I'm not sure I believe he's 39. He looks 59. A year or so back he used to wear a T-shirt with a picture of Sid James on. A girl who didn't know him that well said:

'Isn't that Jegsy Dodd a big-headed git going round wearing a T-shirt of himself . . .'

His latest escapade involves plastic boots and a Russian hat. Lawd knows what they see in him, unless they want the benefit of his experience – which, at 59, I have to allow, must be *considerable*.

There are only two males, one of whom is the manager, and the girl who's been serving behind the bar left. The manager, whose voice has become slightly camp since the last of his diners departed, comes into the snug.

'Do I hear Scouse axe-sents?' he lisps, sounding like Lily Savage. He used to be manager of Michel Claire, a legendary Liverpool 'alternative' club of the early '80s. He loves Liverpool. He's doing very well up here on the moors, the dining business is phenomenal, but he finds it quite boring. We can stay and have a drink if we want. We want.

Jegsy, who is the David James of namekeeping, tells the

barmaid that Peter Hooton was in The Farm. She scrutinises him.

'He weren't.'

'He was.'

'Nah.'

She points at me.

'HE were in Farm.'

I wasn't. There's much ribaldry and leg-pulling. Jegsy persists about The Farm, in spite of Hooto's furious blushing. The barmaid has the solution.

'All right then, prove it! Sing *Don't You Want Me!*'

This is not unlike asking, say, Kevin Rowland to prove he was in Dexy's by asking him to rattle off *Jackie Wilson Said* – in other words, an ideal moment to leave. The lovely staff tell us we can come back anytime and we promise to do so. We all go to the toilet except Danny, who inexplicably has a pee in the car-park 90 seconds later. Still, three points and a phantom pop-star accusation. Mustn't grumble. Actually looking forward to reading the papers in the morning.

29 AUGUST 1997

Birkenhead Park

Sweltering sunshine. Glorious. Worst turnout for ages. It seems that the better the weather the less devotees turn up. A lot of the younger element, Terry, Wally, Adam and co., prefer to amble down to the beach or just sit around the park drinking cans and ogling girls when the sun comes out. They need to take their careers more seriously, these young lads.

There's a queer rumour, too, that Blackie's 'doing a gig'. The famously workshy Half Man Half Biscuit are notoriously reluctant to 'do gigs' – a couple a year, nicely spread out seems to suffice, but August isn't usually one of their months. Jegsy must've got it wrong.

As it is, we scrape together a five against five, Liverpool v. Birkenhead game. Paul Murphy arrives after 20 minutes with his lad, so we split them one on each side. That extra pair of legs really makes a difference in this heat. It's even-Stevens for ages but Jegs misses some tremendous chances and the pace of the 15-year-old Little Murphy starts to tell. Murphy's boy has a brilliant turn of pace, something he seems to use to best effect when he's not on my side. The new, calmer player I promised I'd become if I ever made it back onto the pitch again after the broken rib scenario is rapidly burning up in the scalding late-August sun. I've tried hard to hold my tongue these past couple of weeks, but it's not easy. Watching from the sidelines all those weeks, I saw the folly of taking our little Friday kickabout at all seriously. If God wills it that I should ever play again, I thought, I shall reward Him by praising and prompting and encouraging my fellow players. I shall not shout. I shall not berate. I shall not. But, God, it's hot today! Jegsy's through for another tap-in. He does a Terry Cooper 'Jus' Lak That!' thing with his hands and approaches the ball, slowly and carefully, as though he's going to do something sensational with it. He makes a strange banana shape out of his foot and, steadying himself, all the time in the world, pats effetely at the ball with the curved outside of his foot. His shot goes approximately six feet wide.

'Need to stick those away, Jegs!' I mutter, face blisteringly red, brain pounding.

It's still seven-all. There's about five minutes left, but with Boulter in charge of timekeeping you might as well allow for ten so that his side can win. Jegs refuses to come back and play in goal. It's killingly hot. He smokes 20 a day and two or three per night. He's knackered. He's never going to score. Not if he keeps bending his foot like that and pushing it at the ball like it's going to electrocute him.

We cave in. I try a cross-field, defence-immobilising pass which falls directly to Peter Hooton. He exchanges passes with Little Murphy and sends Treeman the wrong way. Liverpool win 11–8 and I end up screaming Schmeichel-style at my fatigued team-mates – always a sign that I've had a crap game. It's good to be back. The sides were: Liverpool – Roy, Peter, Liam, Mick Duffy, Mick Potter and Little Murphy against Birkenhead – Jegs, Charlie, Dool, Treeman, Murphy and me. Danny, still working on the new Conway Park train station and unable to play regularly, trots up at full time and tells us Liverpool have drawn Celtic in the UEFA Cup. What a draw! Jegs and I, still arguing over which of us should never run out onto a football pitch ever again, jump for joy and envelop each other in hugs. Fuck the Friday kickabout – Celtic, away! The first leg's on 16 September. Can't wait!

31 AUGUST 1997

Newcastle, home

How did I allow this to happen? I'll tell you how. A stupid cock-up over dates is how, devilishly conjured by the evil Roy Boulter. It is Saturday, 30 August and, having set off at 6 ay em, I am now in Polperro, Cornwall, dangling a crab-line into a rockpool and listening to David Mellor's marvellous *Six-o-Six* in the still-warm slow-burning sunshine of the last weekend in August. Say what you want about David Mellor, but his phone-in is head, shoulders and dandruff above the rest of the competition. Being a national show has its advantages, of course – you get a better spread of nutters calling in to complain about Gillingham's cold pies and F.C. Globo Marlborough's cynical ticket pricing for away fans – but, most importantly, Mellor himself is a brilliant host. He's a good combination of chummy, pompous, serious and witty. And I love the way he says Manshunited. In other circumstances, this would be paradise. In circumstances, say, where Liverpool were not playing a crucial fixture for which I've been diddled out of my ticket.

Tomorrow Liverpool play Newcastle at home. I shall miss the match. I shall be here in Cornwall, the victim of a devious plot to trick me out of my ticket by Roy Boulter and his scheming pal John the Geordie. John the Geordie will be in my seat, watching one of the annual highlights of the League calendar. What price another 4–3 sizzler? Meanwhile, I shall be terrorising the crab colonies of the south-west, hell-bent on revenge for Roy's mischief.

I remember his necromancy well. It came after I'd stood smouldering on the sidelines through a hot, stuffy 9–7 win for Birkenhead one Friday back in June. We were sat in the perfumed gardens of The Shrewsbury pub in Birkenhead's elegant Oxton district. Roy and I were trying to work out the weird stop-start first couple of months of the new League fixtures calendar and, importantly, trying to work out where holidays could be squeezed in.

'Yes,' he'd said. Or '*yep*'. It was 'yep'.

That was how he got me. 'Yep'. Simple, but devastating in the hands of a master ticket-swindler. I was hot and confused, trying to make sense of when games would take place and when they'd be postponed. It struck me that I could work backwards from England's fixtures. If England were playing, the programme for the weekend before would be postponed. That's the way it goes, isn't it? But I was certain I'd read that England were playing their last home qualifier on a Saturday, to guarantee a full and noisy Wembley. Roy used this to full and devastating advantage.

'England play Moldova on the . . . 6 September, right?'

'Yep,' said Roy. He was definite. He said it with unshakeable self-assurance. Thief.

'So who do we play the game before that?'

'Newcastle,' said Roy, sucking me into his trap.

'So Newcastle'll be postponed, won't it?'

I don't know how he controlled himself. How he managed to prevent himself from jumping up on the table and shouting:

'Ye-ess!! Gotcha!! Swiped your ticket for John the Geordie!!'

Instead he stayed dead-calm and said:

'Yep.'

So I went and booked a week in the beautifully appointed Treble B Caravan Park near Looe, Cornwall, from 30 August, only to discover much, much later that Liverpool would indeed play Newcastle in front of a slavering TV audience on Sunday 31st. The England squad would assemble immediately afterwards to commence preparations for their game against Moldova on Wednesday, the thieving, robbing, conniving, no-good, hard faced, cheeky 10th of September.

So I'm listening to the *Six–o–Six* with extra poignancy. This must be what it's like for loads and loads of fans who love football but can't get to games, for whatever reason. They must cling to weekly events like Mellor's show, *Match of the Day* and *Football Focus* to satisfy their craving. It's awful. You're so far away, so helpless. I'll never be mean about out-of-town supporters again. I'll be actively nice to them – so long as they don't boo. And as for you, John the Geordie, sitting in my seat tomorrow, I hope we stuff you 5–0.

I watch *Match of the Day*, sober, and cringe at the new opening sequence which I'm seeing, really, for the first time. Whose idea was that? Embarrassingly long close-ups of Teddy Sheringham, Sol Campbell and our own sainted Robbie Fowler staring moodily into the lens. This is a horrible new trait, this Cult of Close-up. I have to look away. It's uncomfortable enough on Sky's *Super Sunday Football* when they sneak up to the dugout and hold the camera up to the side of Jim Smith's head for one entire, endless, excruciating minute as he tries to pretend they're not there by chewing more intently and scrutinising a Christian Dailly back-pass as though it would reveal secret naked breasts if he stared a bit harder. But this new *MOTD* sequence is truly unwatchable. It's only safe to pop your head from under the cushion once Nice Des Lynam is well into his third alliterative sentence.

I sleep fitfully, scoring only one hat-trick against Newcastle and a scrambled winner from a saved penalty against Man. U. If you're going to dream, you might as well dream big. I get up to watch the early morning re-run of *Match of the Day*, minus the titles. Weird. BBC are showing not the highlights of Blighty's finest in footballing combat, but one still-life of a billowing field of daffodils underscored by elegiac violins. Then the caption comes up. All programmes suspended. Princess Diana was killed earlier this morning. It takes a moment to sink in. The wording makes it sound like she's been assassinated. I flick round the channels for more detail, but there's nothing. My mind's a riot. I allow dark thought after dark thought, culminating in one shameful, deliciously shameful notion. And it's this: maybe today's game will be postponed. Maybe it will. I mean, it *could* be. I spend the period between 4.00 p.m. and 6.59 p.m. in a state of near hyperventilation, trying to get the commentary on Radio 5. All I get is a gut-curdling selection of Her favourite music. Each to their own and that, but she didn't half listen to some cack. At seven bells, finally, they put me out of my misery. Someone mentions as an aside during the news bulletin that today's programme of sporting events has been postponed out of respect. Tremendous. Every cloud has a silver lining.

13 SEPTEMBER 1997

Sheffield Wednesday, home

So. England hammered Moldova 4–0. Easy. Could've been more. And poor, feeble Italy could only draw with Georgia. Very, very interesting. Sets it up nicely for the decider in Rome. England need only draw to qualify, but Incey and co. are giving out bullish interviews saying we'll be going there for a win. Good luck.

For now, though, it's the fantastically average prospect of a dull, routine, almost event-free one-goal victory against Sheffield Wednesday, as happens every year. We only ever beat them by one goal at home, and the game is always crap. To safeguard this foregone conclusion, however, I need to take various precautions. One is that I'm giving up pre-match betting. I don't know why I didn't do this earlier. When you bet on the outcome, the score or the first goalscorer, you find yourself watching the match *willing* certain individuals to miss. You're actually militating against your own team. And if you've bet, say, a final score of 3–0 and McManaman's bearing down the right flank with Riedle and Owen unmarked in the box and the score's still sitting nicely at 3–0, you're thinking terrible, dire things. You'd rather the likes of David Unsworth – a horrible footballer – gets in one of his unnecessarily robust slide tackles and the undeserved acclaim that goes with it than see McManaman bodyswerve him, leave him on his rhinoceros-like backside and pull the ball back perfectly for little Owen to score. In short, in spite of yourself, you find yourself compromised if you bet. So I'm not betting, today or any other day. I don't care who scores first. Just so long as it's us.

Lots of mad things have happened since we last played. Jason McAteer has been told he can leave – provided it's to a suitable (i.e. overseas) team – then declared his future to Liverpool. This is good news. McAteer never has a bad game.

He loves playing for Liverpool. He had some sidetracking worries last season, family problems, but he still gave his all. He's the sort we definitely want in the team.

Meanwhile, Ravanelli, after travelling to Goodison to be bamboozled by their state-of-the-art training facilities – Howard Kendall was certain that Bellfield's gravel running-track'd be the ace in the pack that'd convince Ravanelli of Everton's Big Thinking – has turned down the Toffees. They're not a big enough club. He's off to Marseille.

Liverpool, on the advice of Paul Ince, have tried and failed to sign Massimo Paganin from Inter. Paganin has opted for a move to Bologna, justifying it thus:

'Bologna came in and put the money on a plate for me.'

May he enjoy every mouthful and may he be nutmegged humiliatingly by Steve 'New Five Year Contract' McManaman in next year's Champions League Final, a manoeuvre that leads directly to Liverpool's winning goal. Not that Bologna'll get anywhere near the Champions League.

One who *has* signed for Liverpool, allegedly, is Oyvind Leonhardsen. This is a player who was coveted by every Premier League team last season. Alex Ferguson speaks in glowing terms of him – but then most of Alex's words glow from the heat of his BIG RED NOSE. There was widespread relief and joyousness when we finally signed The Energiser to fill one of the vacant berths in our new, all-hustling midfield. But that was the last we ever heard of him. Not only has he traipsed from one niggling injury to another – always snaggy, six-week jobs: strains, pulls, bruises – but his very presence here at the temple of the four times European Champions is now causing much mirth and headscratching over in his homeland. One Oslo-based journalist, quoted in the *Guardian*, suggests that Liverpool have signed a hearty but ineffectual player who will struggle to make the Norway squad for the World Cup. Thanks, buddy. We don't care what you think. Leonhardsen is going to be a revelation for Liverpool.

Without bets to place, we're in our seats early. The Nuisance apart, there's a nice crowd in the seats immediately around us. Behind Roy sits Nice Scottish Man, an astute football-watcher who doesn't shout too much one way or the other. He doesn't barrack. He doesn't really cheer, either. When he does make a comment, he gets it right. Next to me sit The Boffins. There can be no ambiguity, here. These boys work in computers. They're both about 28, although they have the open, bespectacled faces of 18-year-olds. The only thing that gives the game away is that they're bald as osprey eggs. There's no way they don't work in computers. Nice lads.

Next to Roy sits The Bon Viveur and his two twenty-something sons. The Bon Viveur has an instantly likeable face. Ruddy, ironic, ready with a quip, he's about 50, silver-haired and very, very fat. He always looks as though he has just completed, or is just about to tuck into a medieval banquet, with lashings of red wine staining his neat Guy Fawkes beard. His lips are permanently moist with duck grease, or through his regular licking of them as he contemplates his next meal. He's a fellow who'd be at home with a side of venison; he'd know how to set about a crab or a lobster. He wouldn't mind spilling a bit on his cashmere coat. And that's another thing about The Bon Viveur – he must have a few bob. On five separate occasions in the past year his boys – very pleasant kids, don't get me wrong – have been accompanied to the match by supermodels. What we're saying here is that these are, you know, ordinary-looking boys on the arms of staggering, long-legged killer babes – and there has to be some rationale for that. The boys are . . . great fun. They are. They're funny. But their girls . . . their girls are spectacular. These lads aren't *that* funny. It takes a lot to distract Roy from the feast on the field, but it's fair to say he nearly choked the first time the Sons of Bon swanned in with their molls.

I mean, how can I put this . . . their dad's fat, right. He's very jolly, great company, very rotund. And his boys take after him in all of that. Quite often The Bon Viveur will jump up in the air waving his betting slip, shouting YISS!!, very enthusiastically. He'll then reveal that he's put £100 on Mark Wright to score the first goal. He does this regularly. He's. Not. Skint. Yes? They're. His. Sons. Get the picture? Ah, forget it. His two rich, fat, plain sons were again in the company of porno stars for the Sheffield Wednesday game.

David Pleat has sent out a team hell-bent on frustration. It worked a treat for Wednesday last year, when Peter Atherton – I think it was him – followed McManaman everywhere, tugging his shorts down if he managed to get past him. It works a treat this time, too, until Ince prods home a rebound from a scrappy flurry of boots. We're more relaxed now and on 70 minutes Michael Thomas sweeps in a gorgeous first time left-footer to make it 2–0. We're actually 2–0 up at home to Sheffield Wednesday, with 20 minutes still to play. We should take them apart now. They're a beaten team. There's no point sitting back against a team like Wednesday because they're not going to come at us, anyway. We may as well do our goal difference a favour.

But no. We succumb to the recent ailment. We stop pressurising Wednesday and, unable to believe their good fortune at being let off the rack, they mount a half-hearted sortie into our half. With eight minutes remaining Wayne Allison pulls a goal back. 2–1. It's a long, tense, final 15 minutes – there are hardly any stoppages for injury but we play 97 minutes for good measure – and the relief that greets the final whistle is palpable. Another win, then. Two in a row. We've been utterly unconvincing today, but we're starting to chalk up a few points and move up the table. If we can keep the momentum going until Fowler, Redknapp and Leonhardsen come back then things might warm up a little. For now, I'll take the points and forget about this one. It's Celtic on Tuesday.

14 SEPTEMBER 1997

Ashton Park, West Kirby

I'm enjoying the privilege afforded to parents the world over, the Sunday morning kickabout with my wee boy, Joe, who's seven, and his pal Tommy Russell. Actually I'm not enjoying it one little bit. Tom, a ringer for an Evertonian Milky Bar Kid in his blue kit and specs, is grinning joyfully:

'Liverpool got beat at home by Leicester! Liverpool are rubbish!'

'Ho-ho, Tom. Don't be silly! It's early days, yet! Besides, isn't that Everton I see propping up the League table? Good to see them taking up their traditional position good and early, this year . . .'

'Everton always beat Liverpool! Liverpool are rubbish!'

He goes to dribble past me and is sent sprawling into the mud by a body-check Garrincha would've been proud of.

16 SEPTEMBER 1997

Celtic, away (UEFA Cup, 1st Round, 1st Leg)

Ah, the silliness of it all. The pure, wonderful, inexplicable silliness of being old enough to know better, old enough to do sensible, responsible, grown-up things but to still be turned on and psyched-up to meltdown point by the prospect of Liverpool's latest European jaunt. I love these trips. I live for them. Okay, Glasgow is hardly the exotic destination of Euro fantasy games. You live in hope of a latter-round tussle with Lazio or Atletico Madrid, but any game against Celtic, in any competition, is a Big Game. It's one to get the pulse throbbing and it's one we've been looking forward to like impatient children.

It's a full turnout for this trip. Among the impatient children assembled in the Costa coffee shop, Lime Street station concourse, in good time for the 7.38 (change at Wigan North Western) are Danny, Jegsy, Peter Hooton, Mick Potter, Roy and Gag. There's nothing to match those first few moments of a big away trip when everybody's meeting up, there's a new arrival every minute, jokes and tall stories are flying around and everybody is everybody else's best friend. It's like going on holiday. Real life is put on hold for a short while.

The train journey flies by. Gag, so called because he's a great laugh, impresses me with his knowledge of different types of fresh water fishing bait (I told him about the Blackburn trout-mesmerising cult), while Mick Potter harps on about his disastrous love life. Finding himself unexpectedly single has taken its toll on this hopeless romantic. Potter is an ex-hardman who wants to buy women flowers and recite poetry to them – but all they seem to want is a tough guy who'll look after them. He's tried the Reg Holdsworth look, to no avail – the cravat gave him an even more menacing demeanour. He's thinking of becoming a tough guy again.

We arrive at Glasgow Central, check into The Charing Cross Tower Hotel and dive over the road to The Baby Grand for a quick pint while the rain subsides. The rain doesn't subside. It gets heavier. We stay in The Baby Grand for an early scran – plenty of potatoes for me, a notorious lightweight when it comes to all-day drinking. Murphy and Clive arrive to raucous applause. They've driven up in three hours flat, which is nifty jockeying indeed. Jegsy hangs his banner from wall to wall – it's about 15 feet long, a good old Liver Bird flag in the finest traditions. Mick and Danny succumb to the Jameson's at twenty past one. They start singing at five to two.

I know I'm getting tipsy. I enter into an involved debate with Clive about Liverpool's defensive formation. He's a fan of

4–4–2, so we're not too far apart on that – I prefer 4–1–3–2 – but Clive is a devout Kvarme fan. I'm not one for disowning or campaigning against individual players. As fans, whoever the manager picks, you have to get on with it and support the team. Privately, I fear young Kvarme needs to take more responsibility. You start to win things when most of your team are capable of taking the fate of the game into their own hands – taking responsibility. This is the point I'm drunkenly preaching to Clive. He started the conversation and he can't move until he agrees with me. Using cigarette butts as players I illustrate to the poor lad, whose time is precious, how Kvarme's unwillingness to bring the ball forward leads to Liverpool putting themselves under needless pressure. He is, in fact, guilty of Tommy Vialli Syndrome, giving onrushing opposing forwards hope of some crumb of comfort. They know it's worth their while pressurising him. Clive submits out of sheer boredom and makes good his escape.

Jegsy is lugging round a portable DAT recorder, hoping for some rousing pre-match golden oldies for his Red Anthems CD. Unfortunately he has neglected to find out how this complex piece of apparatus works. In a rare outbreak of foresight, I see that not only will he never get the contraption going, but he will be burdened with it all day and will, in all probability, leave it in a snug somewhere in east Glasgow. I persuade him to return his devilish machinery to the hotel and settle, instead, to the task of roaring on The Reds.

We take cabs down to Baird's bar in the Gallowgate. The driver tells us that the match may yet be postponed. The rain is unstinting, the ground is under an inch of water and there's going to be a 5 p.m. pitch inspection. It's about 4 p.m. now.

Baird's is a time-served, dyed green Celtic bar, as great a part of the Glasgow Celtic tradition as The Albert on Walton Breck Road is a part of Liverpool's folklore. Nobody 'takes' Baird's, not even with friendly fire, and, regardless of the good relations between Liverpool and Celtic fans, it's not recommended to go singing the songs of other teams in this place.

So what we do is we go in, The Deficient Seven, hang the flag between two wall lights, and sing many-versed songs about the Liver Bird upon our chests. It takes less than a minute for an ice-cube to whistle past Potter's head, and another minute for a diminutive, genuinely outraged barman to march over and remove the flag from the wall. A game of cat and mouse ensues. We wait for him to get right back behind the bar then shove the flag back up again. A minute later he comes back over and pulls it down. In between times, when we're singing, he sends ultrasonic ice-cubes socking into the back of our heads. The local boys, who outnumber us ten to one even at this early stage, eye us with suspicion. They give us a few minutes to get it all out of our systems then drown us out while they find their range with a couple of old standards.

'We are Celtic supporters, we will follow you . . .'

They're loud. We're drunk. It seems like a good time for some of the old European numbers, just to remind the Celts that they're in the company of Greatness here – four European Cups to their paltry lone success. So there we are, harmonising 'A Scouser In Gay Paree' when, 'allo 'allo – he's here! It's our first Tune-In of the season. Hello, Tommy, and welcome! Tommy Tune-In is a person, almost always alone, who just . . . *joins* your gang. One minute he's not there, the next he's your leader, right in the thick of it, leading the singing – almost always, too, with the wrong words. Today's Tune-In is an excellent fellow, a young lad in a Liverpool shirt who's ready to stand up on tables for the cause and take his share of nuclear ice-cubes. The angry barman gets him right on the side of his ear, causing him to howl with pain and dance a raindance, hopping from one foot to another, as if it'd miraculously cause an ear graft. Tommy Tune-In is gone as quickly and as mysteriously as he arrived.

Baird's is heaving. Hooton goes next door to find his friend

Sandy, a piper in the popular Peatdiggers ensemble. Sandy brings news that the match is definitely on, and is enveloped with sloppy hugs and kisses and offers of drinks. He points out, very practically, that we're a good two miles from the ground and taxis, at this time on match night, are an impossibility. He suggests we walk to a less-packed bar about 15 minutes away, a sort of halfway house where we can take stock and cater to our individual needs with things like pies and soothing unctions for ice-cube welts. We wave a cheery farewell to Mr Angry and head off to This Bar.

Standing with Jegs outside This Bar in the now tropical rain – no idea what the place was called, very inebriated indeed – I witness a surreal sight. Mick Potter, Danny and Murphy are walking by on the other side of the road, singing lustily. It's them. It is. I'd recognise Danny's walk anywhere, Murphy always sings out of the side of his mouth and Potter always has his telescopic chin in Cagney position. And yet . . . how can it be them when they're here, with me, in this halfway-to-paradise bar?

'Zegs,' I say, tugging at Jegs. 'There's Potterandat . . .'

He shouts them over. It is them. They are not with me in This Bar and have not, indeed, been in our company since they left Baird's in search of a chippy an hour ago. They point out that the game starts in 40 minutes. Sheltering from the downpour under the flag, we trudge through mudflats and paddy-fields until we reach Celtic Park and designate an after-match meeting place, for the very likely eventuality that we get split up from each other.

Mick and Danny head for a different turnstile to the rest of us. It is to be Mick's last few moments of liberty in Glasgow. Stopped in a random check-up by the match police, he's asked if he has been drinking. Mick laughs.

'Of course I have!'

The officer asks him if he knows it's an offence to be intoxicated at a football match in Scotland.

'You must be awful busy,' quips Potter. This is more than enough for the zealous copper, who hauls Mick off to repent in the cells at leisure.

There are 3,700 Reds inside the ground – our full allocation – in full, tonsilitic throttle. The Celtic crowd, notoriously partisan, are a bit subdued until the teams step out onto the pitch. But then, suddenly, what a noise! It truly does feel as though your eardrums are going to burst. The new Celtic Park is not fully up to capacity yet, but there's over 40,000 here and it's an atmosphere without parallel. There's no way that, say, Barca v. Real, even with 120,000 in the stadium, can generate more noise than this. We start off *You'll Never Walk Alone* but the Celts drown it out with their own passionate version. They sing it a bit too quick, so they're finished before us. We just keep it going, nice and slowly, thousands of red scarves and flags lighting up that corner of the ground. It's one of the most beautiful renditions of the anthem I've ever heard. McManaman applauds when it's over. Kick-off time. A roar to put the fear of Satan into anyone, and we're off.

The match is bizarre. If anything the crowd's volume seems to paralyse Celtic, instead of Liverpool. We're quickly into our stride, knocking the ball about and running into space. The overwhelming impression from that first half is of vast expanses of green space for Owen and Macca to drift through, unchallenged. It turned out to be a quintessential game of contrasts, although those busy Glasgow revisionists, past-masters of self-delusion, have long since re-packaged this, and the return leg at Anfield, as an all-time TOJ (Travesty Of Justice). It seems they hammered Liverpool from the first to the 180th minute, with ne'ery a let-up in their pulverising, attacking football.

Not quite. We murder Celtic first half. Michael Owen speeds through the Celtic backline as though they're not there, to score with now typical aplomb. We're denied a penalty and we're cutting through their defence at will. McManaman can do whatever he wants. The Celtic crowd are stunned into absolute silence while we dance and sing in the rain. This is fantastic. This is why you get up at 4.30 a.m. to come to games like this. You dream of nights in Europe when your team are, by any standards, a class apart. This is one of those nights. Everyone around me is delirious. Celtic are relieved to hear the half-time whistle.

At half-time I run around the refreshment area, bumping into people I haven't seen for ages, exchanging bear-hugs and assuring each other that this is the team that's going to lift us out of the doldrums. Michael Owen is compared to Jairzinho. The team is compared to France's 1984 side. Everybody is, of course, completely, marvellously pissed. I find Peter and Jegs, who think there might be unoccupied seats on the front row, right in front of the goal we're attacking. We head down there and drape Jegsy's flag over the front. It's a bit exposed, which is obviously why there are seats vacant, but the rain has now stopped and we're going to be in prime position for Liverpool's second half avalanche.

Which doesn't come. Celtic come out growling. This time it's us, team and fans, who are battered into submission. Celtic go close twice before Simon Donnelly's brought down by Matteo. Penalty. It looks an outrageous decision from our end of the ground, but when we see it again on TV it's pretty cut and dried. It's a penno. And they equalise. It's now a completely different game. Celtic are laying siege to our goal and the crowd noise is cranked up to unbearable volume. It's only a matter of time before they score again, Burley hooking in a difficult volley. Now, having looked like Didier Six's France, we look like Doncaster Rovers.

Somehow we weather the worst of the storm, due to a combination of heroic defending, two tremendous saves by David James and a couple of glaring misses. You can sense that Celtic have nothing left to offer. They've run themselves ragged. We're back making space, playing our football again. If there's going to be any further goals in the last five minutes, it'll be us doing the scoring. It's uncanny the way you develop a feel for these sorts of situations. Both Jegsy and I are utterly stone-cold certain that we're going to equalise. So certain are we, that we shuffle along the row to give ourselves a chance of hugging the triumphant goalscorer when he runs to celebrate with the crowd.

McManaman receives the ball in his own half. Everyone has seen the wonder goal a hundred times and everyone still marvels at it – grace, skill, tenacity and athleticism shaped into 12 fluent, determined, wonderful seconds of our lives. What McManaman did in those 12 seconds added something to people's lives. You can pay him no higher compliment. Each time I look back on that goal, I'm struck by the moment he decides, on the halfway line, to flick the ball on and let it do the work for him. That's the crucial moment of genius. If he'd stopped to control the ball and have a look at what was on for him, the game might have caught up with him. But he didn't. His instinct was to keep the ball moving, even though he wasn't sure how many men were back behind him. In doing that – and turning at the same time – he took out two Celtic defenders, both expecting him to kill the ball, each leaving the closing-down to the other. McManaman ghosted between the pair of them, accelerated away like a jaguar and, without needing to beat anyone else one-to-one he drifted on and past them all, cutting left and keeping left, getting a sight of goal and curling that delicious, spinning shot inside the goalie's right-hand post. What a fucking goal. Unbelievable.

We can't contain ourselves. Hugging each other just is not enough. We have to get to McManaman. So, it seems, do about 100 other jubilant Koppites. In slow motion, McManaman runs behind the goal, eyes crazed. He knows this is a Big Moment, not just in personal terms but for everyone who's here. He knows this goal, this moment, this feeling will be talked about for decades. We've got to get to him, get him on our shoulders, share the ecstasy with him. Jegsy bursts past the cordon of stewards. Four or five of them go after him, leaving me with a clear run on Macca. I'm over the asphalt perimeter track. McManaman's being mobbed by team-mates. They're maybe 20 feet away. I can do it! I can be the one who thanked Steve McManaman (Crap finisher. One-off.) for his wonder goal. Head down, I go into Six Million Dollar Man slow-motion, slipping on the wet grass but driving on towards my target. I can't hear anything. I'm vaguely aware of Jegsy getting hauled away, laughing hysterically, but my mind and my eye is on The Prize. Just a quick pat on the back for Stevie then . . . BOOMFF!! Where the ruddy heck did that come from??! It feels like I've been hit from the side by a runaway train. I fall heavily, poleaxed, slam-dunked onto the greasy turf by a hefty copper's high-velocity rugby tackle. He comes with me, all 16 stone of him landing hard on top of my ribcage. OOFF!! I can't breathe. He says something witty to me – honestly, he says something really funny, but I can't, no matter how often I try, recall what he said because at that moment another policeman comes over with my mangled spectacles, yet another asks me if I'm all right and another still points out that they're going to have to eject me. All of this seems to have taken a quarter of an hour, but as they run me down the ramp, shouting for the stewards to open the gates, Jegsy is only just ahead getting the same treatment. We collapse upon each other, laughing in the rain. Not because we think we've done anything heroic – we feel utterly stupid, especially as we're now missing out on the big party sing-song the travelling hordes are now enjoying. No, we're laughing out of delayed, shocked euphoria that McManaman has scored *that* goal right in front of our noses. We were here to see it. In our small, pathetic way, we've been part of another little bit of Liverpool history tonight.

We wait outside for the others. Peter has forgotten to bring the flag. I'm allowed back inside to look for it, but it's been zapped. We'll have to keep an eye out for it at the next home game and make a plucky citizen's seizure. Meanwhile, there's the small matter of Mick Potter, custodian of the constabulary. We make a few calls, but each telephonist tells us a different story. Mick knows where we're staying. Either he'll make it back there or he'll contact us himself.

The remainder of the evening is spent on Sauchiehall Street and in the hotel bar, reliving the spectacle of Liverpool's most hopeless finisher scoring one of the best goals any of us has ever seen. He'll never do it again, of course. But even if he doesn't score again all season – which he won't, for sure – he's given us something to treasure. Thank you, and goodnight, Mr Mac.

19 SEPTEMBER 1997

Birkenhead Park

Agony. Agony in triplicate.

(1) Having got back to a passable state of fitness after the broken ribs saga, I was hoping to last for more than three games. But no. The burly, rugby-tackling Glasgow cop has done for me good and proper. My quack seemed to take a perverse delight in telling me I've splintered open the healed-over cracked ribs again. It's going to take longer to heal them, this time. He won't specify how long. I could be out for the rest of the year. Verily, I am the Mark Wright of sub-standard park football.

(2) Sitting on the touchline, quite enjoying a not-bad game but feeling the jag of my ribs each time I draw breath deep

enough to shout, I flick through this morning's *Mirror*. Oh, Lordy. Will he ever learn? Stan Collymore, a man who truly was worshipped uncritically and unreservedly at Anfield, has come out, with immaculate timing just prior to Monday night's game against Villa, to tell the world about the pressures of conforming to the Liverpool way of life.

'I felt like I had to be some sort of Spice Boy', opined Stan. Dear, oh dear. We had him here for two years. He hadn't even played a game for us before he was marking out a niche for himself as Liverpool's Number One. Two weeks after signing in – a protracted, undignified spectacle in itself – from Nottingham Forest he was hosting a press conference at the ground for his new range of sportswear and leisure clothing. This new label would stand alongside Lacoste's crocodile and Nike's swoosh as a symbol of international verve and culture. These must-have garments were to be the epitome of casual sophistication, and would have a *soigné* brand-name to match, a name that would stand for elegance, style and class. They would call this range . . . Stan the Man.

Peter Hooton went along to the press launch of Stan the Man, hopeful of perhaps ending the day in one of their stylish cap-sleeved T-shirts. Steve McManaman, one of Stan's supposed mates from the England camp and one of the deciding factors in his signing for Liverpool, sat at the back with Robbie Fowler, giggling. It was good-natured mickey taking, Peter said, the sort of treatment anyone in Liverpool would expect from their pals. Stan, however, was unamused. He walked right past them at the end of the session, seemingly pretending he hadn't seen them, or else too angry at their childish behaviour to acknowledge them. So, before he'd even kicked a ball for Liverpool, he'd made a bed of nails for himself. He was a classic Bigtime Charlie and he was already on a collision course with his new team-mates.

Of course, the Liverpool fans loved him. He cost £8.5

million, didn't he, so while Rushie was still breaking every goalscoring record known to man and Robbie was slotting 30 goals a season with his eyes closed, Collymore was being lauded to the roof of The Kop. His was always the first name to be sung. No player ever received more encouragement. Even when things were going obviously, horribly wrong for him in the wake of his scrap with Tony Warner in Ireland, the crowd was with him. The body language between Stan and the team was saddening. On the rare occasions Stan scored, McManaman could hardly bring himself to make eye-to-eye contact, offering a curt handshake or a pat on the back. He had to go, Collymore. Although Roy Evans' comparisons with Ronaldo are far from fanciful – Collymore is pure dynamite when he's in full flow, bursting through defences, charging past challenge after challenge as though they're infant-school tackles – it seems evident that wherever Stan has played, his team-mates end up resenting him. Team spirit was non-existent during the supposed charge for the Championship last season. If we'd still had Rush and Fowler up front, there's no way we'd have been capitulating to the likes of Coventry at home. But Collymore's ailment affected everybody, eventually. No one wanted to play with him. And still the crowd chanted his name.

Today, he has made a major, major mistake. It sums up the infuriating thick-headedness of the man. We, Liverpool, play his team, Aston Villa, at our ground on Monday night. And today, Friday, he's launching an attack against Liverpool. He praises the fans for our support, too, and wishes he could have done more for us. But . . . what an idiot! Does he not know that by attacking the players and the culture of the city of Liverpool, he's attacking each and every one of us, too? It's agony to read. He's going to get murder on Monday night.

(3) And murder is how my ribs feel. I've just bent down to retrieve a runaway ball and I actually felt the click as well as

heard it. I'm stuck in a laughable puppet position, unable to straighten. I am almost crying, half with laughter, half through pain. If I ever play again, this time I WILL NOT SHOUT. That's now an official promise. And as for driving to Southampton tomorrow – forget it.

22 SEPTEMBER 1997

Aston Villa, home

I spend this game fluctuating from intense pain to near unconsciousness, so let's stick to the bare facts. We drew 1–1 at Southampton on Saturday after taking the lead through a Riedle flying header. Southampton should've won. Kevin Davies was superb. Robbie Fowler made his long-awaited return, coming on after an hour and very nearly scoring, but we swapped him for Mark Wright, who twisted his knee in the process of being turned inside out by Davies. It's a bad one. He'll be out until the New Year. Our search for a dominant central defender must now become the club's number one priority. If we don't bring someone in soon, we'll be facing the likes of Everton (Ferguson), Man. U (Sheringham) and West Ham (Hartson) with the most short-arsed defence in history.

It's 0–0 at half time tonight. Collymore's very few touches (he wishes he was back in Cannock) are booed, but not passionately. There's more of a sullen general feeling of having been let down by him. Danny Murphy, starting his first game, is excellent. He has a telepathic understanding with Owen, the sort which can't be honed on the training ground. It's just there. I'd give Murphy a start whenever Michael Owen plays. He's mustard. And Phil Babb, back in the side again, looks rock solid in his true position at left-central defence. Villa aren't going to get through us, tonight. All we need is that first goal and we'll marmalise them.

Robbie Fowler slots home after 56 minutes, neatly set up by Owen. 1–0. And then, what's this? Old shit-finisher's at it again. McManaman takes delivery just inside Villa's half and glides past two, three defenders, curling a low shot around the static, disbelieving Bosnich. How did he do that? Macca will definitely not score again this season. We must prepare ourselves for those staggering missed sitters which are undoubtedly just around the corner. We must be ready to be generous, even when he misses from two yards when we play Everton in a couple of weeks. We must remember his two glory goals this week and be thankful.

Owen, with devastating turn of pace and precocious manoeuvring and ball control inside a tiny scrap of space, takes the ball past Alan Wright – no mug! – and slips the ball back for Riedle to score. 3–0. Riedle's grin says it all – he's delighted to score, but he knows he's in the presence of genius with Owen. He didn't score tonight but he was electric. He's started the season expecting to be one of the extras rather than an ever-present star player. But he's as good as any of them. Robbie Fowler remains the most brilliant instinctive footballer I've seen since Dalglish. Fowler is breathtaking – there's nothing he can't do with a ball. But Owen is different again. He's like a combination of Dalglish and Rush. He has Dalglish's almost unearthly control over the ball, bending it to his will in impossibly pressurised situations, and Rush's devastating speed of thought along with his cool, dead-eyed certainty in front of goal. Give Owen a chance and he will score. It's as simple as that.

I feel sorry for Collymore trudging off, dispirited, and for Brian Little, who always interviews well and whose team is not far off being a great side. Draper's a class player. He's Quality.

If they build a team around him, instead of pandering to Stan the Man, they won't go far wrong. It's not just the touchy ribs making me sensitive, either. I do genuinely hope that Collymore makes something of his extravagant talent. But to achieve anything like his potential, you feel, he has to start owning, and then mastering his demons. Interviewed later, Collymore describes his treatment by the crowd tonight as his lowest moment in football. He's baffling. He won't understand or accept that he, in some way, has contributed to his own downfall. It's not fair. It's not his fault. In his own tortured mind he gave us everything he had as a Liverpool player. But he didn't. He never did. It's infuriating that he won't acknowledge any of this. Regardless, you can't help feeling for the fallen idol.

30 SEPTEMBER 1997

Celtic, home (UEFA Cup, 1st Round, 2nd Leg)

Saturday was the most disappointing result of the season. West Ham looked lively, but once Robbie Fowler equalised Hartson's tap-in, there was only going to be one winner. We hammered the Hammers, chance after chance went begging. Riedle flung himself into a diving header that had everyone out of their seats before the ball bent, at the last second, just around the post. You have to tuck your chances away and it was no real surprise when Berkovic went down the other end and planted a beauty from 20 yards. 2–1 to the Hammers. Two defeats already and we're not out of September yet. Leeds beat Man. U today, which is something, but Arsenal and Blackburn are both still undefeated. We're falling behind. We need to finish the Celtic job then put together a proper, Championship-winning run. We need to go from now to Christmas undefeated – and that means getting results against Chelsea, Arsenal and Manchester United.

But the depression of Saturday has lifted by Tuesday morning. This is one of those Big Game days, when you wake up in the morning knowing, through the fog of your sleep, that something enormous is happening today. The Match! Celtic! Brilliant! It's a feeling that doesn't diminish with old age. Unable to control my excitement and impatient to get the day started I find myself in The Carnarvon Castle, one of Liverpool's oldest and smallest pubs, at midday, chatting to the usual array of L.F.C. veterans and bar-room pundits who seem to be there at all hours, any day of the week. One old boy, touching 80 for sure and wearing a lovely, almost faded hand-knitted bar scarf, tells me he couldn't sleep last night. He was willing the dark to turn into light so that he could get up, make his wife a pot of tea, go out for the newspaper and start the countdown. I shake hands with him and tell him I feel guilty because it took me two seconds after I woke up to realise why I was feeling so full of anticipation. I'm due to meet the gang in Kitty O'Shea's at 2 o'clock. Peter Hooton has arranged a pre-match gig for The Peatdiggers – everyone's going.

I while away a lovely hour nattering to the old boy about players I barely remember. He tells me all about Willie Stevenson, who he rates as one of the all-time greats, and Albert Stubbins. He reckons that Alun Evans was one of the most wasted talents ever to come to Liverpool and mourns the day he was allowed to leave – and he concurs with my dad. Bobby Graham was a latter-day Stan Collymore. He'd turn it on if he was in the mood. I try to put up a fight for my hero, but for every distant memory I can dredge up he gives me a detailed account of Graham 'going missing' when he was needed.

'Put it this way, lad,' he says. 'What did we win between 1967 and 1973?'

'Er . . . nothing.'

'You're right.'

I want him to come and meet the crew, they'd love him, but he's meeting his own pals. It's 2.10 p.m.

When I get to Kitty's there's an iron-grille gate barring entry and two nervy bouncers saying nothing. On the short walk up from The Carnarvon to Hanover Street I've passed a couple of Celtic supporters, magnificently intoxicated, but they're hardly overrunning the city centre. What's going on? Mono, Gram and Lovely Jeff Brittles are outside. Jeff is Lovely Jeff because he looks like Robert Mitchum on a permanent MDMA drip, always happy, always having a grin. Mono, on the other hand, is far from happy. We can't get in. The place is rammed with Celtic fans who've heard The Peatdiggers – Glasgow Celtic's house band, in many respects – are playing. This has become the focal point for Celtic's travelling support and we've got no chance. Jegsy appears on the other side of the grille. He's allowed out to speak to us, like a prisoner on day-release. He tells us Danny, Roy, Peter, Gag and Mick Potter are all inside, having sensibly arrived at midday. Jegsy, unable to sleep, has been there since 11.00. It's a Big One. The bouncer tells us to try again in an hour. He promises he'll let us in, but with dozens of besozzled Celts now congregating outside he can't do anything just yet.

We walk down to The Hanover, meeting Fat Eddie and Ally, two of Jegsy's oldest friends, en route. There are more Halewood boys inside The Hanover, plus some of the Huyton contingent from the train back from Wimbledon.

'Whatever happened to Stoneycroft . . .' I start.

We make it back up to Kitty's and it's worth it. There's a crackling atmosphere in there. In the upstairs bar, where the bands appear, the sweat is dripping from the ceiling. It's almost impossible to move more than a foot or two, either way. The

Celtic fans have taken over the small dance-floor, while the Liverpool congregation are all up by the bar. Both sets of supporters are singing madly, trying to drown each other out.

I open up the emergency exit to let some air in, only to be traumatised by a sight I shall never forget. Squatting over an imaginary lavatory, ginger buttocks exposed to the elements, a hopeless drunk conjures out a Number Two from between his thighs at just the moment I heave the door ajar. Sensing that he is not alone, the dishevelled shitter cranks his head 270 degrees and gurns at me, three browny-yellow stumps punctuating his gummy, happy face:

'Ap dah Shauwtsh!!' (Up the Celts) he slobbers, turns, and gets on with it. I stagger back inside, speechless.

'Don't go out there,' I stammer. 'Whatever you do.'

The charged, friendly Big Match atmosphere continues. Pint after pint is swallee'd. Jegsy is made to tell and re-tell the top-secret tale of the girl in glasses from RJ's Nitespot. We barrell on about Great European Nights, the noise on The Kop against St Etienne . . . Bruges . . . Barcelona. Mono points out that there was probably more noise, more concerted, energetic support at the recent-ish Auxerre match than at any of the more fabled nights. Suddenly the boys from The Kop are defenders of The Tradition. John Garner has slipped into a telephone box and re-emerged as Kopman, our spiritual leader. It's nothing to do with the gargle, of course. We just want another legendary Liverpool night in Europe, and we all want to play our part. We can't let these green and white hordes descend upon Anfield and sing their team to unlikely glory. We must show the way! We must holler and yell for 90 minutes! Yes, 90 whole minutes and that means . . . YOU. All faces, all of a sudden, are smirking redly and drunkenly at Roy and me. We, of course, are the Upper Centenary swankers, too posh to get involved in the proletarian rituals of vocal support. Those chappies down on The Kop are there for our enjoyment – can't they sing up a bit and wave their scarves?

Where's all this atmosphere they sold us in the brochure? Of course we won't be singing. No way.

We taxi from Kitty O'Shea's to Sam Dodd's and wobble from there to the shrine, ready and more than willing to adore Them.

Inside the ground I resist a powerful urge to bet. I bound up the steps, flight after flight, ignoring the snagging from my ribcage. I'm like a schoolboy attending his first game. I swoop for a kingsize sausage roll – the perfect, the only accompaniment to pre-match lager – and almost run to my seat to take in the build-up to kick-off. Roy's managed to sneak off to the lounge for another three-course meal with clotted cream on the side. The singing, from both sets of supporters, is tearjerking. I just stand there and marvel at the noise. The Celtic fans are belting out *Fields of Athenry*, a song we've annexed over recent years, and re-branded as *Fields of Anfield Road*. The Kop are singing back at them and the whole stadium is rocking. I can't help it. It's all too much. A big, unswallowable lump is swelling up in my throat, my eyes are watering and my lips are quivering. This is magic.

The teams march out, side by side. The noise is unbelievable. A swaying massif of red scarves and flags one end, and a canvas of green the other as *You'll Never Walk Alone* goes up. The businessmen in City overcoats in front of me stand, impassive, studying their match programmes. I can feel the words of the song rising up and through me, moving me, again, to tears. I'm singing along at full force, really singing, so loud that one or two business types are turning round.

'SHING YAH BASHDEDSH!! THISH ISH OUR SHONG!! ARE YOU REDS OR WHAT!!'

One afternoon on the gargle and much hope in heart has transformed Roy, and more particularly, me, into Upper Centenary Nuisances. To his abject terror and disgust, I proceed to grasp the Peter York lookalike guy in front and sway him from side to side like an inflatable doll – just to heighten his sense of participation in the match and build up a rapport with my fellow supporters. Once the ordeal's over he looks down at his coat, as though he's been slimed by Timmy Mallett (see *Dramatis Personae*).

Kick-off. Celtic are straight into us, having a real go. It's thrilling, end-to-end stuff for 10 minutes and I haven't even paused to think about Nuisance. But then I hear him.

'Oh brilliant, Jesse, fookin' brilliant – why don't you just give it to the fookin guy . . .'

'And why don't you get off his back, you beaut!!'

I can't believe this is me. And Roy, now. We're standing up, turning round, caught up in the tension and drama – and quite drunk, too – telling Upper Centenary Nuisance to get behind the team. We're quite constructive, I think. I manage to ask him how his barrage of heckling is going to help any player's confidence. He puts up quite a spirited defence, too, arguing that we shouldn't let players get away with anything other than 100 per cent effort. If the manager won't jump on them, then we, as supporters, have a duty to give them a rocket. He doesn't badger the team for the whole of the second half, though, and lets out a yelp of joy on the final whistle when, thanks to a 0–0 draw, we scrape through to the next round on the away goal rule. We nod at each other, but stop short of hugging.

They played well, the Celts. Wim Jansen seems to be turning things around. When we meet in the Champions League next year it might be a different story – but for now we're through, they're out and that's that. Rangers lost, too. To Strasbourg. *Strasbourg*, I ask you! Tonight I dream luridly. My Friday afternoon team – who are actually in Liverpool kits, playing at Anfield and *are* Liverpool – are losing to Strasbourg. I'm berating my team-mates violently. Upper Centenary Nuisance, the match referee, takes me to one side and patiently explains that shouting at individuals isn't conducive to good team spirit. Strasbourg win 3–0. Thankfully, that could never happen in real life.

1 OCTOBER 1997

Relentless hangover and undiluted self-loathing (home)

Well, that was a hoot last night, wasn't it? The Reds got through, everybody was friends, Murphy got up on the stage and gave a quavering rendition of *Liver Bird Upon My Chest* to great acclaim from the Celtic fans and . . . oh, NO!! NO!! Those poor people who have to sit by us!! Were we okay with them? All I can see, now, in my mind's tantalising eye is reaction shots. The facial expressions of the decent folk who sit in the Upper Centenary, who were subjected to abuse from certain quarters, lectured upon how to support a football team, then patronised by the culprits as they suffered from a second-half guilt binge. I have to close my eyes to get away from these faces. They look stunned. They're thinking . . . we love the team every bit as much as you. We don't sing and we don't get worked up – we just don't *do* that. But we don't deserve to be ridiculed just because we're not as sickeningly sentimental as you are about this bunch of imposters in red shirts. Their facial expressions say all that. They really do.

I rake over it all again in my mind. No, we were fine. Everyone was laughing. I took issue with a Celtic fan for applauding a reckless, violent challenge from Alan Stubbs, asked him why he thought that a career-threatening lunge was worthy of applause, but most of the match was spent biting nails and willing the ref to blow for time.

So why do their faces look so shocked whenever I think of them? Dunno. Who cares? Not me.

5 OCTOBER 1997

Chelsea, home

Who the ruddy heck is Staap Jam? Apparently we're trying to sign him but PSV Eindhoven want 8 million quids for him. Now, 8 million quids is not such a fantastical sum of money for an international footballer anymore – but for a defender? And a defender who, as far as I can make out, is not an automatic choice for his national team? Staap Jam and the wonderful-but-worrying news that we've drawn Strasbourg in the next round was the talk of Birkenhead Park. I, of course, could not play and now that Tuesday night's lager anaesthetic has worn off I am feeling every bone in my scrawny ribcage. Serves me right for giving Fat Eddie a shoulder ride. Everybody seemed pleased we've drawn Strasbourg. They're struggling badly this season. They beat Kev's XI in his troubled dreams on Tuesday night but they're having difficulty grinding out a result against the likes of Montpellier. The win against Rangers shocked even their most tunnel-visioned supporters. We should make progress against Strasbourg without breaking too much sweat, and it's easy-peasy to get to.

Great draw. Except that I'm terrified. Oh, for a Lazio, a big, historical, in-form team. The sort of team commentators used to call 'crack' – especially when referring to dour, Iron Curtain army teams. Give us 'Crack Italian Aristos' Inter Milan and we'll play like worldbeaters. Strasbourg, though . . . I hope I'm wrong, but this is the sort of team Liverpool will always underestimate, no matter who our manager may be. We'll always hear the same platitudes about how seriously everyone's taking the threat and so on – but in truth, anyone can see that Liverpool expect to stroll through these games. Maybe we will.

I have a worry yet more pressing. Today is Chelsea at home. Roy and I will have to face the tormented citizens of the Upper Centenary with Tuesday's shenanigans still stale in their minds. I can't think of anything particularly grotesque that happened. The brief altercation with UCN might turn out for the best, and the Peter York bonding session was harmless enough. So long as the Boffins saw the funny side of having their spectacles removed every five minutes, there's nothing to worry about.

It'd be good to thrash Chelsea. Really take them apart. There is one extremely good reason why it'd be good for English football if Liverpool were to destroy Chelsea. Ruud Gullit. This is one of the finest footballers ever to strut the turf, but one, also, who has left all his grace and artistry out on the field. He really is a most annoying gentleman, and those stupid love-beads dangling below his furrowed brow are only the starting point. What rankles about Ruud, as he tosses his pigtails and pauses to make yet another outstandingly arrogant remark, is that he cannot give credit to anybody. He barely gives credit to his own team – there's a sense that he's eternally disappointed that they'll never aspire to his magisterial standards – and the Netherlands will turn into the Highlands before he'll bring himself to praise an English player. Ruud's whole demeanour, his every throwaway comment, is redolent with a dismissive 'maybe-in-England' prejudice. He loves the sophistication and the glamour of London, yet he seems to resent his own affection for the place. It's as though he's wanted to come over here and find that London is just as boorish as he dreaded, and is disappointed to find that, as world capital cities go, London leaves Amsterdam looking like a backwards hick town. Ruud is here to teach us a lesson. Show us how it's done. I wish someone would – but the first stop is to learn some manners.

Ruud Gullit is an astonishingly blinkered man and a

graceless loser. Last season Liverpool caned Chelsea. It ended 5–1, but it should've been 10–0. After the match, Gullit gave no credit to Liverpool for sussing out his crabby, counter-attacking match plan and hoisting him regally with his own petard. He gave no credit to Robbie Fowler for two utterly top drawer strikes, or to Steve McManaman for playing party tricks on Michael Duberry (no mug!). Instead he tossed his beaded fringe, frowned a lot and blamed the referee for handing Liverpool the initiative (if anyone handed Liverpool the initiative it was Duberry himself with a stunning headed own-goal and Gianluca Vialli, whose tantrums finished off a rapidly eroding team spirit). Gullit has got to get used to the idea that there are some very fine players in England. We hammered Holland last time we played them. There are now several English players who have genuine world class, and some of them play for Liverpool. He needs to get off his throne and stop living in the past or he'll be history himself.

My other worry is that Jegsy has booked a recording studio for after the match in order to nail this Red Anthems CD once and for all. Obviously I want the record to be a rip-roaring bestseller, but the last thing I want to do on a Sunday evening is to stand for hours in a studio arguing over the words to an old tub-thumper. I'll delay the final decision until full time. If we annihilate them, and the ribs feel okay, the recording session might turn into a party.

Nobody frowns at us when we take our seats. Instead, there's quite a nice, familiar, morning-after-the-party feel to our part of the ground. Peter York crinkles at me but, just as quickly, jerks his head back to gaze in fascination at the completely empty pitch.

The game kicks off and Liverpool are immediately busy. There are a few half-chances before Berger outsprints Chelsea's flat defence in pursuit of a craftily floated Ince through-ball. He leaves his markers for dead and, drawing de Goey from his line, lifts it up, up over his head and, surely the ball's going over the bar! Where is it!? Will it ever come down again? It drops, almost languorously, inside de Goey's left-hand post, giving us the lead.

Within a minute mayhem reigns. Fighting for a loose ball just inside our half, Mark Hughes throws Kvarme to the floor. It's a pretty unambiguous gesture. Many would call it a foul and those who didn't would call it assault. The ref calls it neither. He waves play on. A disbelieving Zola, who along with everyone else in Liverpool's half has stopped in anticipation of a free-kick, picks up again and sprints on goal unchallenged. 1–1. The outraged crowd bays for reprisals.

Fortunately, the hapless Lambourde is present to pacify the hordes. Already booked for a tug on Fowler, he trips McManaman who has beaten him deftly on the touchline. It seems harsh on him, but it's unquestionably a second bookable offence and he has to be dismissed. These are now the rules of the game, all over the world and in Holland, too. A now-promising scenario for Liverpool is confirmed by the rampant egomania of the Chelsea manager.

Ruud Gullit brings himself on but, staggeringly, takes Zola off. Zola is the one Chelsea player who has been giving Liverpool something to think about. He's looked sharp and cunning, drifting into clever space and constantly showing for the ball. It's a relief he's gone, but it's a disappointment, too. He's a pleasure to watch, Zola.

With, effectively, two extra men – the defence have very little to occupy themselves – Liverpool push forward. Berger is thriving in these conditions. Without a packed midfield snapping at his every move he can run at the Chelsea defence and shoot from all angles and distances. He sidefoots a second on 35 minutes and the goal he scores for his hat-trick results from a sublime, one-touch move starting deep in Liverpool's own half. This is us. This is Liverpool. Ten-man Chelsea albeit, but we're pulling them all over the place and Gullit has run out of ideas. Berger sets up Fowler for the fourth and there could not be a more delighted scorer on the pitch. He looks chuffed to bits. Game, set and match, surely?

Not before Chelsea have the last laugh, literally, as well as the last say. Gullit, determined to prove that he is the greatest player on the pitch, the greatest player ever, ever, in the world, ever and worth three of his next-best Chelsea compadres, sets off on a run so mazy, so directionless and so lacking in any threat whatsoever that Liverpool stand back, scratching their heads collectively. McManaman goes after him but Gullit cuts inside. Belatedly, red shirts start to trot after him, but their half-hearted tackles are shrugged off by the fuming player-manager. The steam coming out of his ears is propelling him in on goal. Lawks! He's one on one with James! How did that happen?

We needn't worry. Tommy Smith's invisible doppelganger is out there, ready to pounce. As Gullit draws back his foot to score he slips and falls flat on his face in front of The Kop. It's hilarious. The whole crowd is laughing at him. He's utterly humiliated. He doesn't know what to do. He can't blame anyone else. He stands up and examines the pitch. The lush, green playing surface is perfectly flat (unlike, say, Ajax's). And he can't shout for a penalty because there's no one within five yards of him. Apart from Tommy Smith's invisible doppel-ganger, who whipped his standing foot from under him just as he was about to score. The home crowd is jubilant, rubbing salt into the wound by goading Vialli into a temper tantrum after he miscontrols the simplest of passes. Any other team would go on to trounce Chelsea 6 or 7–1, but not Liverpool. We think the job's done and lazily give away a penalty five minutes from time, which Poyet slots.

4–2. We race down to catch Gullit's after-match interview. Two things are certain. He will believe that Chelsea were the better side. And he will imply that it is some strange English idiosyncrasy which has cost his team the game – some cloddish tradition which still goes on over here but has long since been replaced in more progressive countries.

'Oh, yah, sure – shcoring more goalsh than your oppo-
nentsh shtill meansh a lot in thish country. You shtill have
shome catching up to do.'

Gullit is, predictably, mean in his analysis of the game. He
doesn't mention Chelsea's farcical equaliser. He's shrugging
and flicking his beads, just as though he's pleading with the ref
for a penalty. The air is heavy with his hurt implications that
English referees are not as good as referees from every other
country in the world.

'With eleven men it's a different game,' he observes.

So don't get sent off, you smug, goofy, once-great dickhead.

I time my run to the recording studio to perfection – they're
just finishing. It has not been a harmonious session. The rank
and file have imposed a sing-to-rule after the management
reneged on their promise of 'limitless free booze'. This turned
out to be a can of Kestrel each, bought under duress by the
free-spending record label. But Jegs thinks that, eventually,
they got nine or ten good songs down where everyone sang
the same words. Whatever – a good win today. Next time
we're slogging it out for Premiership points it'll be at
Goodison against the Toffees.

18 OCTOBER 1997

Everton, away

It's like the first day of the season, and it's not just that nervous
excitement. The sun is demonically hot at 10 ay em, and I'm
kicking my heels, willing the clock to tick round faster.
Danny's doing a morning shift on Conway Park station and
I'm on my fifth cup of tea in Dooley's, post-Breakfast Special.

There's nothing like mopping up your egg and tomato juice with a good hunk of bread while you mull over Mark Lawrenson's 'Where the Game Will Be Won (and Lost)' column in the *Daily Post* on the morning of a Big Match. The Dool brings over a succession of new newspapers and asks how Fowler looked the other night.

We had to go to West Brom for our first sortie in the Coca Cola on Wednesday – the Wednesday following England's marvellous result in Italy. Paul Ince, the bandaged, bloodied, heroic Lion of Rome, was rested to give him a chance to recover for the Everton game, but, strike a light, a shadowy figure called Oyvind Leonhardsen was available for selection. Lummee, guv!

More baffling was the presence in the side of one Neil Ruddock, jester, columnist in the *Liverpool Echo*, big-hearted, funny guy – and not good enough to play for Liverpool. Ruddock thinks he's wrongly portrayed as a solid centre-half. He thinks he's a cultured central defender with a range of passing, long and short, second only to Jamie Redknapp. It's true to say that he can, given time on the ball, ping a 40-yard pass with stunning accuracy from left to right. Given time on the ball. He rarely passes it short and, if pressurised by opponents, will hoof the ball anywhere. He's a great team-player and seems to be someone the squad loves to have around. He's always got a smile on his face, and this is part of the problem. Everyone loves Neil Ruddock, players and fans alike – but he's become a liability. At the highest level – and we have to keep on believing that Liverpool are a team who'll have to play Inter Milan sooner rather than later – he will always be found out. He's another who gives opponents confidence. They'll always have a go at him, try to beat him, and that is unsettling for any defence which tries to play its football from the back.

Ruddock's a dominating character. He demands the ball and sees more of it than his ability merits. Straight from kick-off against West Brom the ball is played back to him and he balloons it out of play. But we're slick and fast going forward tonight. Berger links well with McManaman and Fowler, who's starting to approach his best form again. Leonhardsen looks busy without being especially penetrative. He seems to check back a lot, though that'll just be first game nerves. He's more concerned with not embarrassing himself with a misplaced pass than winning the plaudits for his bold, adventurous play. We win 2–0 and, apart from a spell in the second half where Kevin Kilbane regularly flays Bjornebye and Ruddock, it's a canter for Liverpool.

More joy is to follow when we get back and watch the highlights on TV. Everton have been stuffed 4–1 at Coventry, but this is almost irrelevant next to the spectacle which unfolds on the final whistle. Howard Kendall strides out onto the pitch, livid, and squares up to his players. He seems to be screaming at them. Craig Short appears to have a go back at him. Duncan Ferguson pulls ironic faces at the camera.

Kendall later explains his outburst. It transpires that this sort of behaviour is quite normal in Goodison circles. He was merely requesting that his squad perform the humiliating ritual known as The Warm-Down. The Warm-Down is a thinly-veiled punishment dished out after particularly inept performances. Everton are becoming quite familiar with these after-match aerobics sessions. They are palpably the worst team in the Premiership, kept off the bottom rung only by Barnsley's stage-fright. Once the likes of Barnsley and Bolton acclimatise themselves, Everton will struggle to stay out of the bottom three. Morale is at an all-time low. Nobody of any *quality* wants to join the club, while three of their diminishing band of internationals – Speed, Barmby and Hinchcliffe – are rumoured to be moving away. The only players Kendall seems capable of bringing in are the likes of Gareth Farrelly, an Aston Villa reserve, and John Oster, a shockingly ugly adolescent from Cleethorpes. We can't lose to this Everton today unless we *lose* to them.

I'm starting to get butterflies. No Danny. For all I know he's been on the swallee last night, hasn't turned in for work and is sitting in The Albert right now. At 11 bells I decide to cut and run. I've got to call for Roy first, anyway.

Ambling to the station, I wonder if Jegs got a ticket. It'll be interesting if he did because he and Mono have been at war since the studio session after the Chelsea game. The stuff they recorded was unusable, but Mono has had second thoughts about the whole thing anyway. He's phoned Jegsy to try the diplomatic route, suggesting that they do the thing properly, without the influence of drink and without some of the unsavoury anti-Everton songs they did the other week, but for Jegsy, that's the final straw. He thinks Mono was a disruptive influence in the studio and now envisages a project dogged by the demands of his diminutive baritone. They've kissed and made up in the last few days, but not before threatening each other with The Lads.

It would've been comical if it had come to anything. The Lads they've threatened each other with are all the same people. They'd be standing there on the classic, pre-appointed piece of 'scrubland', each with their squad. It'd be like picking teams in the playground at school.

'I'll have Tony McClelland.'

'You can't have Jagger. He's *my* mate.'

'I went to school with him.'

'I went to see The Jam with him at Manchester Apollo when there was only six of us in a big crowd of Man. U . . .'

Then someone else would butt in.

'Er . . . if you're having Tony, I'll have to go on your side. I can't fight against me old mate Mick Jagger, can I?'

It's good that they've buried the hatchet in time for the Derby. Jegsy Dodd is 40 next month. Mono's 39, going on 19. We can do without spats like this at our advanced stage in life.

Up until yesterday I've been so certain that we'll win this Derby, win it magnificently, that I've been busy worrying about other things. Like Strasbourg, for example. How are we getting to Strasbourg? It's too late to book on Jimmy Flowers' coach – he's leaving on Sunday and he's full. Roy can't decide if he's going or not. Danny doesn't know if he fancies the one-night or the two-night stay. We usually book with Mike Ross of Premier Events, a London-based agent who puts together excellent, affordable packages. He generally offers a range of options, from day-trips to two- or three-night stopovers. This time he's offering one-night and two-night stays in Colmar, a 30-minute coach ride from Strasbourg, with a full stopover in the town on the day of the match. The trips are £249 and £279. It's usually Danny, Roy, myself and Jegs who hanker after the European away trips. As of today, Jegsy can't rustle up the funds. He's keeping his powder dry for the later rounds, plus he's planning a trip to Amsterdam to celebrate his 40th. We've been caught out in the past, waiting for more exotic destinations than Brondby and getting knocked out with a sucker punch, so I'm definitely going. It's pricey, though – no two ways about it. Much dearer than anyone expected for a jaunt across the Channel.

Another trip crops up during the week, via a company called Sports Comm who are advertising one night in a four-star hotel for the very reasonable sum of £199, flying from Manchester. It's an Ulster number, but when I call, which I do four times the day after the West Brom game, there's an unconvincing answerphone message suggesting that you book RIGHT NOW as space is limited. They want you to leave credit card details on the answering-service, something I'm reluctant to do. It seems weird that no one's there to answer queries at such a busy time. The advert looks convincing enough – they stipulate that applicants have to be members of the International Supporters Club, but I reckon we'll pay a little bit more and stick with Rossy. Roy promises a final

doomed. There's not much point going to Roy's or meeting the crew in The Albert. I may as well get rid of my ticket, now, and go to West Kirby beach and walk out and keep on walking until I'm submerged. Because it's All My Fault. And then I look at the teams. Ince. McManaman. Berger. Riedle. Fowler. Against Howard Kendall's Warmdown XI. Fie!! Show me as many 13s as you want, clocks of Liverpool! Nothing would stop me from being at Goodison today when we beat the Toffees 4–0. Maybe 3. Yeah, 3–0 is about right.

I get to Roy's. The debate about the Italian *carabinieri*'s treatment of the England fans in Rome is still crackling on, with David Mellor now getting involved. It's not a cut and dried case, this. It's futile to suggest that England fans were innocent victims, just as it's futile to continually refer to Rome as a 'city of culture'. Great city, with more desperate smackheads per square metre than you'll find outside of Naples. Any tourist visiting Rome stands a good chance of being harassed in any number of ways. Mugging is high on the list for a lucrative quick-fix, while any group of non-Roman men are immediately seen as invaders. They're a challenge to the local *panineri*, who will spend hours circling on mopeds and scooters before picking their moment to attack – as Liverpool fans found when we played AS Roma, in Rome in the 1984 European Cup Final. The scale and the gravity of violence after that game was never widely reported in the wake of Liverpool's superhuman victory and fourth European Cup, but it was a brutal night. It seemed as though the attacks would never end. Depraved Romans were swarming out of the bushes, out of the parks, smashing up vehicles, hurling lumps of concrete, attacking anyone in Liverpool colours, women and children included. The police were nowhere to be seen. They, like the Italian media, are in denial about their country's social schisms. If they're to be believed, they don't have a problem with football violence. Those sustained battles you see most weeks on *Football Italia* are theatrically staged affairs to give the British viewer something to identify with. The police mainly turn a blind eye.

But they were everywhere before the game. Large groups of people who are not citizens of Roma congregating in the Eternal City for a football match represent a direct challenge to the police, requiring direct action. They see Rome as a bastion of fashion and culture, requiring protection from these pink-skinned vikings. (If the wearing of checked peg slacks with a pastel-coloured Pringle sweater slung over your shoulders year in, year out is fashionable, then Rome beats the pants off boring old London, any day.) The *carabinieri* patrol, batons in hand, guns in holsters, in groups, trying to make eye-contact, trying to provoke a response. There will always be somebody to oblige, some pest who's drunk too much wine, whose pickled brain is still functioning well enough to realise he's being victimised but not well enough to realise that there's nothing he can do about it. Once he answers back to the police, he's had it – and it only takes one unfair, heavy-handed arrest to spark off trouble.

It's likely that something similar happened prior to the big group decider against Italy in Rome. England's fans will have been boisterous and annoying, singing outside cafés and shouting at passers-by. But it's unlikely they'll have done anything serious enough to warrant the baton charges many of them say took place. It was plain to see that by the time they got inside the ground they despised the local police and felt they were justified in fighting back. To his credit, David Mellor is on *Grandstand* now defending the England fans or, more specifically, condemning the Italian police for flagrant provocation. Too often government officials have leapt to condemn this country's football supporters before waiting to find out the facts behind the headlines. Hillsborough is one humbling example. It's great to see a figurehead like Mellor taking such an unconventional stance.

My guess is that enough English supporters behaved badly

enough to give the *carabinieri* licence to lay into the others. They probably went to extremes to mete out their skewed justice. Unfortunately, you should never be surprised by incidents like this if you're following a team like England in a place like Italy.

Roy lives by Newsham Park. After *Football Focus* we stroll, shirt-sleeved in the sunshine, across the park, wittering on about this and that. We've both noticed how referees seem to get in the way so much more and how commentators seem to get basic, obvious things wrong. Like they'll shout 'excellent save from Bosnich' when the ball has clearly *clearly* hit the post. And the referees *are* worse. This season more than any we can recall they're getting major decisions wrong. It must be all the increased attention they're getting in light of the debate about action-replays or a cricket-style second ref in the TV room. I favour neither myself. Football's all about immediacy, for better and for worse. So long as the refs share out their disastrous, myopic cock-ups equally, who cares? It all adds to the sound and fury of football, doesn't it?

We meet up with Danny (drunk) and Mono, John Garner, Lovely Jeff and company (not yet drunk). Not content with putting the Indian sign on Liverpool down in the tube station at midday, I do it all over again. One thing we've learned as Liverpool fans over the years is never to be smug before the event. Never count your Liver Birds before they hatch. The road to oblivion is paved with the famous last words of foolish managers and petulant fans. Any fan who sings 'what a waste of money' at the opposition's new star signing – especially in the first half, when anything can still happen – can confidently expect a chastening slap with a wet towel when that player goes on to score a hat-trick against them, as he is bound to do. Any team who unfurls a banner reading 'Fourth Place in a Two Horse Race' at an FA Cup fifth round tie in the month of February can look forward to being dumped out of same competition instantly and having their interest in Europe curtailed pretty smartish too. The smugs don't work, as I should know by now. So why do I suggest to all present that, when we're 3–0 up with five minutes left, we should conga around Goodison singing: 'Let's All Have a Warm-Down'? What folly! What a stupid, stupid, stupid thing to say! That's obviously what did for us. That, and the tube-station clock.

The butterflies really kick in when we get to Goodison. Up until now I've only seen Liverpool fans, but here we are, right outside the seat of broken dreams, and the hatred hangs putrid in the air. Goodison is the third most dilapidated ground in the Premiership and makes a perfect backdrop for their theatre of hate against Liverpool. Let's get this right. Evertonians *hate* Liverpool. They've always hated us, but since 1985 the Bluenoses have been almost deranged with contempt for The Red Shite, as they call us.

Here's the reason. In 1985, Everton had the best team they've known at Goodison since the great team of '66–70. In 1985, Everton won the League and the European Cup Winners' Cup. They missed out on the Double courtesy of Norman Whiteside's bending grasscutter in the FA Cup Final. A couple of weeks later, as a result of the Heysel Stadium tragedy, all English clubs were banned from European competition. Everton were deprived of their place in the European Cup.

Given the astonishingly good record, up until then, of English clubs winning the European Cup, it's not deluded for Everton fans to believe they could have added their name to the list. But instead of joining the elite of Europe, they argue, their great team simply broke up and went away. They've never recovered from it. That part of the argument doesn't stand up especially well to close scrutiny. The following season they added Gary Lineker to an already fine squad. They would've won the Double that year had not Liverpool won the League and the FA Cup. They won the League again in

1987, so clearly the fall-out from Heysel wasn't hitting them too badly.

Another factor the Blues conveniently overlook is the effect that the European ban had on another team. Liverpool. It's beyond dispute that Liverpool's team between 1987 and 1990 was one of the finest assembled anytime, anywhere. The team of Barnes, Houghton, Beardsley, Aldridge and McMahon was lauded by Sir Tom Finney as the greatest ever. It's hard to see how they could have failed to win the European Cup, qualifying either as winners or as English League Champions, in each of those four years, giving Liverpool a highest all-time total of eight wins. Everton might well have won the trophy in 1986, but thereafter Liverpool would have dominated. In those years, 1987 to 1990, the competition was won by such superpowers as Steaua Bucharest, Red Star Belgrade and Olympique Marseille (who had to give it back because they cheated). To suggest that Liverpool would not have overcome teams like that is patent nonsense. Had we not been barred from Europe in 1985, Liverpool would by now have won the European Cup more times than any other club in the competition's history. Everton have a reasonable beef, but the real vicitms of the ban were us. Liverpool Football Club.

But Everton still despise us. Men in Everton shirts congregate outside the Bluehouse with kids on their shoulders, flicking V-signs at passing Reds. Part of the problem, part of what makes it unbearable for Evertonians is that we don't hate them back quite as much. We wish them nothing but the worst, for sure. We hope passionately that they lose their annual struggle against relegation. But they're not worthy of our unmitigated contempt any more than Manchester City are deserving of more than passing malevolence from United. Quite simply, they're not worth it. They're a sideshow, an occasional source of fun when their pre-season promises turn rapidly to the reality of another dogfight.

Twice a year, though, they're an irritant. Somehow, their troupe of has-beens and never-will-bes transforms itself into the gutsiest, most focused, committed, powerful unit our team will have to face all season. Everton are pure bottled aggression, let out of the canister for 90 minutes in which they steamroller Liverpool with their greater desire to win the game. Many an Everton manager of recent years has been left scratching his head in the dole-queue, still befuddled that a team which can fight so effectively against Liverpool can surrender so tamely against York City, Portsmouth, Port Vale, Bradford . . .

We take up our seats in the Upper Bullens Road stand. The one thing Everton have in common with Manchester United – apart from the fact that both teams are regularly trounced by York City – is the way they place visiting supporters in parts of the ground where they can least effectively encourage their team. United stick you away in that little corner, nowhere near the pitch or your team. So, too, do Everton. The bulk of our tickets are for the Upper Bullens, a twat of a spec in a twat of a ground. Small wonder they're moving to Widnes.

We start well enough. Graham Stuart is trying to snap at Ince, Berger, McManaman, anyone – but he's like a dog chasing his tail. Ironic cheers from the Liverpool fans as he chases his lost cause and we pass the ball around only make him more determined. He wins a few tussles with Ince, who's playing quite deep. But we're seeing a lot of the ball. Berger gets free down the left a couple of times and McManaman is beating Earl Barrett at will. From one such dribble Macca pulls the ball back across the Everton penalty area, inviting Riedle to shoot. He steadies himself, pulls the trigger and . . . THWACK!! He kicks Patrik Berger on the shin. Berger must have had his 75 per cent appearance mandate on his mind:

'Work permit! Work permit! Work permit!'

Like Father Jack in search of a drink, Berger has but one

thing on his mind as he comes screaming in for Riedle's ball. The ball rolls invitingly for either player to blast home. Berger charges in and shapes to shoot and, just as he's about to hit it, Riedle brings his foot down for his own shot. The two of them kick each other, shout at each other and the ball trickles harmlessly away.

Everton are playing ugly pipsqueak Pugsley Oster on the right wing, with young Danny Cadamarteri on the left. On the rare occasions they receive the ball they look dangerous against a ponderous Ruddock and a nervy Kvarme. From a dangerous raid by Pugsley, Everton get a corner. This gives the Goodison crowd new hope. Liverpool are always prone to flap at corners and, in Duncan Ferguson, they have perhaps the most dangerous aerial targetman in the division. One bonus about having Ruddock in the team is that he's quite commanding in the air. He'll relish this tussle with Ferguson. It's the sort of scrap he thrives on. Except that, it seems, young Kvarme has been detailed to counter the aerial threat of Ferguson. How naive of us not to have seen the logic of it earlier! It's genius! Slight, fairminded Kvarme'll take huge, powerful thug Ferguson while sluggish Ruddock will shadow cheetah-swift Cadamarteri. What crap. 1–0 to them.

The corner's taken. Ferguson flicks it on and the ball ricochets off Ruddock into the net. It's nobody's fault, least of all Neil Ruddock's. It's a freak goal – but a goal nonetheless.

Everton are going to be hard to break down, now. McManaman beats Barrett again, but this time – and for the remainder of the game – Graham Stuart is backing him up. McManaman has to squeeze inside or outside four flailing legs and eventually runs the ball out of play. Stuart and Barrett high-five each other by the corner flag. The very sight of these two dogs – no disrespect to two honest, hardworking journeymen but Chubby Brown has more class – hailing each other as though they're Napoleon and Montgomery trotting back from another satisfying game of Campaign is enough to drive you mad. Why it doesn't drive our team mad, I don't know. If I was Macca I'd want the ball again, immediately, and I'd want to put it through Stuart's legs and beat Barrett twice before rolling it back for Robbie to blast an Exocet in. Maybe they don't want to be goaded into any horseplay by Everton, but right now play of any sort would be most welcome.

I see Keith from Doncaster at half time, glassy-eyed yet perfectly sober, standing outside the lavatories counting people for no obvious reason. It's starting to get to some people, following this team.

Second half follows a similar pattern. Ince, who's had an anonymous first half, is getting forward a bit more, trying to drive the team on. From a corner he powers a header down and into the net and . . . no! *Not* into the net! Smack into Earl Barrett's hand. Barrett clearly controls the ball with his hand! Penalty! We're on our feet screaming at the linesman, the referee, anyone who is prepared to parp on his whistle and point to the spot. But nobody out on Goodison Park fits that description. They're not going to award us a penalty simply on the grounds that an Everton player controlled the ball with his hand inside his own penalty area. Yet again a well-placed referee gets a crucial, a *crucial* decision completely wrong. Oh, for an action-replay facility! Why can't we take a lead from cricket and have a second ref up in the TV room, wired up to the ref on the pitch to tell him what he needs to know? There's too much at stake in football today for these well-meaning fools in black fancy-dress to fuck things up every week! The F.A. has got to get its act together . . .

Everton punt a long ball clear, thankful for any respite from Liverpool's bombardment. Kvarme has plenty of time to control the ball and start the attack moving again. He does that skip of his, as though he's about to hit it long, then changes his mind and looks for a six-foot, sideways option. Nobody wants to know. He's forced to go forward, tentatively, nervously, not having the faintest idea what he's going to do with the ball. In these circumstances Matteo should always be there to take the ball off the defence, beat a man and play someone into space. It's dead simple, and Matteo's made for that role. In his absence, Ince or McManaman or Leonhardsen should just track back and take the ball off Kvarme – take responsibility. Instead the kid's left in no-man's land, shuffling forward with no one showing for him. Cadamarteri, fast and enjoying himself today, runs towards Kvarme in the hope of making him play a hasty ball. His prospecting earns him gold. Kvarme gets caught in two minds and slips, fielding the ball tamely to Cadamarteri who sprints past him. Kvarme tries desperately to make up ground. Ruddock tries to cut off his route, but he's so slow. How can anyone so slow be a professional footballer? Cadamarteri could hitch a ride on a pensioner's shopping trolley and still beat him for pace. He cuts back inside him and, with all the composure of a Derby-day veteran, rifles past James from ten yards. It wasn't a difficult chance after the space he made for himself, but it would've been easy to miss. He's understandably delirious, running to Everton's jubilant fans in the Park End. They turn towards us in one joyous, disbelieving mass and bounce up and down singing:

'You're not very good, you're not very good . . .' to the tune of *Knees Up Mother Brown*. So much for our conga.

The lad next to me shakes his head:

'These'll be the points that keep the twats up, as well!'

Losing 2–0 to Everton. This is emphatically the worst feeling, ever. Far from conga-ing joyously around Goodison, we are shuffling out, heads down, hoping against hope itself that we don't run into anyone we know. A couple of seasons ago, after another 2–0 reverse at Goodison, I spotted John Potter heading towards me in Goodison Road, singing. He hadn't seen me. I ducked down behind a car and, as he got closer, wriggled underneath. For a minute I thought I'd escaped but Potter, joined now by Tony Sage and Andrew Streuth, grabbed me by the ankles and dragged me out, joyfully declaring that I was coming to The Royal Oak with them. It was bad. I want to get home as quickly as possible today.

I spy Tony McClelland, one of the founder-editors of *The End*. I haven't seen Tony for a long time and these are hardly the circumstances for a reunion. We persuade each other to go for one drink in The Albert. The post-mortem is in full swing when we arrive. Everybody's getting stick. Obviously Roy Evans and Neil Ruddock are the main targets for the hanging judges. I can hear Danny lecturing Bucko from Bootle on Roy Evans' tactical weaknesses.

'He's on glue! I'm telling you, lad! He's on fucken glue!'

Others are criticising Fowler for his brattish habit of strolling back at his own pace after an attack breaks down. I don't fancy the witch-hunt. The whole day needs to be lopped off above the knee before the gangrene sets in. I'm out of here.

19 OCTOBER 1997

Tom Russell, home (9.15 a.m.)

Sunday morning and I'm just glad I haven't booked for Strasbourg. It's one of those days, utterly, numbingly depressing, that you just have to get through. I avoid the newspapers, but I can't avoid the sudden proliferation of Everton shirts on the street. Either they've been keeping themselves well hidden up until now or there was a timely fire-sale at the Toffee Shop after yesterday's match. There's worse, though.

'Jane. Can you call it off with Tom, today?'

Anyone mention hubris? Last week, anticipating a huge win over Everton, I, in my boundless wisdom, thought it'd be a nice idea to take Joe and Tom to play football today. Tom's dad must've been even more confident than me. He offered to bring him to ours himself.

'No! Of course not! He's looking forward to it . . .'

Their car pulls up outside. I hide in the airing cupboard, sending my body temperature racing past the 100 mark as I have to listen to my wife downstairs telling Tom's dad I've popped out for the papers.

'Tell him to stay away from the back page,' I hear him chortle.

I have to come out sooner or later. I'm not prepared to die for Liverpool. Not this fucking team, anyway. I hobble downstairs for desperately needed Kia-Ora, to be greeted by a grinning, bespectacled boy of 8 dressed in full Everton kit.

'HA-HA!! 2–0!! 2–0!! YOU WERE RUBBISH!! 2–0!! 2–0!! 2–0!!'

I try to smile gamely. There's no let up. His style reflects his team's approach to Derby games – unsubtle, but very effective.

'2–0!! 2–0!! HA-HA-HA-HA!! 2–0!! YOU'RE NOT VERY GOOD . . . YOU'RE NOT VERY GOOD!!'

'Tee-hee, Tom. But you don't get any prizes for winning Derby games. It might keep you away from the trap-door for another week, though . . .'

This is what my team have reduced me to. Bickering unconvincingly with an 8-year-old. How could we lose to Everton? *That* Everton, an assembly of kids and no-marks, no better equipped to stay in the top league than Burnley. Where was our fight, our skill, our pride? Where was Paul Ince, the Lion of Rome a week ago, bought specifically to counter the direct approach of teams like Everton? He was being mugged by Danny bloody Williamson is where. I hate this Liverpool team for making me feel so low. I hate them. Thank Christ I haven't laid out another 300 rips to go and see them lark about on the continent, mindless and careless of the traditions and the reputation of the club they play for. I hate them. I don't want to see this lot ever again.

19 OCTOBER 1997

Home (7.32 p.m.)

I'm pining for them. I get to thinking about Jimmy Flowers' coach, already making the Channel crossing and not due to arrive in Strasbourg until Tuesday morning. I'm thinking that now, of all times, is the moment to stand up and be counted. These are the games where you have to show your face and get behind the lads. If everybody just folded at the first signs of a bad run we'd be nowhere. Besides, we'll never play that badly again. After a defeat like that, suffered so meekly at the hands of our city subordinates, everybody'll be chomping at the bit, desperate to make amends. I need to be there with them.

21 OCTOBER 1997

Strasbourg, away
(UEFA Cup 2nd Round, 1st Leg)

Monday morning is spent, amazingly, being kept on hold and then told that there's no room at the inn. Now, even the day-trips are fully booked. We're going to have about 3,000 fans in Strasbourg but that's no consolation to me. I look at the feasibility of Eurostar, but it's too dicey. The slightest delay en route and I'll miss the match.

The *Echo* comes to the rescue. Towns Travel are offering a day-trip from Liverpool airport – at £185. It's not much cheaper than one of Mike Ross's two-day stopover trips. I should've just booked for all four of us when Premier's mailshot came through the post, paid the deposits and offered my wavering pals no choice in the matter. But wavering they are. Not about the team or the match or the principle – they just don't think a half-day trip to Strasbourg is a good way to spend that amount of money. Danny and Roy, my last two remaining travelling butties, are pulling out. So it's just me. I'm even more determined to go.

The Towns Travel itinerary, I must confess, smacks of officialdom. Towns are one of L.F.C.'s official travel operators, but this is just *too* official. It's all escorts and guides and tabulated time and motion. I can sympathise with Liverpool F.C.'s appointed travel agent wanting to ensure that none of their customers is involved in anything unsavoury, but these overplanned tours often lead to the sort of build-up of tension and resentment that can lead to trouble. I went to Genoa a few years back in similar circumstances. Day-trip from Liverpool airport. Met off the plane at Genoa by an armed police escort. Marched onto a coach and driven around the city ring road for two hours. Stopped at a rocky car-park overlooking the sea, where four other coaches full of fans were parked up. All allowed off the coach for 15 minutes to stretch our legs. Police watched intently, rifles cocked, from a distance. Somebody commented that it's like the exercise yard in *The Great Escape* and that's where it all started. Twos and threes started drifting away, flagging down cars and taxis. Then more. It was *Escape To Victory*, a general, if half-hearted, charge towards the dual carriageway involving 60 or 70 fed-up fans, pursued by the gun-toting *carabinieri*. The police rounded up the escapees and jostled them back to the coaches. Everyone was herded back on board for another scenic tour of the outskirts of Genoa. These were ordinary, decent fans who only wanted to see a bit of the place they were, literally, paying a visit. It was no surprise when Liverpool lost 2–0 that night. It was probably down in the small print on the itinerary.

If I book this trip, I should do it expecting nothing – *nothing* – for my money. I am going to Strasbourg because it's something I have to do. If they drive us around all day then make us go inside the stadium three hours before kick-off, so be it. It's all part of the sentence. It's Extra Time.

I get through to Towns after many, many attempts and am almost relieved when they tell me they're fully booked. That's it, then. I'm not going. Some supporter you are, Mr Sampson. When the call came, where were you? Watching your telly, with all the other part-time supporters.

And what of the match? Too dispiriting to recall, even now, the morning after. It makes no sense at all. I don't know whether I'm partially pleased because I didn't shell out hundreds to go and see Liverpool's most gutless performance in Europe ever (the players were abused by fans waiting in the airport for flights after the game); or depressed because I feel I should've been there. I'm going to just blot this week out. No recriminations. No scapegoats. We lost 3–0, but it could've been six. We were shite. If only Robbie Fowler's brilliant 40-yard volleyed lob had gone in, though.

25 OCTOBER 1997

Derby County, home

Back to the drawing board. I'm over the worst of the crushing disappointment of the past seven days. Only a week ago it was the morning of the Everton game. Hope sprang eternal. More than hope – confidence, expectation, anticipation of great things over the next two games. Now, a week on, it looks as though we're out of Europe and our plans of winning the

League are the delusions of madmen. Three defeats and we're not yet into November.

The sun's still shining, though. It's still hot enough to sit out and catch a nice, red stripe across your nose. I've got to *do* something about this team of mine. Maybe it's time I went back to basics. I decide I'm going to do a Les Tour, today. I'm going to break from my usual routine and go to the match, alone, taking the route I used to go with my dad. So I get the 14C from the pierhead towards Breck Road, and get off at the corner of Breckfield Road, walking in the direction of The Derry Club. This is the way we used to come, cutting down Salisbury Street to The Little Salisbury. There's another, better known Salisbury just along from The Albert, but The Little Salisbury is where Les used to pop in for a quick pre-match half. So I pop in for a pre-match half. The walls are still bedecked with scarves and souvenirs and a collection of photographs which would honour the finest galleries. A lot of drinkers are standing outside, enjoying the sunshine, but inside, half-empty, the pub still feels cosy.

I head over to the ground. It's a quarter-to-two, but I want to take in the whole first game trip. I'm going to close my eyes and pretend it's 1969 again. Even at two o'clock, the noise from The Kop then would be outrageous. I'd leave my dad in the canteen and go down to his seat – they used to let the kids sit on their old man's knee so long as they weren't taking up too much room. I could stand there, on the chunky wooden seat in the Kemlyn, and just watch The Kop in awe. It was a tumult. It didn't last much longer like that. Nostalgic Koppites of my own generation like to think it was still a hotbed until the '80s, but in truth The Kop became a special-occasion crowd as long ago as 1975. It was still a terrifically noisy, passionate, witty gathering, capable of petrifying opponents and squeezing one last attack, a last-minute goal out of a lost cause. But the pre-match singing got later and later. The mass of scarves which decked out The Kop from one side to the other for *You'll Never Walk Alone* started to thin out at both sides, and by 1975, apart from the big, special-occasion games, the vibrant, vocal support was concentrated between the two stanchions in the middle. These days we need special flag days, to remind ourselves how awesome we used to be. But today, I'm going in the ground at two o'clock, I'm going to watch the team warm up and I'm going to screw my eyes up and summon up the spirit of perpetual excitement that used to take me over each time I clicked through that turnstile. Maybe, along with the shivers down my spine, will come the inevitable 3–0 thumping of the opposition which always seemed to follow.

It doesn't work. I'm bored stupid after 20 minutes of watching Sammy Lee's pass-and-go triangles. One interesting sideshow is a three-way game of keep-up between Fowler, McManaman and McAteer. Each of them is pulling a ludicrous 'goofy' face, like the school dunce, and is deliberately shinning the ball high into the air. Yet they're doing it under complete control. They can control the pace and direction of the ball perfectly, even with their shinbones. It's the sort of thing you'd expect to see on the beach in Rio, maybe, but not before a match at Anfield. I'm shocked, too, I admit it, at how natural McAteer is on the ball. I always think of him as a 'heart' player, someone who compensates for less than optimum technique with total commitment to the cause. But look at him, out there. He's the most gifted of the three. He's Pele. They keep it up for ten whole minutes. They're laughing their heads off, shinning it up to the next one who shins it up to the next one. The ball is never out of reach. It never touches the ground. Karlheinz Riedle watches, laughing, but he doesn't join the goof-circle.

To hell with it! A curse on this superstition! I'm bloody well going to have a bet. It can't ruin the game for me any more than Liverpool's gutless performance will. I trudge back to the Ladbroke kiosk and while away a pleasant ten minutes considering, then rejecting, outlandish bets. Jacob Laursen of Derby has predicted a 6–0 win for The Rams. I almost stick a quid on 6–0 to us, just because we always hammer somebody at least once a season, but I go for a much more conservative double of Robbie Fowler and 3–0. I also pop a little side bet on, to cover myself.

We start nervously, confidence obviously shattered from Tuesday night. Dominic Matteo is in for Neil Ruddock but, having seen the stick Ruddock took after Strasbourg it's not right that only he should carry the can. Steve Harkness, too, was dangerously at fault. He doesn't appear to have recaptured the pace and timing in the tackle he had before his horrific injury at Coventry, which kept him out for a year. Prior to that, he was looking like an England centre-back, but now . . . As supporters our memories and tolerance are short. No matter how great the legend or how well a player did last week, it's today that counts. We're all appreciative of Harkness' bravery and his sacrifices for Liverpool, but he's got to get his act together again. He's got this infuriating habit of backpedalling with his head turned back over his shoulder, like a dog chasing his tail. Not surprisingly, opposing attackers find it easy to drift past a marker who has his back to them. He was doing it all night against Strasbourg.

Just when we need it most, Robbie Fowler pops up with a goal. Great! Two more and I've won 56 quid! Fowler and Michael Owen are gelling well together. Owen's a little bit in awe of Fowler. He seems eager to please him, pulling chances back so Fowler can shoot when he was probably in with a better chance himself, but he's so full of mischief that he can't fail to create opportunities, whoever sticks them away. Jamie Redknapp, one of our few successes when he returned to the team against Strasbourg, is creating a lot of space for the pair of them. Just look at the talent out there! Redknapp. McManaman. Ince. Fowler. Matteo, and now Michael Owen, so bloody brilliant that the bloke who won the European Cup last season can't get in the team. We should be winning every trophy in sight with all this quality out there. Maybe it's not too late.

Fowler bags a second and Leonhardsen, who still instinctively turns back towards the goal as soon as he receives the ball, rolls the third in nicely from 12 yards. That's it, 3–0. Now, if they'll kindly pull their usual stunt of relaxing for the last ten minutes – but not so much that Derby come back into the game – little Kev'll be getting the drinks after the game. 56 quid. Not bad for a £2 double. Everyone's happy. I show the Boffins my betting slip which, of course, is fatal. The Bon Viveur, a betmeister of the highest order who doesn't consider anything less than a £50 stake to be a bet, chuckles generously and shakes his head.

We get a last-minute corner. No danger, we never score from corners. There's only Riedle who scores with any regularity with his head and he's not playing. I may as well go and queue for my payout. Redknapp bends in a beauty from the corner flag and there, hahahahah!, there goes McManaman making a run for it. Hohohohoh! McManaman!! McManaman's going in for a header! Heeheeheehee, good job we're 3–0 up! Good job we're not relying on Steve 'Bullet Head' McManaman to bury a late winner with that laser-guided nodder of his. In he goes. Completely unchallenged. Come on Stimac, get up with him! Stimac, you've lost your man, he's . . . WHAM! Goal!

Bastard!

McManaman goes running to The Kop, jumping up and heading thin air, grinning massively. Once everyone around me has finished jumping all over each other, the Sons of Bon Viveur turn to me, sympathetically.

'Never mind, eh? You'd've settled for 4–0 before the game, wouldn't you?'

'Two quid for a 4–0 win, eh? You'd've give that, wouldn't you?'

'Not quite,' I reply, producing another slip from my pocket. A pound on Liverpool to win 4–0. No Fowler double but it's still worth £18. Moods enhanced by a convincing win, they're all laughing and shaking my hand. Derby stream down the other end straight from the kick-off.

'Oh, here we go!' chuckles Son of Bon (2).

'Never get your ticket out until . . .'

Powell is through. What the ruddy heck is HE doing there! Out comes James, sprawls at Powell's feet, the ball ricochets around the penalty area and we clear. Phew! The ref blows up for full time. Double phew!! Maybe I'll just get lost in the crowd, pocket my winnings and slip away, rich as Croesus. A well-fleshed hand reaches over countless vile bodies and collars me.

'Drinks all round then, Sammy?'

And drinks all round it was.

1 NOVEMBER 1997

Bolton, away

We seem to be lost. It was going fine until we got past Wigan and then the road signs stopped. It's probably as good a time as any to stop for a drink. We pull up in a village called Adlington, which has no fewer than five social clubs, working out at roughly one per six villagers. There's a pub, too, to which Danny, myself and his mate off the building site hasten. His mate is called Eggeye, Danny tells me, while he's at the bar.

'I can't call him that!'

'Why not?!'

'Well – his eyes! They're like boiled eggs . . .'

'Why d'you think we call him Eggeye . . .?'

It's a funny old to-do, this pub. There seem to be two rival functions taking place at either end of the establishment. In one corner, happy as muck, is a wedding party. The bride is radiant, and very, very ugly. I don't know why women, women like my own dear mum, are suddenly afflicted by myopia when any old pudding of a girl pulls on a wedding dress. She'll give a sharp intake of breath, my mum. She'll be genuinely, properly taken aback.

'Oooh!' she'll gasp, tears of joy pricking her eyelids. 'Doesn't she look lovely?!'

Well this one doesn't. She's a bonny, healthy, unremarkable-looking girl, except for one outstanding blemish. She has this growth on her chin. You couldn't call it a wart – it covers too much ground, this specimen, and it's dark brown and perfectly covered with coarse, horse-type hair. It's fascinating – you can't help sneaking a little look at it – and repulsive – you can't help looking away. She's right next to me at the bar, but I'm not going to stare in horror at her. No way. I just wouldn't do that on her wedding day.

They're all very jolly, this party. The father-in-law comes over and gently points out that this is a private function, strictly speaking, but he's no objections if we want to stay. But could we use the other side of the room?

'Sound, lad,' says Danny. 'No problem.'

Danny's been calling taxi drivers, ticket inspectors and other octogenarian men 'lad' since he was 15. From the day he was made an Apprentice Brickie to when he was sworn in as a Timeserved Master Bricklayer, he used to carry his tool-box everywhere with him, calling grown men 'lad'. Only a few more years to go, Dan. You'll be a fella soon. The father-in-law picks up on his accent.

'Scousers, eh? Off to match? I could've done with you boys in week. Ah needed set of hub-caps for Peugeot 205!'

He's bowled over by his own wit. I wonder what he

would've said if I'd asked him if someone had stolen his definite articles, too. But it's hard to take offence against the old wheeltapper, particularly as his son – a total gawp – is now besottedly kissing the bride. His nose is actually rubbing against the growth. I wonder if it'll become stimulated and start to quiver like a manitou. Maybe he just hasn't noticed it. Maybe he'll wake up tomorrow morning, blissfully happy, turn to his beloved and suddenly see the thing for the first time. He'll sit up straight and point at it accusingly.

'Chuffinell, Mary!! You never telt us about THAT!!'

We cross to the other side of the pub, where more madness awaits. Here sit three women, all dressed in black. They look, to all intents and purposes, like a funeral gathering. They're not the most animated group, indeed they haven't uttered a word to each other since we came in. They're just staring straight ahead. Surely the pub landlord couldn't be so insensitive as to book a wedding party and a wake into his establishment on the same day? Danny's friend Eggeye starts tittering silently.

'The witches of Pendle!' he whispers. We are actually within sight of the deathly Pendle Hill of black legend and forsooth, it was All-Hallows Eve yesterday. Maybe these three witches are remnants of some unspeakable satanic ritual which took place on the hill last night. Just as I'm thinking it's probably time to sup up our beer and collect our fags, Danny, who's been watching the three cloaked ladies with interest, pipes up:

'Anyone close?'

They stare back, totally mystified.

'The funeral, like? Anyone close?'

I'm looking for the nearest exit when the youngest of the three starts laughing. No, no, no, she tells us. No. They're part of the local amateur dramatics group. They rehearse in the upstairs room of the pub on Saturdays. They're just waiting for the others to arrive. It's with almost embarrassed relief and gratitude that I ask them for the best route to Horwich, home of the new Reebok Stadium and Bolton Wanderers.

'Funny how there's always a Tesco in it somewhere,' muses Eggeye, mystically, as we drive towards Horwich.

'Eh?!'

'When you ask directions to the ground. It used to be, you know, turn left at The King's Head, didn't it? Now it's always first left after the Big Tesco Superstore.'

He's too right. When we can see the Reebok way down below us, we park up at a pub in Grimeford. It's full of Liverpool fans. They reckon the ground is about a two-mile walk from here. I've drunk my strict when-driving limit of one pre-match pint so I don't care, but the others are insistent on at least one more drink before kick-off. We're still in the pub at quarter-to-three. There's no choice. I'll have to brave Bolton's already infamous car-park.

Tony Sage and Gary Hart, friends of ours who follow Everton, have already warned me about the Reebok car-park.

'Don't,' they pleaded, 'under any circumstances be tempted to use the official car-parks!'

Their eyes widen as they tell of its terrors.

'Take it from us. You'd rather park five miles away and walk it than get stuck in there. In fact you'll still get home quicker if you *do* park five miles away.'

I know Bolton have had a bit of a tasty firm in their day, especially when they're playing Man. U – but I'll eat my hat if they've got an active mob who bash up away supporters in the car-park. Not in 1997. Surely not?

'It's nothing to do with the Bolton fans . . . they suffer just as much. It's . . . The Car-Park. Just don't do it, no matter what the temptation. If you do . . .'

Gary, who had been nodding solemnly, completed the story.

'. . . you'll never get out again.'

So I'd had every intention of leaving the car at the pub. But, of course, my non-driving, non-thinking, selfish, thirsty, don't-worry-it'll-be-fine bricklaying comrades know better, don't they? Back into the car we jump. Out of our lovely, cosy little parking spec and down the hill towards the Reebok. Loads of people are filing down little alleyways and over pathways across fields, taking shortcuts to the new stadium. Too late I spot a gap in a line of cars parked up on the grass verge. That would've been perfect, but there's too much traffic behind to reverse, now. We're round the roundabout, left again and we're there. I must say, the stadium looks fantastic but the words of Tony Sage, Evertonian, are haunting me as a whole tribe of gesticulating stewards try to point me into their own little section of the Notorious Bolton Wanderers Car-Park.

'Just don't do it, no matter what the temptation.'

Ah, well. I've done it now. It's five-to-three. Better leg it. We stop to natter to various faces outside the ground. Each time we stop, an amazing spectacle unfolds. Bolton have their own *carabinieri*. They do. I can't be sure whether they're a special unit within the Greater Manchester police force or whether they're private security, but their uniforms are terrifying. They have black, knee-length jackboots, cropped, tightly belted black jackets and hard-hat riding-style helmets. From their belts hang two deadly weapons. On one side, a long riot stick. It's too long and thin to be a regular truncheon – unless I'm still working to the Enid Blyton stereotype. No, this hard black baton is a riot stick. On the other side of the belt is a fastened holster. Presumably it contains a revolver of some description. Just what are the Bolton police expecting, today? All I know for sure is that each time we stop to let on to someone we know they move in on us. They're polite enough with it, but they won't have groups of away fans building up in a stationary position. They want to keep everyone moving.

We find our turnstile and get inside the ground. Big roar. Kick-off. Unfortunately oxygen isn't provided upon entry.

After jogging up flight after flight after flight of stairs we're still only in the canteen. There's a huge noise from our end. We've scored! Brilliant! Shit! Missed it!

Terry Miles and Frank Banner and Nicky Holt wave us over to a television in the corner of the canteen. We watch the action replay of the goal, a lovely strike from Robbie Fowler who's now back in the groove, scoring instinctively and regularly.

We find our seats, which are on the very back row. If we had known then what we now know about the car-park, we'd have used our position next to the exit to better advantage. Instead we sit back and watch Jamie Pollock commit scandals, atrocities and vicious woundings all over the middle of the park. He has a good kick at everyone, but we manage to keep our shape. Later, Roy Evans will complain that Pollock had 'carnage on his mind'.

At half time I spy a figure who is vaguely familiar. I don't immediately place her but then it all comes scuttling back. Sitting right in front of us, right in the next row, within ruffling distance of her carefully sprayed hair is Danny's 'cracker' from Blackburn. The one with the parka and the Patrik Berger plate badge. It's her! Danny's gone down to the toilet to offload all that greedy, selfish beer he took on board before the match, while I was sipping orangeade and saying:

'We should get off, you know.'

I reckon that if, when he gets back to his seat, he finds I've nipped off somewhere, he won't be able to resist chatting to that certain little lady. He always has to be talking to someone, Danny. So I shuffle around the perimeter gangway until I spot someone I know. Ah-hah! There's Little Tracy and her mum.

We met Little Tracy and her mum in Sion a few seasons ago. Tracy's not actually very little. She's a beautiful, willowy brunette who everyone fancies madly, but our abject inability to deal with women on an equal basis coupled with Tracy's youth has led to the patronising nickname we've saddled her with. (Sorry about that, Little Tracy.) I rabbit on, vaguely remembering seeing them before the Celtic game, and in two shakes of a lamb's tail it's the second half. I clamber back to see how Danny's progressing.

Now, this is what is meant by a sight for sore eyes. It's so beautiful I could cry. The woman is fully turned round to face Danny, animated and laughing at his patter. Danny, for his part, is beaming ruddily, pleased as punch that he's succeeding so well in pulling off this Scouse Card act. There's a Ready Brek aura engulfing them. Anyone remember the scene at the end of the James Bond film where Jaws, the one with metal gnashers, finds a pigtailed girl with corrective braces on her teeth? They smile devotedly at each other. That's these two. At least it will be once I've had a chance to prompt them a little. They're just a bit shy, right now. But this it. This is Lurve.

The second half consists of Bolton chasing the game, Liverpool waiting patiently to spring them on the break and Jamie Pollock, a man with a concave face, still harbouring thoughts of carnage. These three factors converge in one fateful minute to decide the outcome of the game – and perhaps influence Robbie Fowler's season.

Fowler is played through with a precise McManaman daisycutter. He's away from the defence and one-on-one with the keeper. It's McManaman at Blackburn all over again. Fowler has so much time that option after option opens up in front of him. Everyone's up on their feet, shrieking their own advice.

'Go round him, Robbie! Don't even think about anything else! Go round him!'

Unfortunately he does. Or, rather, he tries to. He throws a spellbinding little disco two-step which is meant to send Branagan diving the wrong way. He doesn't buy the dummy. He reaches out instead, and whips the ball from under Fowler's feet. Robbie is beside himself with rage. He screws up his face and looks up to the dark skies. There's only 20 minutes to go. Let's hope this miss is not too costly. No disrespect intended, but anything less than three points at Bolton is a disaster.

Robbie Fowler must still be fuming from his miss because, a minute later, after an innocuous-looking challenge from Per Frandsen, Fowler poleaxes him with a backwards sweep of his forearm. Frandsen makes it look bad, rolling over and playing dead, but whatever the Bolton player did or said to Fowler, it's worked. He's off. The difference a few minutes in football make, hey? Robbie could've been celebrating another brace, three points and the start of a real, bountiful run for both himself and Liverpool. Instead he's looking at a three-match ban and Liverpool have all hands to the pump to try and preserve our flimsy lead. We nearly manage it. The finishing line is within sight when, with a couple of minutes remaining, Nathan Blake rises above everybody to nod home a free-kick. How many times have we seen that, this season? The situation where we survive a lucky scrape, concede a corner or a free-kick but, far from being jolted into some form of galvanised rearguard action by the near-miss, we carry on slumbering and give them another bite at the cherry. How many times will it have to happen before Roy Evans concedes that there's something badly wrong with our defence?

1–1. In the end, though, we're grateful to hold on for a point. Bolton go close twice in the last minute, but it's a bitter, angry mob that piles out of the Reebok. I momentarily lose Danny, but then I spot him up ahead. I can't miss him with that Ready Brek glow shining out like a beacon.

Eggeye's already waiting by the car. We're in, engine running, Radio 5 churning out the bad news, when we realise that nothing, *nobody* is moving. We are completely gridlocked. Approximately 5,000 cars – there's no other way of getting to this mall – are all trying to exit the four vast car-parks at once. 5,000 times 5 quid parking fee. That's £25,000 in parking tolls every home game, and they can't organise a flow system.

Traffic lights'd be a good start. And where are all those pointing, waving, go-this-way stewards who were jumping all over us before the match?

The scores have been and gone. Halifax are top of the Vauxhall Conference. Not one car has moved one inch in all that time. Only after 25 minutes of this do I twig and turn off the ignition. We're not going anywhere. This is what Tony and Gary were warning me about. The Black Hole of Horwich – once entered, never seen again. Just what we need to cap a miserable afternoon.

We're well into David Mellor's first hour before we even start to edge towards the exit. Fist fights are breaking out all over the car-park as impatient drivers try to cut in ahead of each other. Oh for a mobile phone. I'd get Mellor on the line and let him listen to sounds of organised chaos. Sort it out, Bolton. You deserve to go down for treating your customers so badly.

I drop Eggeye first, then pull in to drop Danny, as usual, by The Cross, one of central Birkenhead's biggest drinking areas.

'Going to see her again, then?'

He taps his nose and beams.

'She knows the '74 Cup-winning team.'

I find this strangely cheering. All those victims out there, all those disparate lives so intricately influenced by the fate of the Men In Red. Danny, as always, raps twice on the roof with his knuckles to speed me on my way. I don't feel so bad, after all.

4 NOVEMBER 1997

Strasbourg, home
(UEFA Cup 2nd Round, 2nd Leg)

It's 4 o'clock. I'm in The Carnarvon Castle reading the *Echo*,
hardly taking it in. I keep drifting off into a daydream. In this
daydream Liverpool race out of the starting blocks and into a
2–0 half-time lead. We need to beat Strasbourg by four clear
goals. As tension mounts and the second half ticks away,
Michael Owen slips his markers, shimmies round the goalkeeper and it's 3–0! 15 minutes left. Will it be extra time or can
someone pop up with a winner? We're pushing too many men
forward. We need to stay solid at the back. Strasbourg venture
on a rare raid into our half, punt it long and . . . oh no!
They've scored! Liverpool's players are dropping to their knees
in despair. There's about eight minutes left. Straight from kick-
off McManaman beats four Strasbourg players and pulls back
for Fowler to notch his hat-trick. Seven minutes left. It's win
or bust. Roy Evans takes Harkness off and sends on Karlheinz
Riedle, still struggling with a thigh strain. We bombard the
Strasbourg goal. The support from all sides of the ground is
brain curdling. Strasbourg hold strong. Time is just about up.
We force a corner. Redknapp flights it in, hovering the ball
over the penalty spot on its own air-current. In comes Riedle.
Up goes Riedle. Gets a good connection on it and . . .

'GOAL! YES! YES! YESYESYES!! WE'VE DONE IT!!
WE'VE FUCKINWELL FUCKOFFMANYOU DUN-
NIT!!'

As daydreams go, it's a pretty potent one.

Danny's not due until 4.30, so I slip round to Stanley
Racing. I've got to put some money on 5–1. What'll the odds
be on that? 60 to 1? Somehow, during the short walk, I cool
on the idea. This game is just not going to produce a 5–1
scoreline. Even if I only throw a quid on it, it's money down
the pan. I reckon 3–0 to us is more than possible. Maybe even

4–0. 4–0 is 18 to 1, so I pop a couple of pounds on that, and another deuce on 3–0.

Up ahead I spy the Gargling Bricklayer, marching purposefully towards Matthew Street. I run and catch up in time to see him sneaking into Flannagan's. This puzzles me somewhat, as he's due to be meeting me in The Carnarvon in, ooh . . . three minutes. And then it dawns on me. I know what I'm going to see before I get inside there. The Ready Brek floodlight is visible from outside. I discover a better judgement I wasn't previously aware of having, and decide not to interrupt his date. I trudge back to The Carnarvon. Stood up. Stood up by Danny Giles.

Back in The Carnarvon, two old Liverpool boys are ribbing two hoary old Evertonians about the ease of Southampton's demolition of the Blues at Goodison on Sunday.

'Normal service resumed, eh?' crows one. 'Youse've had your Cup Final now.'

He's right about Everton fading into their bad old ways after trouncing Liverpool so spectacularly the other week. But some credit has be due to Southampton. They were superb. Kevin Davies scored a solo goal of mesmeric quality. He's another who we watched and watched when he was at Chesterfield, but it was Souness who had the nerve to go out and buy him for Southampton. For £750,000. He's worth £5 million, now. He scores exceptional goals, all the time. But he wasn't Man of the Match. That honour must be reserved for an even more stunning performance from the Southampton midfield. Kevin Richardson was tireless and unbeatable, but next to him was a player of unique grace, speed, vision, tenacity and anticipation. He read everything. He was by far the best player on the pitch and he was Carlton Palmer. Carlton Palmer. The name has become a by-word for bungling, gangling mediocrity. But what a player he was on Sunday! Maybe he's come out the other side of his Tunnel of Trouble wanting to prove a point. If so, he did it in good style in front of the Sky millions on

Sunday. I'll never refer to him in the same breath as Ravanelli again.

I'm just finishing off my pint and trying to decide whether it's too early to go up to the ground when Danny the Stud walks in. He looks pretty pleased with himself. I don't want to let it slip that I've been spying on him, so I don't mention his Date. And neither does he. It's agony. I want to know everything.

Instead we find ourselves talking about bets. He persuades me that I have to put a little side bet on 5–1, so we walk down to William Hill and get a miserly 40 to 1 on it. I have to stake two rips to make it worthwhile. We stop at deCoubertins, the most relaxed and stylish of sports bars, and spend half an hour wandering round their classic photo gallery. Still he doesn't mention Parka Woman. I'm just going to have to drop it. Shred all recollection of her. It's driving me mad.

We jump a cab – but not literally. Only Duncan McKenzie can do that. We get a taxi to take us to The Little Salisbury. I'm keen to keep the other Saturday's good habits going. I'm doing my bit by retracing my steps. All we need is for Liverpool to do likewise. Another 4–0 would do ever so nicely, thanks.

We've been drinking at a nice pace. I've had five slow pints and I'm approaching optimum yodelling level. Too much, and I can't hit the low notes but I'm just peaking for a nice, mellow sing-song. Off to the ground, then.

Electric is an oft-used word to describe that sensation of tense, crackling anticipation when you step into the crowd before an enormous game like this. But it is. The night is electric. It's 7.30 and The Kop is awash with flags. Thousands of them. The stadium's almost full already and the volume has been turned right up. The noise has that slightly drunken intensity that you get at the away games. There's a good chorus of *Liver Bird Upon My Chest* going, and that hardly ever gets sung at home. As the teams run out you can feel the players' hair stand up. If Liverpool can't be moved by adoration like this, then they can't be moved. And if the French team aren't terrified, then they're robots.

Roy pitches up. He's working too hard. He's had to miss out on all the recent aways and now, even at the home games, he's arriving just before kick-off. We wish each other luck and settle back for a minimum of 90 minutes of unbridled tension. Well, no. I don't settle back at all. I sit right on the edge of my seat, hunched forward, urging them on. Strasbourg pack the midfield and defend strongly, keeping chances to a minimum. In an identical position against Paris St Germain last season, needing four on the night, Robbie Fowler scored a cracker after about a quarter of an hour. We thought it was going to be one of those magical nights. But tonight – we scarcely get a shot on goal in the opening half-hour tonight. Strasbourg are growing in confidence. The noise tumbling down from the crowd is less spontaneous. We need a break. Just before half time, just as he did over there, Fowler makes room out of nowhere to curl an audacious chip over the keeper. Somehow he manages to bend himself double and flip backwards to touch it over the bar. It would've been an incredible goal, but not tonight. Tonight it's a marvellous save. o–o at half time.

Ince, who has had a good first half, comes out fighting. He's inspirational. The crowd senses something and wills the team on. Ince drives forward on the hour and cracks a rasping shot in. The keeper dives low but spills it. Michael Owen is first to react, darting in on the loose ball. Surely this is it! Defenders converge and, although he manages to get a shot in, they do enough to put him off. It's not a decisive strike. Our best chance yet has gone begging. Maybe this is just not going to happen.

But before we have a chance to get too despondent, we're 1–o up. Owen gets felled in the box, there's no dissent about the ref's decision and Fowler places his penalty coolly past the

Strasbourg keeper. There's about 25 minutes left. Riedle's on, now, and he's making a difference. Strasbourg have abandoned any thoughts of hitting us on the break and are throwing every man behind the ball. Ince urges his team-mates forward. We carve out half-chances but Strasbourg are getting the run of the ball. It looks beyond us.

From yet another corner, Riedle gets up miraculously and despatches a Yozzer Hughes headbutt into the net!! 2–0!! Incredible scenes of rejoicing. I have both Boffins in my arms, dancing round and round in circles. How long left?! How long left?!

There's still six or seven minutes to go. We can do this. Strasbourg's collective arse has gone. They're hoofing the ball anywhere, everywhere, slicing it up in the air and putting themselves under unbearable pressure. Surely they'll fold, now. The Kop blasts out its support as McManaman and Ince exchange passes. McManaman's away! This is it. He's bamboozled his closest marker and is now behind the defence, heading for the box. Four red shirts are screaming for the pull back. It bobbles through to Fowler who, if he does anything wrong, tries to bring the ball under control too hastily and gets the ball stuck under his feet. He digs out a shot which is blocked by three sets of thighs and flies out for our 200th corner.

We've played 95 minutes. The Strasbourg coach is pacing up and down by the dugout, remonstrating with the linesman. Come on Karlheinz Riedle! Another Bundesliga Bullet and we're there! But almost inevitably the corner is a poor one, Strasbourg clear and manage to hold on to the ball for long enough for the ref to decide that that's enough throbbing pulses for one night. The crowd rises as one to applaud both teams and Liverpool are able to leave the battleground with their heads held high. Later, furious friends of mine will complain that we're too used to playing the role of gallant losers. But I really can't complain about tonight. It was tremendous. We were great.

Danny and me end up on the last train back to Birkenhead. Finally I crack and enquire, ever so gently, whether he has any intention of seeing 'that bird' again. He taps his nose and beams.

8 NOVEMBER 1997

Tottenham, home

Just what we need. I'm sitting in Dooley's enjoying a lovely egg and Ulster-fry on toast, digesting every word of Mark Lawrenson's column. And then I see it. A Mad Statistic. You can guarantee that whenever one of these statistics is dusted down it'll be used as a stick to beat you with. I remember a few years back, one of the local radio stations smarmily pointed out that Chelsea hadn't won at Anfield in their last 37 visits or something. Whatever the statistic, it was just asking for it. Nobody knew or cared that Chelsea hadn't won at Anfield for donkey's years (or, indeed, for dogsdays). But as soon as this jackanapes pointed it out, obviously we were on a hiding to nothing. Chelsea won. And now, right next to Lawrenson's thoughts are those little It's a Fact boxes, containing meaningless, useless snippets of football trivia. Mad Statistics. Such as this. Tottenham have only won once in the League at Anfield in 71 years. I mean, who needs to know *that*?! It's just asking for it, isn't it? I eat up, shout ta-ra to The Dool and jog to Hamilton Square. Danny, mysteriously, is vague about his plans today. I'm still in a lather over the statistic. I make dashed sure that no platform clocks sneak a 13 on me this time.

First half is dire. There's nothing out on the pitch which is remotely as entertaining as Gerry Francis' barnet. What is the man playing at! It's a throwback swede, throwing Gerry back to the days when he was an apprentice boilermaker in 1973. His hair is as follows: bald yet still spiked on top; cut blunt above his ears; long and bushing out at the back. How the players can take instruction from a man who looks like Wayne in *Auf Wiedersehein Pet*'s dad is beyond me. Maybe he's harking back to the golden years of Hoddle 'n' Waddle, circa *Diamond Lights*. That's Hoddle as in Glenn. The England manager. The image-conscious disciplinarian.

Tottenham are marginally the less bad of the two teams, and the game is bluntly poised at 0–0 as the teams troop off for their hot toddies. We're looking good for that second League defeat in 71 years. A stroke of luck in the first couple of minutes of the second half comes to our assistance, however. It's about time we had some luck. First, McManaman scores a prod-in from a spilled Redknapp shot. What a predator that McManaman is! Everything he hits goes in! One of the most lethal natural goalscorers I've ever seen. Just as we're recovering from the shock of yet another Stevie Mac strike, up toddles Oyvind Anonymous to follow up a half-parried Fowler shot. 2–0 after 47 minutes! I'd forgotten Leonhardsen was playing until then. Folk around me are saying the jury's still out on Leo, but my own personal Judge Dredd is ready to return his verdict. For his own good, he needs to be dropped. Leonhardsen is overawed by playing for Liverpool. He knows what the pressure is like, now, and he knows what's expected. It'll be different for him watching from the sidelines now that he's had a decent run, different to watching when you're injured. He can analyse the game so that when he gets back in the team he's better able to make a telling contribution. But for now, though, I'd leave him out. Danny Murphy and Patrik Berger are both well overdue a run in the team.

Jamie Redknapp, who's brought his shooting boots today, blasts in a beauty from 25 yards, then Michael Owen seals an unlikely rout with a devastating burst of pace in the last few minutes. 4–0. Who'd have thought it.

There's no Danny in The Albert after the game, either. He was seen headed towards the bus stops with 'some auld bird'. Who'd have thought that, either.

21 NOVEMBER 1997

Birkenhead Park

The incredible healing ribcage hasn't given me any bother all week. I should probably give it another couple of weeks to bond properly, but what the heck? It's a lovely, muddy day and I haven't played for years.

In fact, nothing has happened for years. Arsenal beat Man. U 3–2 with a last-minute header from David Platt, and England beat Cameroon 2–0. Robbie Fowler scored a cute little nod-in to make the game safe, which'll be a relief to him. Hoddle made it clear in the summer that Fowler and McManaman had put themselves in the Naughty Corner by booking themselves in for operations rather than playing in Le Tournoi. The likes of Paul Scholes, who had a good tournament, and Ian Wright bumped themselves up the queue for France '98.

Both McManaman and Fowler have since pleaded that their operations were essential and that they liaised with Hoddle over the scheduling of them, yet the England manager issued an embarrassing 'I don't get mad, I get even' threat. It was a poignant moment seeing the two Reds on the bench in Rome, trying to look committed in their supporting role but knowing that they should've been out there. They ran onto the pitch for the celebrations at the end, tracksuits on, while bare-chested Ince and Ian Wright were doing a lap of honour. They must have felt awful, knowing that less good players were now firmly ahead of them in Hoddle's troubled mind. It's good that Robbie is back in the frame for England. He's got such breathtaking ability, Hoddle shouldn't even think about it. He should be an automatic choice. But he's scored, anyway, it's his second goal for England and it doesn't matter whether it's Cameroon or Germany. It was a nice way for him to go out.

He started his three-match ban, for the Bolton incident, after that. Fortunately, two of those games are home bankers. Grimsby, who we despatched 3–0 on Tuesday night, and Barnsley tomorrow. Easy. Teams are queuing up to boost their goal-difference against Barnsley. They've conceded seven, six and five in their last three games, so we should be good for two or three, even on our current weird form. But after Barnsley it's Arsenal, away, a game I will miss due to a prior date in Amsterdam for Mr Dodd's 40th. Our plan, when Arsenal was a Saturday game, was to fly straight out after the game and have Saturday and Sunday night in The Dam. When it was switched to Sunday, Jegsy broke the news.

'Everyone else is up for going on Friday, now . . .'

'Even Danny?'

'Even Danny.'

I'm surprised. Arsenal, away, is a game Danny would never want to miss. Whatever, we ended up booking Jegsy's weekend for Friday, 28 November. Next week.

This week, now, I must play football. I get there a bit late, but even on this chilly, sloppy day it's a heart-warming turnout. Puffa is there with a full car-load. Peter Hooton has brought songwriting partner Steve Grimes, along with Liam Streuth and Mick Potter, so that's eight from Liverpool. Roy is just arriving, so that's nine. And here's Double D, The Dool himself, squeezing his famous white delivery van onto the end of the row. Also present from the posh side of town are

Treeman, Blackie, Charlie, Jegsy, Colin Chopadopalis and Simon From The Pub. Eight including myself. We'll see how it goes up until half time and maybe rejig the sides after the break.

It's a hard first half, in every sense. The pitch is boggy, the ball soon becomes heavy and Puffa's accomplices today are Jimmy Fowler and Baby Bucko, two very spirited competitors, along with Bucko himself, who plays like he broke a leg in Paris last year. Mick Potter is always a hard opponent, too. He's got great skill, he's pretty strong but . . . well . . . he plays with his elbows out.

On balance, we're just about the faster side. Baby Bucko is lightning, Jimmy is fast but the rest of them rely on other weaponry. Steve can dribble, Peter and Puffa are exquisite passers of the ball and Roy scores four or five every week. From extremely close range. But their team isn't overstocked with sprinters. For an 18-year-old who used to outrun whippets a year ago, Liam has gone terribly slow. He's either discovered booze, girls, cocaine or all three.

On our side Blackie is fast, skilful and very clever. He sees things early. Charlie is quick, selfish and always good for a hat-trick. Dool, Colin, Jegs and Simon are all slow, but compensate with great timing in the tackle, good anticipation and a good range of tricks. Jegsy's great in the air. Treeman's a brilliant goalkeeper who should never play outfield. When he runs, he looks like a baby giraffe whose legs are about to splay out from under him. I just go bright red, whatever the weather, and shout a lot.

We go 2–0 up quite quickly, but that means nothing. What means more is that Treeman, enjoying his traditional 20 minutes' playing out before taking his place in goal, misses three glorious chances in quick succession. Straight from the third, Peter flights the ball over our midfield with enough backspin for it to sit up for Jimmy Fowler. He takes it forward with two touches and plants it. Open sesame, floodgates!

For the remainder of the half we survive a mauling only by virtue of courageous and inspired goalkeeping by the Treeman and abysmal finishing from Liverpool. We actually extend our lead to 3–1 at one point, but by half time it's 5–3 to them. There's no such thing as a half-time team talk. Everyone just sits together and talks about whoever isn't there. Feeling immediately guilty as soon as I've blurted it out, I say:

'What about Danny and this mystery woman of his, eh?'

So shocked is Puffa by the story that, still reeling at the start of the second-half, he lets me nick the ball off his toe and weave through the stationary Liverpool defence to make it 5–4. For much of the second-half we lead 8–6, largely due to tired legs all round and a staggering, surely-impossible volley from Blackie. He lifts his left foot up somewhere above his shoulder as though it were another hand and, with his right foot still firmly on the floor, hammers a ferocious, unstoppable missile past Hooton in goal. Most players in the Premier League can't volley like that. We played in a charity game last year against a knockabout team whose cumbersome midfield included one John Barnes. Blackie scored one of those volleys and chipped their keeper for another. A week or two later I bumped into Barnes, shopping in Chester, and was shameless enough to stop him and talk about the game as though it had some bearing on the outcome of the Championship.

'Who's the kid who scored the volley?' asked Barnes, shaking his head in wonder at the recollection of it.

Kid? He must be 32! Trying to disguise my envy as modesty I looked at the pavement, kicked my heels awkwardly and allowed an embarrassed grin to spread all over my face.

'That was me, actually, John,' I gushed.

He shook his head again, this time in pity, and went on his way.

Blackie's volley makes it 8–6 to us, then I miss a chance so easy that, if I'd had a blunderbuss like Hank's in *The Three Bears* I'd have shot myself in the thigh with hardened bacon rind. 9–6 and it would've been over, but as so often happens, the missed chance reminds them that they're still in it. With Roy Boulter as timekeeper they're always in with a chance of sneaking a last-ditch equaliser and that's exactly what happens. I'm purple in the face with fury – fury at myself, of course, dressed up as disgust with Roy for adding on nine minutes. He looks incredibly upset that anyone could call him a cheat.

Nobody's ever discussed it, but we never allow ourselves an honourable draw. It's always next goal wins. We surge upfield, me, Charlie and Blackie interchanging passes. Blackie fires in a cross-cum-shot. Jimmy, in goal, drops it. The ball bobbles along the non-existent line. I just have to touch it in. Lick it. Get a hair on it. Anything. What I end up getting on it is worse than useless. I wave my right foot at it. My right foot is as powerful and as accurate as a lilac fart. Jimmy hoofs it clear and smug, jubilant, infuriating Hooton runs in on an unguarded goal to score the winner. He runs around the pitch with his arms in the air, putting on one of his ridiculous commentator's voices.

'Oh yes! Sensational! Maradona has stolen it for Argentina with the last kick of the match!'

I run to catch up with him.

'Argentina my arse! That was shite!'

A major incident is prevented by the sight of Danny Giles heading across the cricket square towards us.

'Fuckinell!' shouts Bucko. 'It's Studs Terkel!'

The one running to the trees for a timely piddle was me.

22 NOVEMBER 1997

Barnsley, home

It's 7.10, evening of the game, and I'm staring into an abyss. Yet again, I shall be unable to watch *Match of the Day*. In fact, I shall be unable, or unwilling, to move. I feel numb. I don't want to do anything. With feelings of enormous disloyalty to Roy Evans, I lie there, close my eyes and let it happen. It's this season's first visitation. It's time for ... YOU – THE MANAGER.

I'm weird about this. Everyone must do it, surely? Speculate about what they'd do if their team's chairman got to hear about their unerringly accurate assessment of team matters and, in a stroke of blind panic-stricken inspiration, appointed YOU – THE MANAGER. Money is no object. The chairman'll back you to the hilt. You can go out and buy whoever want, regardless of whether they're available and regardless of whether Alessandro Del Piero has any ambition to join Darlington. You can do whatever you want inside the comfort zone of your own demented head.

But I do it a bit different. I do the whole thing for real, every time. I conjure up this entire fantastic scenario that makes the whole thing almost possible. Here's what happens. Gag, who works in the rightly renowned Bar Flava in Southport, is talking to one of the distant relatives of David Moores, Liverpool's Chairman, who sometimes drinks in there. They're talking about how, often, the fans see things that the management miss. Gag mentions that his good friend, Kevin Sampson, is a very shrewd judge of a player. Completely out of the blue, just like that, David Moores steps out from around the corner where he's been sitting alone, listening. He hands Gag his mobile phone:

'I think it's about time I met this Kevin ...'

And that's how it starts. He calls me in, tells me he has

nothing but the greatest respect for Roy Evans but desperate times require courageous decisions. The job's mine, if I want it. I kiss his hand and tell him he won't regret this. I am the man to lead Liverpool out of the doldrums and back to the pinnacle!

I then have all these conversations with Moores about balancing the books, how the job is about all-round skilful asset-management. I do all this, lying on my bed, as though the whole thing is a kissing-cousin of reality. Only then does the fun start. Out go half the squad – 'ripping the whole thing apart', as Roy Evans calls this reactionary process – and in come Chris Perry, Matthew Elliott, Rio Ferdinand and Steve Staunton. I flirt with names like Juninho, Kinkladze, even Nemec, the Czech left-back.

I go further. I bring John Barnes in to run the Reserve Team. Liverpool Reserves used to win every single game they played. Last season we needed to beat Everton in the last game of the season just to stay in the top flight. This season we're fourth from bottom. Part of the problem is that the Reserve team is being used as a kind of Sin Bin for out-of-favour players, instead of a talent pool to feed the first team squad. On the couch tonight in my session as manager, I bring John Barnes in to coach the Reserves, and give him his own budget of £3 million to sign players from the lower leagues. He is to run the team like a first team in miniature. His brief is to develop the talent that steps up from the youth teams, but also to go out and buy the most promising teenagers around, all over the world.

Back with my own squad, I buy Robbie Keane from Wolves, Carl Serrant of Oldham, Damien Duff from Blackburn, Richard Wright of Ipswich and Kevin Davies from Southampton, but I'm buying them for the future. I always end up with the following team. The formation is 4–1–3–2, with Matteo playing in front of the back four.

James

Carragher   Elliott   Babb   Staunton

Matteo

McAteer   Ince   Murphy

Owen   Fowler

Here are two Depressing Theories and a Fact:

Fact: you can be Real Madrid and buy the 11 most gifted players in the world, but they won't make a team. A team that wins trophies, year after year, has heart and spirit. The team above contains winners in every position, and more ability than you can shake a stick at to go with it.

Depressing Theory 1: McManaman wants to leave Liverpool. His carefully worded statements to the contrary are rife with get-out clauses, comments like:

'All my friends and family are here – it'd be senseless for me to leave Liverpool at the moment.'

There's no point in putting him in my team when his heart has already left Liverpool.

Depressing Theory 2: Jamie Redknapp, who lives and breathes Liverpool, will never turn out to be a key player for us. He's got everything as a player, Jamie Redknapp, except perhaps that final ingredient of committed, passionate application – hatred, almost – that all winners possess. What you want from your players, especially your playmakers, is the ability to change the face of a game. To make a difference. To be the type who, when the chips are down, is out there scheming, planning how he can take things into his own feet and make something happen. To me, Redknapp goes missing in games like that. He's the most beautiful, extravagant talent when we're 3–0 up, but when it's Everton and we're suddenly two goals down, he's not the one who's going to turn it round. He won't be demanding the ball. You can tell an awful lot from players by the way they show for the ball – or don't. From throw-ins, for example, you'll get the type who make darting little runs, trying to make space, and you'll get those who shake their head, signal with their hands that they don't want the ball and point to someone else. That's Jamie. I've watched him for years, willing him to fulfil all that glorious potential. My view – as The Manager, lest we forget – is that that is what it'll remain. Potential. It goes without saying that every other critic in the country thinks Redknapp should have Paul Gascoigne's berth in the England midfield, that he's a maestro and a matchwinner and I hope desperately that they're right and I'm wrong. But I can't help myself. I see it like this – he's been our central midfielder for six years now and we've won absolutely fuck all. I'd try something else.

So there we have it. We've been beaten at home today by the worst team in the Premiership and I have spent Saturday evening lying on my bed, fantasising, doing deplorable things in my mind with people I've never met. I feel terribly guilty once it's all over.

Our next games are away, at Arsenal, then at home, to Manchester United. We started this season convinced, absolutely certain that this was going to be the year. After false dawns last year and the year before, this team was going to be the one to bring the Championship back for the first time since 1990. We're still in November and we've been beaten – by Leicester, West Ham, Everton and now Barnsley – four times.

Beaten four times already in our Championship season. We might need a little extra time.

29 NOVEMBER 1997

Amsterdam, away

It suddenly strikes me, just before we land at Schiphol, that everything is going to be fine. Starting this weekend. Liverpool, without Robbie Fowler, are playing Arsenal, with Dennis Bergkamp back and raring to go after injury. Towards the end of last season, when Bruce Rioch was still manager at Arsenal, there was talk that he was trying to set up a swap deal to bring McManaman and Redknapp to Highbury with Bergkamp and cash going to Liverpool. It never came off, and Wenger would never contemplate the move, now – it'd mean bringing two English players to Highbury – but what a dilemma! Imagine Bergkamp, Fowler and Owen together . . .

Games like Sunday's, when one side is hitting a tricky patch and the other is motoring, seldom go the way of form in the Premiership. This is something we have to acclimatise ourselves to. No team is going to terrify another with their reputation any more. For the foreseeable future, no team is going to be supremely better than the rest. No team will embark upon 12-game winning runs. Nobody is unbeatable. Leicester, say, are more than capable of beating Manchester United. Liverpool will lose at home to Barnsley one week and win at Highbury the next. This is the way it's going to be, all season. We'll probably lose another four or five, and still win the Championship. Starting on Sunday. This is the almost evangelical calling which hits me, as we're circling Amsterdam, awaiting our go-ahead to land. We're going to win at Arsenal on Sunday, and win the League. Oh, Lordy! It's a good job the only God I believe in wears Liverpool's Number 9 shirt.

Of the travelling party of 13, we have four Evertonians on board. In order to save them from further embarrassment, I have changed their names. They shall be known as Micky Musker, Clid, Markoosh and TC. They make a pathetic deputation to me as soon as our first drink is in our hands.

'Listen, Kev. It's Jegsy's weekend, right? We don't want to ruin it for him with all the usual stuff, eh?'

The usual stuff is me and TC arguing fervently, with fulsome enjoyment, from the first minute of the night to the last, about whether or not Everton will succumb to their destiny to play in Division One next season. He's pretty easy to get going. You just tell him that Liverpool fans don't care either way what happens to Everton. They're not really our rivals any more, so who cares? Of course we all really, really, really want them to go down and rot in the stinking mediocrity of Division One and play teams like Bury and Crewe and Stockport. But we don't really care . . . Markoosh joins in.

'What d'you reckon? Truce for the weekend?'

I reckon I can manage it if they can. We shake on it.

The truce lasts approximately three hours. Emboldened by a vicious combination of skunk and Amstel, the four kamikazes proceed to stand in front of the hurtling express train of fate and taunt it with bare fists.

'2–0!! We beat The Shite 2–0!!' they sing lustily to the tune of *Blue Moon*. I'd love to be able to say that we winced at each other out of pure embarrassment for them, but that wouldn't be strictly true. Rather, it was the signal we'd been expecting, the starting pistol for a night of very petty backbiting. But they started it.

So it was that, with enormous satisfaction on Saturday, 29 November, we crowded into Markoosh's room to witness unbelievable pictures being beamed live from Goodison Park.

The natives were restless. They were not happy. They wore pinched, pained, humiliated expressions. They had just seen their team (Everton, that is) being humbled by the mighty Tottenham Hotspur, a team in an even worse mess – or so it seemed – than Everton. Tottenham won 2–0, but according to this report, now, they wiped the floor with a woeful, dispirited Everton. The fans have stayed behind in the ground, en masse, shouting for the head of their Chairman, Peter Johnson. They want to stick it on the end of a big sharp spike on the gates of Goodison Park and send out an SOS. To who? Doctor David Marsh?

We say nothing to the Blues. We're too busy trying to keep our faces straight. This antagonises TC beyond the realms of human belief. He throws himself across the bed, jugular veins standing out, shrieking:

'Come on then!! Let's get it over with!!'

At first I think he's challenging me to a bout of cudgels in the nearby Vondelpark. But no. A scene yet more curious than that on the TV screen unfolds. He lies flat on his back, arms stretched into a crucifix.

'Come on!! Let's have all your pathetic, horrible, predictable Red Shite jibes out of youse now, 'cos I'm not letting this ruin MY night!!'

I look down on him with unhidden astonishment and step over his prostrate body, stopping by the bedroom door to make certain that this actually happened. He's still lying there, arms splayed out, a tortured man staring at the ceiling for hope. I can still hear him wailing as I sprint down the corridor as though a tidal wave is about to appear behind my shoulder.

'Youse'll laugh the other side of your faces when Arsenal twat youse tomorrow!!'

Poor lad, relying on other teams for his jollies so early in the season. Tragic.

Down in the hotel bar, Danny is terrifying four air-hostesses from the Croydon area. He's a faithless bastard, Danny. No sooner is he away from his lovely, snorkel parka'ed ladyfriend than he's wooing someone else with that silken tongue of his. I don't know what he's saying to them, but the four girls are simultaneously trying to back into a space the size of an overnight bag at one end of the bar. I bound back upstairs to Jegsy's room. He's still red-faced and tear-stained with laughter over the Goodison report.

'Quick! Get down to the bar! Danny's about to go down for manslaughter. He's talking these girls to death . . .'

We go down and talk to them, too. There's Carole, tall and beautiful, the only one with a current boyfriend. Marisa with the flashing eyes and dramatic cheekbones. Penny, quiet and a little bit poorly. And then there's Sonya. Sonya is small, blonde, vivacious and funny. She is, let's face it, Baby Spice – and it is she who's under the most immediate threat from Danny's repartee. Her face is an atlas of puzzlement as she strives to understand one single word the existentialist bricklayer is saying to her. She used to live in Chester but she hasn't a clue what Danny's going on about.

'The man with the round stomach climbs two hills while the thin man quickly dies of thirst . . .' he rasps.

Sonya pulls a face behind his back. They're tired. They're going to have a rest before they decide where they're going tonight. Taking the brush-off with all the dignity of a beaten Evertonian we say, no problem – we had plans anyway. We're, er . . . we're going for a great, big, Indonesian banquet. Yeah. That's where we're going.

Which we do. And quite delicious it is, with spicy, aromatic pork and wisp-thin slivers of beef in liquorice sauce. I think that's where my problems started. The beef in liquorice dish has an almost immediate effect upon me – that effect being an instantaneous bellowing from my bowels. My metabolism warns me something's up by making me trump pungently, two or three times. Our banqueting table is a riot of hilarity and theme-from-Toblerone singing, so nobody notices the noxi-ous farting too much. I do, though. It's right under my nose. I go to the toilet and have quite a sloppy time of it.

Waiting outside the restaurant for our taxis, I'm still aware of the smell. More so than before, now we're in the open air. It's deadly. It's not just your ordinary, lingering, smelly old trump gas. This is poison. It's rotten. It reeks. I ask TC and Markoosh – not, on reflection, the most reliable witnesses – whether they've noticed anything, but they reassure me that we all smell of spicy food. Don't worry about it. Have a laugh.

In the taxi, though, there's no escaping it. I'm minging badly. I turn to my brother, Neil, for a verdict. If you can't trust your own brother to tell you whether you've followed through, who can you trust? He gives my kecks a desultory sniff and returns to his conversation about the great chocolate bars of the '70s. Maybe I'm imagining it, but the pong follows me around so doggedly that I have to take myself off into the toilets of a busy drinking establishment to check out the damage once and for all. I'm wearing a pair of off-white (ecru, apparently) Hamnett jeans. When I eventually manage to balance myself on a broiling hot radiator for long enough to be able to get a sight of my backside in the mirror (but not for so long that I suffer anything worse than third-degree burns), I start to get a measure of what's happened here. The evidence is incontrovertible. There's a vagina-shaped yellow-green stain between my buttocks. I've cacked myself.

Suddenly I can't avoid my own stench. Everyone in Old Amsterdam must be able to smell me. I shuffle out of the building, head down, and out onto the teeming streets of the red-light district, sticking close to the canals in the hope that the faint breeze will diffuse the pong. I can't inflict myself upon some poor taxi driver. I hum. I'm going to have to jog back to the hotel, get myself cleaned up and get straight back out again.

The run only takes me 15 minutes. As grateful as I've ever

been for anything, I hurl myself inside the sliding automatic hotel doors and . . .

'Kevin!! Hi!! Come and have a drink!!'

The air-hostesses are back at the bar, drunk. Nothing else explains their unrestrained pleasure at seeing someone they were humouring politely only four hours ago.

'Come on! Come an' have a bevvy with your mates!'

'Well, I've . . .'

'Oh yeah? Not so brave without your pals, eh? Come on. Have a glass of wine.'

Marisa pours out about a half pint of ruinous-looking red wine and pulls me to the little bar by my sleeve. Sod it. They asked for it. If they want a stinky person sitting next to them, here I jolly well am.

They don't seem to notice anything. Maybe the worst of it has dried up. Maybe they're just too drunk, too tired, too merry to care. Penny, who is not feeling at all well, goes to bed. Maybe she caught the whiff full on but didn't like to mention it. Whatever, the rest of us get into a strange conversation about love and, inevitably, sex. I say that kissing is the most underrated sexual skill of all. I tell them all that I am a wonderful kisser. I will happily spend the entire night kissing each and every one of them.

This offer is so tempting that Sonya and Marisa start yawning and stretching. To my considerable consternation, though, our idle jousting seems to have awoken stirrings of desire in willowy Carole. This is tricky. In our two conversations thus far – the first lasting 20 minutes, this one now well into its second hour – I have failed to mention my besottedly happy married status. It just hasn't come up, yet. We're just chit-chatting at the bar and I haven't felt the need to jump up and shout:

'By the way, girls, I should warn you! I'm married, you know!'

There is another matter, too, which could yet prevent me

from capitalising on Carole's tentative interest. I have dried poo encrusted on my thighs, groin and buttocks. She seems to be mouthing a room number at me. Yes, here we go – she's drawing it in thin air, right over the top of her two sleepy chums' heads lest they think badly of her. Crumbs. What'll I do?

45 seconds later I am in my own bedroom, precariously perched on top of the small pedestal washing-basin with my bottom against the mirror, my head craned back over my shoulder and a soapy flannel working assiduously around the soiled area. I pat myself down, root out a clean pair of boxers, slap a palmful of zesty Czech and Speake aftershave onto my squeaky-clean buttocks to stifle any last lingering pong and present myself ship-shape and lips puckered at Room 102. There is no answer. A gentle buzz of snoring is all there is to be heard. I knock a little more loudly.

'Who's there?'

'It's me.'

'Who?'

'The Kisser.'

I smooch kisses through the keyhole. Carole appears at the door, tall, sleepy and a little bit cross.

'What do you want?'

I try to do one of those Carry On Shagging 'what do *I* want??!' sort of faces, but I know straight away it's not working. I hang my head.

'I don't really want anything, to be honest. It's just that you gave me your room number and I thought it'd be a bit rude if I just went off up to bed without pestering you at least a little bit.'

She laughs.

'I didn't.'

'You did.'

'Nice try.'

'Thanks.'

I slink back to my room with my tail between my legs, but with a fantastic-smelling arse. To spare me further humiliation, Carole bumps into Danny at breakfast and tells him she only gave me her room number so that we could invite them all to Jegsy's last-day-in-Amsterdam-birthday-Sunday-brunch today. Which, thinking back, is exactly what she *did* do. I mean, I wasn't going to do anything, was I? It's just very, very bad manners not to present yourself spick and span at a lady's quarters if invited. What might she think of me? She might've turned up for breakfast, all Wonderbra'd and tall, and shouted across the room to Danny and co:

'Gave your mate Kevin me room number last night – but he didn't turn up!'

What might people think *then*? Still, eh? Everton got thumped and we're going to beat Arsenal later on. Mustn't grumble.

Finding myself shunned by polite society – there goes the lad who thought he was 'on' – and finding my back aching from perching too long on minute washing pedastals, I decide to take advantage of one of Old Amsterdam's specialities. A massage. What I have in mind here is a proper, brutal, above-the-counter sports injury massage which will, with luck, relieve my many and niggling ailments. Thigh pulls. Groin strains. Attitude problems.

I ask at the hotel reception in a loud and confident voice if they can recommend such a place, an establishment which specialises in Straight massage.

'Not straight as in, you know . . . heterosexual. I mean, I want a heterosexual massage . . . or, well, more to the point I don't want a . . .'

I'm not doing very well. I try again.

'I just want somewhere that'll give it me . . . Straight.'

'Most places do, sir,' she answers, perplexed.

Shit. What's up with me? Why can't I tell her what I want?

'No, no – I don't mean *that*. I mean . . . what I want is an

ordinary, straightforward massage. Non-kinky, yes? A pum-
melling. An honest, non-kinky massage.'

She's looking at me as though I am the living spirit of the
Mad Englishman of recent lore. I see TC, Markoosh and
Musker coming up the three steps into reception. They start
making farting and rasping sounds and holding their noses. I
give up the massage as a bad job. Stupid bloody idea, anyway.
The Bluenoses look unbelievably smug for a minority
representation of a team who are definitely going down.

'Ready to see The Shite get twatted, are you?'

I give them my best, most patient Alastair Sim look, peering
at them over imaginary half-rim spectacles.

'Boys. Desist from this folly. You support a shit team and
you are in shock. You are in denial. Do not try to resist the
mighty Reds. Instead, embrace Us. It is never too late to see
the light. Do you see it? Do you see the light?'

'Fuck off!'

'Fuck off you! We'll twat Arsenal today!'

And we do. We beat Arsenal. Now regular scorer Steve
McManaman notches another incredibly lucky fluke goal,
wellying the ball aimlessly towards Seaman's goal and jumping
for joy when, to his total amazement, it flies into the net. It's a
marvellous goal, a strike from a player entering his peak. You
just know it, you know – McManaman's going to do things on
a football pitch over the next four or five years that mark him
down in history as one of the greats. Let's just hope that this
isn't his last year doing it for us. And let's also hope that
Hoddle takes the red blinkers off his rheumy, suspicious eyes.

The minibus which carries us from Manchester airport back
to Merseyside is a joyous little wagon. It matters not that those
laugh-a-minute Evertonians spiked me with laxatives last
night. It's all coming out, now – boom-boom! It matters not
that 13 handsome, virile, exotic kissers like ourselves have
returned from Europe's capital of sleaze unblemished by
romance. Even the ones who paid to go with hookers couldn't

rise to the occasion – but, as Evertonians, that was nothing new. None of this matters. It matters not, because today Liverpool beat Arsenal. Yesterday, Tottenham beat Everton. And we're just back from Amsterdam. Weekends don't come much better than this.

Each time I catch TC's eye, his face implores me for mercy. Don't kick a Dog of War when it's down, his eyes beseech. There's no reason in the world why I should show clemency. That animal'd be all over me if the boot was on the other foot. But I let him off, regardless. When I catch his eye I just smirk, hold my hands up and say:

'No, no. Nothing.'

They can't wait to get home. Marcus is called Markoosh because Pilar in *Eldorado* used to call Marcus Tandy '*Markoosh*'. I've been trying to remember the name of the Jesse Birdsall character all weekend and it's the second to last thing that creeps through my mind before I black out on Sunday night. The last thing is that we play Manchester United on Saturday. Win that and we'll win the League.

5 DECEMBER 1997

BICC Social Club, Helsby

Ah, the joy of nets! Full-sized goals and nets! It still has the same effect on me now as it did when Thingwall Primary School first got nets when I was nine. I want to run out onto the pitch with a giddy thrill in my stomach and blast the ball in, time after time, from every conceivable angle. I will never tire of cracking the ball into a real goal with nets. When I can hit the target, that is.

Running out impressively onto the BICC pitch for our

once-a-year game against a real team – this time it's West Cheshire Constabulary – I manage to sprint towards an open goal (everyone else is still in the changing room), take aim and, conscious that a wide-eyed collection of kids has gathered on one touchline mistaking the presence of proper football kits for the presence of proper footballers, curl the ball five yards wide of the furthest goalpost and onto the M56.

It's not a great game. Our team consists of the united might of the two Friday teams. Puffa, Peter, Gary Hart, Tony Sage, Steve and Mick Potter, along with Jegsy in goal, Charlie, The Dool, Colin and me. We lose 5–3, but feel we could've won it. We've never played together as a team, for a start, and the pitch feels enormous. Considering they were 4–1 up after an hour, we didn't do too badly. Another 10 or 15 minutes and we might've done it. Anyway. Real nets. Fabulous. Bring on United.

6 December 1997

Manchester United, home

Why does everybody detest poor old Man. Utd so? University doctorates now exist on the subject, but it's an easy one. They're detestable. Chelsea aren't exactly lovable themselves, but when they play in Europe you want them to win. Everyone does. But when it comes down to spiteful Man. Utd playing arrogant Borussia Dortmund, there can be only one winner for us patriotic Tommies. A nation celebrated when Dortmund caned them, convincingly, home and away. A nation celebrated because Man. Utd make themselves hateful. They have no humility. In short, they suffer from the ultimate in hubris – they have delusions of grandeur.

That arrogance is best represented by Messrs Beckham and Sheringham. Gary 'Mad Eyes' Neville's not far behind, either. They've been led to believe that they're 'winners', that they're players who'll die for the cause. But they're not. They're fakers. They're not even Hard Men. Roy Keane is a Hard Man and an absolutely fantastic player. You'd love to have him in your team. And Ryan Giggs. A genius, but first and foremost a team player. But Beckham? He's dabbling at it. David Beckham will always steer clear of the likes of Neil Redfearn or Kevin Richardson or Patrick Vieira – they scare him. Especially if Father Ted isn't there to back it up for him. Yet he'll go looking for Ginola, Overmars or Zola, trying to make his point. It's a pity. Beckham's blessed with sublime skills, but he's better known for Brylcreem and cupping his hand to his ear. He's going to fuck himself up.

Delusions of grandeur seem endemic to Manchester. The city keeps bidding for the Olympics, bidding for all sorts of international events, competing with the likes of Sydney, Toronto, Amsterdam. This is most bizarre behaviour from Manchester, a characterless industrial town in northern England. It's like Betty Turpin continually applying for the lead romance part opposite Leonardo di Caprio. Get real, Manchester. Who's the odd one out in this list? Sydney. New York. Manchester. Paris. Liverpool. The answer is Manchester. If you showed a foreigner a postcard of any of the other famous cities of the world, they'd recognise it. Manchester's just an ordinary northern town, but arrogance reigns supreme there.

Perhaps they have a right to be cocky, Man. U. For five years now, they've dominated the Premier League – though you'd have to argue that only the 1994 team was truly in a League of its own. They've benefited since then from the levelling out of the competition in general and the consequent incapability of one of their rivals to seize the initiative. But still, no sour grapes. They're the team that keeps winning it and they're the new bench-mark.

This actually makes things a little easier for Liverpool fans. Coming to Liverpool used to be like a trip to hell for United, but the antagonism has lessened – slightly – in inverse proportion to their success. Our complaint used to be that, no matter how successful Liverpool became, no matter how many European Cups, League Championships, Super Cups and new English records we conquered, the media would always favour Man. United. Any sniff of achievement – three wins on the trot or a last-minute equaliser against Norwich – would spark a frenzy of delirious praise for the north-west's perennial under-achievers. They'd always be referred to as Britain's Biggest Team or The Most Famous Club in the World, epithets which were spurious in the extreme. We hated it, and we hated them for the jealous, watchful pretenders they were.

Never was this malevolence more marked than the period when Ron Atkinson was in charge. Ron's reign coincided with two more European Cups for Liverpool, several more League Championships and a meaningless League Cup win over them at Wembley, courtesy of a Ronnie Whelan curler. They were like Everton. They'd raise their game to stymie us in the League, but be unable to hoist themselves higher than third or fourth while we were running away with the prizes, yet again. And still the press shouted their name.

It seems less unjust, now. They win the League with the monotonous regularity of Liverpool teams of old. Old Trafford holds 55,000. They're big. They go to pieces as soon as they step out in the European Cup, but they deserve the praise of the tabloids more than any other team, just now. It seems that, now, we're way down the list of teams who claim the most virulent hatred of United. Leeds, Man. City and Chelsea are all up there, but still Bolton reserve that extra degree of loathing. They hate the Red Devils more passionately than any other. This leaves us free to mock them for their other failings.

For a start, the bumptious Old Trafford hordes are the worst offenders for stealing other clubs' songs – and getting them wrong. In the mid '80s, influenced by our regular excursions into Europe, Liverpool had a ditty that went:

'*Championi, championi, championi Li-ver-pool!!*'

The 'ch' is hard. It's *campioni*. Many years later, the unsophisticated element from Manchester, untroubled by over-exposure to foreign travel, have taken the song as their own, ignoring its Italian origins and giving it a judicious 'Spanish' flavour. It's European, right, and so's Manchester. Dead European. It's European as fuck, is Manchester. Here's how the Man. U version goes: '*Champione, champione, ole, ole, ole!!*'

They pronounce the 'ch' in champione as in 'chuck'. Man. Utd fans, too, are the worst offenders for *Go West* songs – it seems like half their repertoire is based on that tiresome gay anthem. By supporting Man. U, so many unattractive, unimaginative people have come to believe they're a breed apart, but they're a bunch of thieving piemen from the milltowns. They nicked the Ronnie Rosenthal song for Andrei Kanchelskis and the Patrik Berger anthem for Andy Cole. It doesn't even scan.

With this balanced, rational take on our opponents, I approach today's match with confidence and trepidation in equal measure. It's an 11.15 kick-off. I hate 11.15 kick-offs. It doesn't feel like you're going to a match. At around the time you'd be contemplating your first pint of the day, perhaps a nice meat and potato pie and a genteel perusal of the day's fixed-odds coupon you find yourself instead heading out of the ground in despair. We never win morning kick-offs. Even years ago, when we used to have 11.00 a.m. kick-offs on the morning of the Grand National, we'd draw games we'd normally expect to win.

Today is a day that I shall have two breakfasts. Breakfast Number One comes at 8 ay-em in Dooley's. I was up at 6, kicking a rolled-up pair of socks round the kitchen. A chair was placed at either end of the quarry-tiled floor, representing Man. U's goal and Liverpool's. In a last-minute change, unknown park player Kevin Sampson was drafted onto the bench. He's not needed, as everything Liverpool hit went in, but with the score at 7–0 after four minutes, Kevin is brought on to rapturous applause and caps his debut by nutmegging Mad Eyes and chipping Schmeichel from three yards.

As soon as it's feasible I'm out to Dooley's, devouring every newspaper in the house for pre-match reports. Robbie Fowler definitely plays. Hurrah! Three mugs of tea and an egg sandwich with brown sauce later, I'm off to the ground for my main breakfast of the day, the Liverpool F.C. Christmas Buffet-Breakfast (With Surprise Gift). Now, normally this is the sort of stunt Roy and I would avoid like the mange, but as the Man. U game has got nearer and nearer we find ourselves inexplicably tickled by the idea of eating bacon and eggs in the boardroom at 10 o'clock on the morning of the match. And don't forget the Surprise Gift or the automatic free entry into the prize draw.

We meet outside the Centenary Stand. I'm (a) late and (b) stuffed. I couldn't eat a thing. Mercifully, there are liberal quantities of Buck's Fizz – just what the doctor ordered to banish those butterflies. Actually, the Buck's Fizz is not supposed to be liberally dispensed. We only read the menu – which clearly states ONE glass of Buck's Fizz per person – after our sixth glass of bubbly, and by then we're hooked.

Things are going well. The Surprise Gift is rather nice. It's a bone china Liverpool tea mug. Excellent. Quite honestly just what I've always wanted – but no one ever seemed to buy one for me. Furthermore, we've managed to sneak multiple entries into the prize draw. We've done this by repeatedly going to the toilet. Each time we re-enter the room, the slightly myopic lady who is organising the draw asks if we've put our name in the hat, yet. I manage to slip three entries in, while Boulter manages an impressive five. One of us is sure to win. It's only going to be a Liverpool mug, after all. Who's hurting?

The nice lady steps forward with her hatful of names. She's excited for us. She announces that today's prize is a signed Liverpool football. Excited kids shrink their heads into their shoulders and grin at their dads. I blush furiously. You're not supposed to get good prizes. I wouldn't've cheated if I'd've known it was going to be a swanky prize like this. It'd make some kid's Christmas if they won the signed Liverpool football! Anyway. If I win, I'll just the hand the ball, straight away, to the nearest heartbroken 9-year-old. The lady dips into her hatful of numbers. We all strain eagerly at her.

'K. Sandon!'

Everyone looks round. No one comes forward. She squints at the little card again.

'V. Sandon? Simpson!'

Ah, shucks – it's me! I'm just going to have to go up there and collect the damn thing, now. But I'll give it away. I will. Just watch. Ears a sprightly shade of rouge and face twitching with embarrassed pleasure, I step up and accept the beautiful, slightly deflated football. It's gorgeous. I take it back to our table where Roy and I pore over it, deciphering illegible signatures. Kids shuffle over to steal a peek at it. No way is any little brat getting this beauty off me. It's mine.

Liverpool start well. Man. United look tired, wary and totally lacking in invention. They're there for the taking. With Paul Ince simultaneously suspended and injured, Jamie Carragher has slotted into the destructive midfielder's role with relish, letting Beckham and Giggs know he's there immediately. We carve out three good half-chances, the best of which sees Michael Owen kill Pallister for pace and blast into the side-netting from a promising position.

United seem to jolt themselves out of whatever torpor is ailing them and come back at us with their teeth showing. Even without Roy Keane, they've got plenty to offer in midfield. Nicky Butt is someone I've liked since he first came into their side a few years ago, and with Mad Eyes pushing up to support him they're starting to hunt in packs again. They do this extremely effectively, closing teams down quickly and harassing them out of their stride. However, with as many as four United players converging on one opponent at times, it would leave them fatally exposed if their prey managed to slip the ball past or through them. If Redknapp chooses today to show what he's truly capable of, we might just have the answer. They're trying Everton tactics on him at the moment, tearing in on a recently returned invalid to test his mettle. If he can beat off these massed, haranguing challenges and fire off a few 30-yard passes behind their defence we can really open them up. Come on, Jamie. Show us what you're made of. Show me I'm a fool.

At half time it's still 0–0, but we feel as though our necks have been cricked towards the Anfield Road end for most of the game. It's been, more or less, all Liverpool. But not long into the second half we commit the suicide we've all been dreading. Kvarme, under no real threat but with no obvious, instant pass available to him, tries to walk the ball past Andy Cole, 10 yards inside our half. Understandable. Andy Cole is not a ferocious tackler. It's good that Kvarme's taking it on himself to bring the ball out of defence. Matteo shouts at him for the pass. Cole sidles towards Kvarme, dispossesses him and hares in on goal. Matteo tries to make up the ground on Cole. He catches up with him but, just as he's prodding out a foot to flick the ball off his toes, Cole checks inside him cleverly and rifles his shot past James. There's no escaping it. It's a hell of a goal. We're guilty again of sloppy, contributory negligence – but Cole has made a goal out of nothing. He's done it all himself. He's rightly chuffed with himself.

Now United's chests are out. They're starting to crow. And just as they do, we receive a penalty. Mad Eyes hacks down Owen a yard and a bit inside the box, runs screaming his innocence to referee Elleray, but to no avail. Penno. Fowler, without a shred of a second thought, steps up and plants it past Schmeichel. 1–1. Surely, now, the momentum of the goal will carry us past them on a tidal wave.

Er, no. Redknapp, who has done well today without ever completely bossing the midfield, messes around with Carragher down by the Anfield Road end of the Centenary side. He has plenty enough time and opportunity to move the ball upfield – he doesn't even have to launch it – but he plays, instead, a tight little ball to Carragher who has little or no chance of mastering it and gives away a free-kick in a naughty situation. It's in a central position, just outside the penalty area. Well within Beckham's range. Sheringham, too, scored a beauty for Tottenham from this very spot in the F.A. Cup a few years ago. Beckham has a little look, lines it up and, with very little backlift, trims the ball into the net via the crossbar. 2–1. He'll later claim he knew it was in from the moment it left his boot. He's probably right. We were certainly hanging our heads as he trotted into his run-up.

We're now into the last 15 minutes and Liverpool are chasing the game. There was no need to in the first place. Man. U came here for a draw, shit themselves for 20 minutes then realised that Liverpool didn't have the nous to cut them open. But they never went on the offensive. Liverpool could've double-bluffed them and counter-attacked *their* counter-attacks. But now we're throwing all hands forward as though it's the last game of the season and leaving ourselves exposed at the back. *More* exposed at the back. Sheringham, absolutely and utterly unmarked at the near post, flicks on a Beckham corner for Cole to stab home from under the crossbar. It's Man. U's third goal against us directly from a corner in the last two home games.

3–1. I sit motionless in my seat, long after United have danced gleefully off the pitch, waving to their supporters. I can't believe what's happened out there. It's . . . it's nothing less than a scandal. It's a disgrace. We can't keep turning up against teams like Everton and United and Arsenal, teams with canny, elbowy, aerial strikers, and simply hope that they have a bad day, today. You can't concede a key area in the strategy of a football match so tamely. We just don't compete in the air. We close our eyes and hope that we don't get hurt. We don't even set a specific man, regardless of his size, against the likes of Sheringham or Ferguson. We just let them walk into the box and pick off the lofted ball at will. We cannot let this situation continue. Roy Evans MUST buy a defender. He must buy a domineering central defender before we play Newcastle, and the bound-to-return-against-us-and-score-a-headed-hat-trick Alan Shearer, at St James's Park on 28 December. There must be someone out there. Someone, playing in the favelas of São Paulo or the quagmires of the Highland League, must be a better prospect than what we've got. That's all we're asking for, just now. Forget the ball-playing central defender. We'll settle for a Stopper. A fast, young, aggressive Stopper. That'll do us, for now. And all I want *right* now is to spill messily into town and get drunk in The Blob Shop. Bad day. Bad day.

13 DECEMBER 1997

Crystal Palace, away

And this isn't much better. What started as a snuffle a few days ago has escalated into full-blown flu — shivers, hot sweats, headaches, the works. I'm consigned to my pit, sniffling pathetically and going into spasms of multiple sneezing. I conceded yesterday that I wouldn't be going to Palace. I haven't listened to the match live on the radio for years. I send out for *Shoot! Goal! 4–4–2* and *The Kop* and The Lovely Jane brings me a flask of tea and some toasted Marmite butties. Heaven! Better than the bogs at Selhurst Park, any day. All we need now is a thumping win, which other teams have been finding a doddle at Palace. In fact, Palace have not won at home in the League all season. Sounds horribly like a Pointless Statistic to me.

In the interests of absolute impartiality I listen to the first half on independent Radio City and the second on BBC Radio Merseyside. It sounds, again, as though there are more Liverpool fans inside the ground than Palace supporters. Ace striker Steve McManaman scores his inevitable wonder goal while Michael Owen leaves the Palace rearguard for dead to slot the second and Leonhardsen chips in with the third.

Owen is starting to regularly terrorise defences. Last week against Arsenal, Tony Adams was reduced to laughingly body-checking him each time he skated past him – laughingly because even as Owen was crucifying him he seemed to appreciate the irony of the creaky, cunning old dog set against the hungry young cub. Owen got the better of the exchange, though Arsene Wenger preferred to concentrate on the genius of Nicolas Anelka in his after-match interview. But he's really found his feet, young Michael. He's keeping Riedle out of the team on merit. If Owen started the season expecting to be Liverpool's third choice striker, he's exceeded himself. He's starting to put in consistently brilliant performances – all that's been missing are the goals. If he starts scoring regularly, he'll be hard to ignore for the full England team. The happy Liverpudlians play out the last five minutes with a deafening chorus of *O Come All Ye Faithful*, making me feel ten times better – and ten times worse that I didn't ignore my life-threatening temperature and get down to Selhurst. We're still languishing well behind United, but with home games against

Coventry and Leeds coming next, at least we can try to start putting some points on the board.

The excitement is far from over, either. I now have the tension of a live F.A. Cup draw to savour. Anyone at home'll do. Anyone. And that's what we get. Coventry, at home. The sort of uninspiring home banker that can so easily trip you up.

20 DECEMBER 1997

Coventry, home

My birthday. Strangely enough I had my birthday yesterday – but it's not until today. I had my birthday yesterday because people couldn't wait. I'm that popular. Yesterday was the last Birkenhead Park Feast of Friday Football of the year. We're not bothering on Boxing Day due to real matches thoughtlessly being scheduled on the same day. There was half-hearted talk of a morning game, but we all know it has to be 2 p.m. or not at all. So this was going to be it for 1997. We usually go out for a meal followed by laughable disco routines to celebrate our decrepit knees getting us through another year of mortal combat, so with my birthday coinciding there ought to be a good turnout. We'll probably go to some sort of discotheque and dance to all the latest sounds.

The game is a corker. Only seven-a-side, but Puffa, Jimmy, Joey, Christian, Roy, Peter and myself take on Jegsy, Charlie, Dave Dooley, Colin, Blackie, Treeman and Simon from the Pub. I'm eligible for the Liverpool squad because of my dual nationality – born in the Women's Hospital, Liverpool, raised in the teeming projects of the Wirral. They stick me in goal for the first 20 minutes and, in an end-to-end encounter, our side get our noses in front, 3–2. By half time it's 6–2 and when, ten minutes into the second half, we go 9–2 ahead it seems to be all over as a contest. In these Friday games, however, one goal usually leads to another. Charlie beats every player on the pitch (except me) and jammily backheels the ball into the net. His team-mates are already screaming 'NO!!' at him as the ball rolls over the line. Charlie misses at least a double hat-trick of chances every week by over-embellishing the easiest of tap-ins with not-quite-right designer flicks and frippery. He revels in tormenting us until we have to scream:

'JUST PUT THE FUCKING THING IN, WILL YOU!!' then he'll miss, deliberately, and run back grinning. But he putts this one nicely between Jimmy Fowler's legs. This opens things up for the next 15 minutes. They score, then we score. They score, then we score. They have a flurry at the end, but the score finishes something like 15–10 to us. There has been some tremendous togger played, considering we're all ancient and we're all shite. I really fancy a good old drink, now – especially since it's my 'unofficial birthday'. Wonder who's done the organising? Roy, probably. He's good at that.

Half an hour later, in The Shrewsbury Arms, no mention has been made. I know they're just waiting for me to crack and bring up the subject first, and I'm not falling for that old cookie. Mention has been made of the Players of Liverpool Football Club Christmas Party.

They had it on Sunday night. Some players were still staggering around on Monday afternoon. There seems to be a code of honour in football which involves the capacity to drink a great deal but still be able to train like a horse the next morning. Our team has been rumoured to have had a committed drinking core for some years. They were supposedly known as Liverpool Football Pub. You try to ignore it. You think of some of the great players over the years who were legendarily fond of the gargle. But still it rankles. It doesn't seem right that they think so little of the hope and faith that's invested in them. It doesn't seem right that they limit their own ambitions so. Football's a young man's game and it's unrealistic to expect fertile young lads to live a monastic lifestyle. But still, you can't help thinking – if I was playing for the Reds . . .

But I'm not. Other people are. Peter Hooton met some of them, glassy-eyed and incapable of intelligible speech, in The Retro Bar on Monday afternoon. Some of them were boasting of their intention to stay out on 'a mammoth bender' until they were required back into training on Wednesday. These professional athletes were out en masse, intent on softening up their bodies some more, cutting down, gradually, the longevity of their careers with another debilitating night on the sauce. More depressingly, they thought old Hooto would be impressed by this. For now, I'll be impressed if anyone offers to take me on a mammoth bender. It's not funny anymore.

And it's not funny when, an hour later, I'm back home being consoled by The Lovely Jane.

'Maybe they just forgot. It's a busy time of year, you know. There's a lot going on . . .'

'No. They're getting me back for shouting all the time.'

'Don't be stupid! How many times does that phone go every day? It drives me mad! If there's someone more popular than you round here, I'd like to meet them . . .'

'No. They hate me.'

At ten-to-twelve, peeping out of the curtains in case they're all out there, waiting to snap on the H.A.P.P.Y.B.I.R.T.H. D.A.Y. lights at midnight, I slope off to bed. Those drunken bastards had better win 5–0 tomorrow.

We don't, but some amusing things happen. One is that I treat myself to a birthday present. It's freezing today, my ears are throbbing with cold and I'm jolly well going to buy me a Liverpool bobble hat. Without a bobble. It's years since I bought any L.F.C. merchandise, and I find myself feeling unusually self-conscious when it comes to the plunge. Is it obvious, I wonder to myself as I bottle out of approaching yet another street vendor, that I haven't done this before? Can they sniff out my lack of experience? Do they have two prices for their goods? One price for the Toughs, and another, inflated price for the Tourists which they rapidly flip over when they See Us Coming? Or is it just a simple case of going over, pointing to the hat you're after and saying:

'One of them, please, mate.'

It probably is. I've already walked past four or five stalls, so my last chance is coming up. There's always a woman by the gates to the Centenary Stand car-park. I've never even so much as glanced at her display, but I know she's there. I amble over, casual as a crow, and run my eye over the many and varied hats. I can feel a bit of embarrassment coming on, which I manage to fight back down again. My heart is beating fast, but there's something else wrong, too.

The hats. They've got black in them. Some of them are actually black with a red Liver Bird on. Black! Two colours we should never, ever see on any item pertaining to Liverpool F.C. are blue and black. Red and black equals Man United. No matter how progressive football thinks it has become, no matter how 'buoyant' the 'market' and how seemingly endless the public's appetite for new ranges of merchandise, Liverpool should never allow black onto the kit, the scarf, anything. Lord knows, there's plenty enough scope with all the ecrus, greens, yellows and other permutations available. We don't need Man. U hats, thank you very much. This makes the choice easy. Out of a range of six choices, there isn't even one red and white hat. The closest is red and yellow. I buy it. It's 6 quid.

If I was embarrassed buying it, I'm mortified wearing it. As I pull it down over my eyebrows, I feel as though all eyes are on me. That bloke's just bought a hat. Look! How foolish he looks, blushing as though everyone knows he's just bought the hat we're staring at. Oh, look who it is! The guy nobody wanted to go out with last night. On his birthday! No wonder! He looks a right idiot in that hat!

Defiantly, I keep the hat on inside the ground. Roy turns up just before kick-off, laughs like a Disney hyena and points, trying to get the words out. In the end he settles for just one:

'Rampton!!'

The Boffins' seats are unoccupied. It's not unusual for one or both of them to be late, but 20 minutes into the game Boffin 2 arrives with . . . a *woman*. An extremely beautiful woman, too. Breathless, he explains:

'Jeff's just taken up a job in Germany. Had to take it, really. Best paid systems analysts in the world, Germany.'

A-HA!!

Two things, then – if a little belatedly. Boffin 1 goes by the name of 'Jeff'. Not a stereotypically boffinesque name. Not as bad as Nigel, say, or Boris. Jeff. Not bad. Suppose I could've found out earlier by saying something like:

'Anyway, mate, what's your name?'

But the longer we called each other 'mate', the more impossible it became to suddenly say:

'Look! What's your bloomin' name, anyway?'

Now I'll never get the chance. Ah well. I now know that Boffin 1 is Jeff and he unquestionably is a boffin. He's a systems analyst. He works in computers. I knew it all along.

The game starts and finishes. We beat a dreadful, dreadful, Coventry side 1–0, look far from rampant ourselves, some of us look like we were in The Retro Bar all day Monday, and Fowler, for the first time since he broke into the team with a neat goal at Fulham in 1993, has the wrath of an impatient crowd to contend with. Michael Owen, on the other hand, scores another cracker and looks like fused gelignite all afternoon. On the whole, though, we're shabby and lacklustre. I let out a relieved shriek at the end, suddenly overjoyed to have taken another three points.

We skulk in the bar, where Danny joins us with the depressing news that Everton have scored a last-minute penalty winner at Leicester. He asks what I want to drink.

'Nothing, thanks. Got to get home. It's my birthday.'

Roy actually blushes.

'You've got to stay out for a bit! Everyone's waiting in The Albert for you . . .'

He's lying. They hate me. And even if all my hundreds of muckers do want to take me out on 'the piss' it's too late! There's no use in begging me to stay out like that – I've got other plans! See you on Boxing Day!

I head out into the stupefying chill of a late December night. There's a little feel of Christmas in the air. When I was a kid I used to run down the hill all the way to the bus-stop outside the adventure playground, thinking I was Stevie Heighway. What'd I be hoping for, for Christmas? I'd definitely get *The Topical Times* football annual, along with Charles Buchan's *The Rothman's Pocket Almanack* and half-a-dozen other football books. What I asked for, though, forlornly, year after year was a set of junior goalposts, with nets. I knew it was a hopeless request, but I was well-off in so many other ways. I knew for certain that my team'd win on Boxing Day, for one thing – and how many kids could say that? All I want for Christmas now is an ugly, toothless, Scottish centre-half.

Satisfied that I'm far enough away from the ground, I slip my brand-new red and yellow Liverpool hat out of my pocket and over my frost-bitten ears and, head down, hasten down that same hill towards that same bus-stop by that same playground. A Red is for Life – not just for Christmas. Merry Christmas, one and all.

26 DECEMBER 1997

Leeds United, home

Easy. We tank them 3–1. Could've been 10–0, they were that useless. Robbie Fowler still looks sluggish but defies his growing army of critics with a neatly taken double. Michael Owen, almost inevitably, now, scores the other. In a moment of unbelievable skill – unbelievable in that nobody could believe it was happening – Jason McAteer cuts through the Leeds defence, wriggles into the box, beats one, two, three lunging tackles and, having done the hard bit, blazes wildly over the bar when he can see Nigel Martyn's tonsils. Throughout the 20-second incident, people chat nervously among themselves, introduce themselves to complete strangers and hum tunelessly, unable to accept that McAteer is doing what he seems to be doing. He's brilliant. We know he's good. We know he's been consistently played out of position since he came here. But he's brilliant. He's brilliant.

Of course it wouldn't be Liverpool '97 without a couple of blackspots.

Blackspot 1: yet again, we relax for the last ten minutes and allow Alf Inge Hooligan a (shock!) free header from a Kelly free-kick. Instead of pegging back that Man. U goal-difference and notching up a 4 or 5–0 buffer – which would've been easy, it really would have been ours for the reaching out and taking – we go for an early communal bath and end up with a far less convincing 3–1 win.

Blackspot 2: my penis has vanished. It's viciously cold today, and the occasional 'shrivelling' is part and parcel of winter football, but nonetheless – I have to stand at the urinal at half time with my left knee cocked defensively against chance sightings of this freak of nature and my right hand pulling my kecks forward to form a protective tent. It's gone. My chillblained knob has completely disappeared. It's home for a piping hot early bath, for me. No Albert today.

28 DECEMBER 1997

Newcastle, away

I'm outside Mick Potter's house in Kirkdale at 11, beeping the horn and, loveaduck, he's ready! He actually appears at the door within seconds of my apologetic beep, wearing a bright red kagoul and sunglasses. He looks like a nurse-stalker. He scrutinises the sky for telltale clouds and messages from God before disappearing back into the house and re-emerging in a warm, sensible, Joseph fleece jacket.

We're on the M6 by midday. The plan is to stop off somewhere picturesque in the Lake District and help ourselves to large portions of pie. En route we talk of little else but sex. Sex, and the myth of those beery, hospitable Geordies. All these places where you're supposed to get a warm welcome – Newcastle, Barnsley, places like that – end up being a bit hairy, whereas your Chelseas and Tottenhams, the dodgy hoods of yore, are a bit of a doddle these days. I can't think of one trip to Newcastle – this'll be my eighth visit today – when there hasn't been an incident of some sort. Last season Jimmy Flowers, amiable, inoffensive Jimmy, was put on his backside by a passing sheet-metal worker who took exception to his Liverpool sweatshirt. The season before that Sully, a stalwart of many decades' standing, received similar treatment. They just don't like anybody with less than a 40 inch waist or less than three Newcastle United shirts on.

We spot signs for a place called Kirby Lonsdale and decide that this sounds a likely venue for Desperate Dan-style pub grub. We are not disappointed. Just yet. We pull up at a sandstone inn in Lupton – the cunningly named Lupton Arms – and walk into a roomful of cheer. Blazing fires, dozens of thawing fell-walkers and a tipsy landlord taking orders for food. Just the ticket.

We attempt a conversation with four students in hiking boots who are vaguely from Down South, but once it becomes apparent that we don't know our Baxenghyll Gorge from our Ingleborough Cave, the chit-chat flounders. They start taking pictures of one another. I offer to take a group shot of them but, mysteriously, they decline. With the fires, the Speckled Hen ale and the agreeable port-in-a-storm warmth of the place, it's a wrench to have to leave. But it's gone 2 o'clock. Kick-off is 4 o'clock and the Reds need us.

A shock is in store. We had both assured each other that Carlisle is, roughly, in the Lake District, and as we are now in said district of lakes, Carlisle can't be far away. Carlisle to Newcastle is about a 45-minute drive, so we're in plenty of time. Except that, once we navigate ourselves back onto the motorway, a sign is quick to greet to us. It says: Carlisle 63. Cripes! Going to have to pedal a bit faster.

We hit the A69 just after 3 o'clock. We should be fine, provided we don't get stuck behind too many lorries. The A69 is notoriously dangerous for overtaking – much of the winding, hilly route is single-lane traffic – and if you find yourself behind a juggernaut you can forget travelling any faster than 40 mph while you labour in his slipstream up the next hill.

We've got Radio 5 on. Everton are 2–0 up at home to Bolton. Coventry are beating Man. U 1–0. No they're not. Man. U have just equalised. Bastards. But what's this, now? Back to Goodison Park. Stuart Hall is almost oozing out of the radio with twinkling hilarity. Please God, don't let Ferguson have scored again. He hasn't. Bolton have scored two in 30 seconds. It's 2–2. Mick and I squeal with laughter and slap the dashboard. Our amusement is to be shortlived.

Leaving Hexham behind and approaching the final furlong to Newcastle, Mick suddenly slumps back in his seat and pulls that face. The world's greatest method actors can't reproduce this face. You have to actually go through a real-life, stomach-dropping moment to make your face do that. You have to be on your way to the airport for your hard-earned fortnight in San Antonio and realise that the nagging in your guts is nothing to do with fear of flying. You've forgotten your passport. For the next ten seconds your world caves in and your face does what Mick's is doing now. He swapped jackets just before he came out. His match ticket was in the red stalker's kagoul. His ticket is in Kirkdale.

We spend a fruitless run-in to Newcastle trying to contact the club's ticket office but, naturally enough, it's closed on Sundays. We jammily park up at 3.50 right outside the directors' car-park at St James, and leg it round to the main entrance. A steward points to a queue snaking back into the car-park. There's a window open for F.A. Cup tickets – they play Everton at Goodison next Sunday. What use is that? But as we get closer we see another, smaller queue for people picking up tickets for today's game. Knowing how bogus the whole story is going to sound I prepare myself to be sent packing, but the woman in the ticket office is all sympathy. She's like a Geordie Sybil Fawlty:

'Ooh, I know pet, I know. I've done it myself. Infuriating, isn't it? I know.'

Her sympathy doesn't extend to a free replacement ticket, but we can pay for a new ticket and get a refund from Liverpool for the unused original. That'll do for now. Potter shells out £21 and we make it into the ground for kick-off.

We have a tremendous first half. Apart from the fact that Newcastle take the lead – surprisingly Steve Watson gets a free header from a free-kick – Liverpool are all over them. It's only a matter of time before we score. Fowler instinctively controls a flighted crossfield pass on his thigh and, as the ball drops, he swivels and lifts it 30 yards to McManaman. McManaman lets the ball fall in front of him and, looking up once to see where the keeper is, he volleys spectacularly past Hislop, crashing the ball in off the far post. 1–1. For a fraction of a second we're stunned, then depraved celebrations ensue. I fall over four rows of seating, picking up a familiar twinge in the ribcage area. Who cares? Not me. That's the best goal I've ever seen, anywhere. Not just the finish, which is truly world-class, but the approach play, too. Fowler's control and pass will be glossed over when this goal is celebrated and re-told through years to come, but if we were watching Argentina or Brazil, Andy Gray would be shaking his head in amazement and suggesting that only obsessive juggling of Pepsi cans on the Copacabana can produce skills like that. Well he's wrong. You can do it in Toxteth, Liverpool 8, too.

Shortly afterwards, Fowler, Owen and McManaman work the ball quickly through the Newcastle midfield, freeing Owen on the right. He looks up. Macca has stopped his run, pulling back from the Newcastle cover. Owen curls a lovely ball behind the onrushing Magpie backline and McManaman leans into a balletic half-volley, sweeping the ball past the bewildered Hislop. 2–1.

We could have had two more by half-time but McMana-man and Owen, both in good positions, seem to be trying to lay goals on a plate for Fowler. He's in a bit of a rut, Robbie, but he'll still give you moments of pure class like today's. Whatever's going wrong in his life – and the city is awash with stories – he's just got to keep playing his game. A beguiling dark side often comes with the territory of genius. Look no further than Maradona. Fowler's better than Maradona, and he'll go on to prove it. Meanwhile, Owen and Macca should stick their chances away while they can. We're only 2–1 up.

We spot Mono and Jeff at half time who bring news that Coventry beat Man. United. Apparently they've scored twice in the last few minutes and won it 3–2. Some hope. If ever there was a classic half-time rumour, this is it. I'll believe it when I hear it from Gary Lineker. We also get stopped by a tipsy Koppite who has news for us. He's got Jegsy's flag. He's been looking after it since Glasgow. He'll meet us in The Albert after the Coventry game.

Second half is, as expected, a rearguard scrap. Gillespie is tormenting Harkness, who still keeps backpedalling with his head turned round over his shoulder and still keeps getting skinned. Barnes is taken off after about 65 minutes. This is a relief. He was their best player in the first half, trying to prove a point against his old club. Ketsbaia is dangerous, but you'd sooner be up against him than John Barnes. Let's hope Rushie stays on the bench, too. He's just the sort to come on and prod a last-minute equaliser. They carry on the onslaught, but we have plenty of opportunities to extend our lead. In the final, excruciating, never-ending ten minutes Newcastle make enough chances to save the game but we hold out.

Getting out of the ground is weird. With what looks like a large dose of afterthought, the police – six of them and one horse – are holding us back. Penning us against a wall is more like it, while the united wits of wags of Newcastle file past, irate.

'Not one of youse has gorra fooken job!' fires one handsome fellow, the epitome of style with his tartan cap and Biffa Bacon tattoos. If the Newcastle mobs, who are now pouring out of the ground, fancy taking out their anger on us lot, this minimalist police initiative will provide them with no problems. It sums up Newcastle's approach to crowd segregation in general. It's a bit half-hearted. It relies on people's goodwill too much. Inside the ground there are two or three areas where away supporters are flanked by the home crowd. In the scenario of, say, a controversial Cup-tie where the ref has a bad game and Newcastle go out of the competition as a result, it's not difficult to envisage problems in that away section. I glance around and see Little Tracy and her mum. They're worried.

They shouldn't be placed in situations like this. If the police want to revert to 1980 and keep us all in at the end of the game, fine. Out of sight, out of mind perhaps. But penning us in, here, right in the front line is very foolish. Newcastle have just lost 2–1 and the representatives of the team who've beaten them are now being flaunted in front of them like sitting ducks.

We're happy to be back in the car, inching our way out of Newcastle in the after-match queues. There are few things in life to beat the feeling of elation when you're on your way home from a good away win. Four wins on the trot is nosebleed-inducing stuff, and we've finally made inroads on Man. U's lead at the top. Gary Lineker's Sunday show is still on Radio 5. He confirms the score from Highfield Road. Darren Huckerby, it seems, scored a dazzling individualistic goal in the last minute of the match, and we, for once, have taken advantage in the last game of the year. 1998 could be interesting. *Very* interesting.

2 JANUARY 1998

Birkenhead Park

I'm 50–50 about playing today after scraping my ribs over four rows of St James's Park plastic, but the moment I stick my boots in that natty green Tesco Bag For Life I might as well accept I'm playing. And how glad I am that I packed them! When we get to the park there are already 19 eager combatants, impatiently waiting for us to turn up with the ball. All the old faces are there. Pete Naylor. Wally and Danny on a rare day off from the building site. And who's that in the Italian football shirt? Oh YES!! It's Tommy Vialli! Fan-tastic!

If anything, there are too many players today. It must be 13-a-side. There's no room in midfield and, after taking a whack off Christian, one of Puffa's Saturday League team, I drift back into a left defensive position – which is where I used to play before I decided I was a crafty midfield playmaker.

As usual, everyone's on Tommy Vialli's case, yelling at him, panicking him, giving him no encouragement whatsoever. With about ten minutes left of a dour struggle, it's still 4–4. Tommy has just let a howler in under his body and has been banished upfield to see out the last ten minutes goalhanging. This reaps us an instant dividend. With Christian and Mick Potter closing in on me like a pair of rampaging, crop-headed bison, I hoof the ball long. Everyone misses it. Everyone bar Tommy Vialli, that is, who sticks out a toe and diverts the harmlessly rolling ball across the line. He runs the length of the field, face alight, with one finger wagging at the imaginary crowd. He thinks he's scored the goal of the century.

Two minutes later we repeat the tactic. Liverpool fail to take our secret weapon seriously and leave Vialli unmarked in the box. Blackie gets to the by-line and slings a poor cross over. Puffa goes to head clear, but for reasons best known to himself closes his eyes on contact and directs the ball straight to the feet of soccer's most deadly predator. He only needs one chance (several times per game). Wham! He completely mis-kicks it, but from two yards out even a Tommy Vialli daisycutter dribbles into the net. 6–4. It's all over.

Except it isn't. Liverpool put together a lovely, sweeping move, all one-touch passing from defence through the midfield. They must be getting a rush of blood because suddenly everyone's joining in the attack. They've got seven or eight strikers bearing down on goal, with me, Pete Naylor, Colin and The Dool trembling in our boots. Then, there's a glimmer of hope. Peter Hooton slightly over-runs it towards me. I can get there. Embarrassed at letting his amateur footballer team-mates down and spoiling the best move of the game, Peter over-compensates in his efforts to redeem himself. I get to the ball first and nick it out to Charlie. I don't see the rest as Peter, unable to stop, flattens me. I fall hard, straight onto my back from standing, with nothing to break my fall. Whatever wind was inside me is expelled at full force and I'm left gasping, trodden into the mud. There's wild cheering from the other end of the pitch. Later I will hear that Tommy notched the first hat-trick of his life with a diving header from Charlie's cross, but right now all I can hear is birds tweeting. That's me out for another six months.

3 JANUARY 1998

Coventry, home (FA Cup)

If the newly re-cracked ribs and the lump on the back of my head aren't painful enough, Liverpool are torturing us some more, dragging their New Year hangovers onto the pitch and wandering around with a lethargy known only to serial sleepwalkers. Mick Potter has Roy's seat today, and has thoughtfully brought a flask of Scotch with him. Well, Irish to be exact. It's a nice little drop of the Jameson's that he has.

The game goes to plan for a few minutes. Redknapp scores direct from a free-kick then hits the bar with a cute little chip, but Huckerby then runs through our defence with laughable ease just on half time and still has the audacity to squeeze the ball over David James from the most impossibly acute of angles. One all at half time.

Second half is worse. Coventry, realising that Liverpool have run out of attacking ideas, decide to seize the moment. Dublin scores a tap-in, Liverpool don't have a clue how to get back into the game, Danny Murphy comes on for Leonhard-sen, the crowd start getting at Robbie Fowler, Whelan scores a third and it's game over. 3–1 and we're out of the Cup. Thousands have streamed out of the ground after Coventry's third, but those who've remained until the end just sit there, stunned. No booing this time. Just the shamed realisation that we're crap.

There's only one way to take a defeat like this. Gag, Danny, Potter and myself head for The Albert. Once again it's the nerve centre for the Witchfinder General. I find Bucko up on the platform, deconstructing the game with Tony Murphy. They're giving Leonhardsen stick, which he now fully deserves. His allocated time for teething troubles is long gone. He hasn't got any better. He just looks . . . *terrified*. You can't play football with fear in your heart. Roy needs to rest him, now, let him recoil from the culture shock and give Danny Murphy a good run in the team. He's only come on as a sub a couple of times this season, and even then it's been to try and rescue a lost cause. In spite of the frantic circumstances of the games against Barnsley, Wimbledon and today against Coventry, he always looks composed, incisive, inventive and dangerous. I like him.

Over in the corner, Wilcox is having a full-volume row with Lenny Woods about Robbie Fowler's attitude. I can't see them but I can hear them. One or other of them is holding firm, saying that we've got to turn a blind eye because he's the best player in the world. Couldn't have put it better myself. Infuriating though Fowler is at the moment, now is the time to stand by him. The rewards will come in the form of a European Cup-winning hat-trick at the Bernabeu next year.

The pub empties out, leaving a hard-core of optimists and blaggards. Jimmy Flowers, Lenny Woods, Bucko, Danny, Mick Potter. They're all still there trying to trump each other with obscure songs when Gag and I leave at 9 o'clock. As I get to the door I have to check back. Surely I'm hearing things?

From Lenny's corner, a slowly-building song is quavering through The Albert's smog. There's no mistaking it. It's the tune of *Needles and Pins*. But Lenny's changed the words. He's changed the chorus to . . . *Riedle and Ince*. I rake back over the remnants of my mind. Was Lenny Woods on the train back from Wimbledon? He was. He was sat at the two-seater table behind me. I'll be on to the Performing Rights Society first thing on Monday.

4 JANUARY 1998

Watching TV at home

Everton against Newcastle in the Cup. I'm watching this in the certain knowledge that Ian Rush will come on and score the winner for Newcastle. There isn't a string of doubt in my well-strung heart. Rush will score. Rush WILL score.

He does, too. But first, we have to put up with an hour of Alan Parry getting things wrong.

'What's the referee given here? It looks like a corner!'

The patient voice of Trevor Francis comes in.

'I think it's a free-kick, Alan. Gillespie's offside.'

Gillespie doesn't come out for the second half, which is a pity as he's been causing no end of problems down the right. But not to worry. It should happen any minute. Any minute now. Oh look, there's John Barnes on the ball. He's going that way. The Everton defence is going the other way. My word! How did he get a cross in from *there*!? Pity there's no one there to knock it in . . .

But wait! I hear horses! I hear the sound of trampling hooves and . . . YES!! It's the cavalry! It's Mr I. Rush, goalscorer. Here he comes. He's nipped in front of the Everton defence . . . he's

pressed the Extend button on his telescopic boot . . . boiiiiing
. . . his big toe has lengthened to its full extent of ten inches in
'stretch' mode, just long enough to nudge Barnes' cross over
the line! Oh, what a lovely goal! I'm so happy. Goal of the
Year and it's only four days old. This has cheered me so much
that I consider sprinting down to the M53 and applauding Mr
Rush off the motorway as he makes his way home. Tonight I,
THE MANAGER, fall asleep recruiting Ian Rush to be my
assistant manager with John Barnes still in charge of the reserve
team. That way neither of them can score against us in the
Coca Cola Cup on Wednesday night.

10 JANUARY 1998

Wimbledon, home

Roy's still away. I ask Joe, who turned 8 over Christmas, if he
fancies coming to the match, but he prefers the Playstation
version. I'm not going to force it. It'll happen. He'll just walk
in one morning and say the magic words:
'Dad. Can I come to the match with you today?'
I'll try again when he's 9. Perhaps then he'll realise that he's
holding out on one of a father's few real pleasures in life.
Taking his boy to the match. And maybe he'll realise that as
long as he keeps holding out, Liverpool are doomed. We
haven't won the title since he was born. It's all his fault! He *has*
to start coming to the match! But in the meantime, I effect an
elaborate swap that means that Joe's pal Sean and his dad sit in
mine and Roy's seats while I'm consigned to the outer flanks
of the Upper Centenary, Anfield Road end of the ground.
I feel very chipper walking up to the ground. For various
complicated reasons involving ticket swaps and a cast of

dozens, I miss out on all pre-match shenanigans. But I'm glowing with confidence. We beat Newcastle with ease on Wednesday night. Robbie was again lethargic for much of the game but he took his goal like a true predator. This is only partly what he is – he and Shearer are the only real goal poachers in the England frame. Quite why Hoddle can't see this is baffling. It's obvious he prefers Sheringham alongside Shearer. Perhaps he's got a downer on Liverpool dating back to his numerous drubbings at the hands of Messrs. Souness, Dalglish et al. There's some sort of agenda going on for sure, because Goddle's latest anti-Liverpool outbursts include a strange, veiled attack on stainless Michael Owen's character, hinting at but not specifying a sinister dark side to his nature – along with a heartless dropping of David James from his latest squad.

James, who I maintain is one of the three best goalkeepers in the country, has suffered from the lack of reliable cover in front of him. He's had a mini crisis. He wasn't superb against Man. United and now, after much on-off traffic, we have recruited Brad Friedel from the States to provide some competition.

James doesn't need competition, though quality cover is always a good principle. James needs two things and they're two things which go hand-in-hand. He needs confidence and he needs a defence in front of him. And he could probably do without svelte Joe Corrigan as his tutor. What is certain is that Glenn Hoddle's dropping him from the training set-up altogether effectively tells him that there's no way back. A braver manager, one who understood the true relationship between an individual's skill, confidence and team efficacy, would have kept David James involved. He was England's keeper a few months ago and now he's out, straggling behind Ian Walker and Kevin Pressman, two moribund performers by any standard, anywhere. James is so much a better keeper than these two that it's almost a joke, but I doubt whether Jame-o's laughing. He's being pilloried for things which are not strictly his fault – and that's not funny.

Even Schmeichel has runs like this. Last season he was getting mugged by everyone, from all over the pitch. Remember Phillippe Albert's chip at St James's? What about Davor Suker for Croatia in Euro '96? Or Derby County's third at Old Trafford, when Schmeichel ran smack into Pallister and left Sturridge to walk the ball into an empty net? Both David Seaman and Nigel Martyn have gifted goals to the opposition, too. They all have flaws in their technique. None of them has more natural ability than David James. Glenn Hoddle should protect him at a time like this, not hang him out to dry.

So back to Robbie Fowler. He's not on song at the moment, but the same principle applies. You don't drop God. You have to stick with Him, because He will always come up with something out of the ordinary, just when you need it the most.

Just as he did against Newcastle in the Coca Cola quarter-final the other night. We had genius all over the pitch. Michael Owen is Kenny Dalglish. Jamie Redknapp can do whatever he wants with the ball. Does the boy not realise how great he is? Why doesn't he play like this all the time? And as for McManaman . . .

Middlesbrough, who we play next in a two-legged semi, should be quaking in their boots. We were great on Boxing Day against Leeds, great at Newcastle a couple of days later and clinically good against them again during the week to reach the semis of the Coca Cola. But hark! I sense a cliché bubbling under the surface, prickling at me, reminding me that it's there if I want it. And I do! *I do*. I'm reaching for it and . . . yes! Here it is!

'Forget. The FA Cup. We are. Free. To concentrate. On . . .'

No! I can't carry on with it! I can't finish the sentence. We may well be free to concentrate on the League, but that doesn't mean we will. Not Liverpool. And anyway, I'm gutted to be out of the Cup at the same stage as Everton. All I can say is that, as I bound up the 1,203 steps that lead up to the uppermost uppers of the Upper Centenary stand, I feel strangely confident. Man. United have lost a few games themselves, now, and they're drawing games they'd normally win with their eyes closed. Teams like Bolton are taking points off them. If we beat Wimbledon today, we've got a very do-able run of fixtures in the League over the next month or so. Fair enough, you have to go out and win them, but if we want to consider ourselves Championship material, we have to confront the following, expecting nothing less than a full flush of wins:

Leicester (away)
Newcastle (home)
Blackburn (home)
Southampton (home)
Sheffield Wednesday (away)
Everton (home)
Aston Villa (away)

Eight games, including today. We want 20 points from that lot, at least. Maybe a draw against Leicester. Blackburn are pretty tough to break down, too. But we're talking about going out and seizing the Premiership here! Putting Man. U under the sort of pressure they haven't felt since Blackburn took the title off them a few years ago. We've got to win these games. Starting with Wimbledon, today.

If this is the message Roy Evans has drummed into his players then he's drummed it so hard that he's stunned them into submission. It's back to the sort of performance we were trotting out back in the autumn. Lazy, slovenly, clueless. Nobody will take responsibility. There is not one player out there who looks like he wants anything more than to get this over with and get away from here. Fair enough. The crowd are more of a hindrance than a source of inspiration, but it's difficult to feel any kind of affinity for players who act like this. Robbie Fowler is one of several culprits. He just doesn't look interested. The closest he gets to animation is when Leonhardsen plays the wrong ball – as he routinely does – slowing down or breaking up the slightest threat of an attack by Liverpool. If Leonhardsen plays Fowler in too late or Fowler gets caught offside, he trudges back in suspended slow-motion, looking at the floor. In the time it takes for him to get back onside we might – or a good team might – have won the ball back and started another attack moving. Which would be pointless as Robbie Fowler is still in an offside position. WHAT'S UP WITH HIM!!!!?????

The crowd are starting to turn against Fowler, an unthinkable turn of events up until a few months ago. But now there are so many rumours flying around this compact city that most people believe at least some of them. Everybody seems to have a close friend or relative who personally saw Fowler in a compromised situation. Cities like Liverpool thrive on gossip and hearsay, and it's Robbie Fowler's unlucky lot to have to take his turn on the rumour mill. The majority of this stuff is pure bullshit, the invention of bored taxi-drivers and covetous Evertonians. Unfortunate, too, is the timing of Liverpool's talks to commit Fowler to a new contract. He is said to be opening negotiations with a request for £50,000 per week. (Rib-tickling how footballers, a breed who now have least in common with the last of the weekly-paid breadline earners who turn up to adore them, are still quoted as getting their wages 'per week'. The idea of Dennis Bergkamp, Overmars, Seaman and co. queueing up outside Wenger's cramped office while he hands out brown envelopes every Friday is too rum for words.) It's unlikely that Fowler's advisers have asked for anything like £2,500,000 per annum. But even if they have, he's worth it. Liverpool can't buy a replacement for under £15,000,000 – if one exists, which I sincerely doubt – and that's before the replacement's wages of, er ... £50,000 a week.

Most Liverpool fans would happily see us pay, say, Alan Shearer £3 million a year. Or Kinkladze. But we can't pay it to a Scouser. Why should one Scouser be paid so much more than another citizen? That's the skewed logic, here. It's part and parcel of the culture of Liverpool. We want our sons to do well. But not too well. We're always here to remind them where they come from and it doesn't surprise me in the slightest that it all gets a bit too much for them sometimes. I'm convinced that it's already proved too much for Steve McManaman and I wouldn't be surprised if others followed suit.

There's a simple solution, of course. The players just have to go out, every week, and give their all. Most of us don't give two hoots how much they get paid – they're welcome to it – so long as they look as though they care. Care about the game they're playing in. About the fans who, let's face it, absolutely fucking worship them. And about what it all means, what it means to play for and support and be in love with Liverpool Football Club. They don't seem to have too firm a grasp on all of that, and if they do, then they don't show it. Not often enough. Robbie would do himself no harm throughout this rough patch if he were to compensate for poor overall form by showing tireless effort.

No one else is much better. Nobody ever seems to close the goalkeeper down when, as Wimbledon and others always do, defenders play the ball back to him. Why don't we put him under pressure? At least make him play the ball quicker than he'd like, put it out of play or send it straight to a Liverpool shirt. Who knows? Once in a blue moon he might balloon it or completely miscue it straight to Owen or Fowler. But to make him gift us a goal like that, we have to put in the graft. GRAFT. Our boys don't know what it means. They think they're a 'footballing' side. Not against the likes of Wimbledon, they're not. Let's hope they can shake themselves out of it in the second half.

At half time, staring out listlessly over the pitch towards the Main Stand, I become aware of someone watching me. I look down. Kneeling up in the row in front is a young lad of about 5 or 6, sitting with his dad and uncles, all of them in Liverpool shirts. Sikhs. The boy has enormous black-brown eyes which are fixed on me. I wink at him. His face cracks into a huge smile. I give him a thumbs-up. He gives me one back.

'Who's going to score, then?' I ask.

He looks down, embarrassed. His dad chucks him under the chin.

'Hey! The fella's talking to you!'

He's a Scouser.

'Who's gonna score?'

The kid still says nothing. His uncle joins in, now.

'Who's your favourite player, hey?'

The little lad looks up, grinning again.

'Michael Owen scores the goals!'

Everyone starts laughing and the little boy buries his head under his dad's jacket. The teams come out and the game reverts to its first-half pattern. We're showing a little bit more urgency, but Wimbledon hold firm. I haven't worn a watch for years and, with no Roy next to me to tell me how long to go, it's starting to feel as though this goal is not going to come. Fowler's balance seems all cocked up. He keeps falling over, miscontrolling the ball, making simple things into difficult ones. The reaction from many sections of the crowd is savage. Me too, but not at Fowler. At the crowd. How can they turn on him like that? Would they do it to someone we paid out millions for? To Collymore? Of course they wouldn't. They think they have a right to have a go because they've started to take him for granted. He's only a local lad from the youth team, after all.

Just as I'm about to turn round and take up cudgels with some ignorant, garrulous yokel behind me – he keeps shouting 'Bloodyell *Foolorrrrrr*!!' – Redknapp snaps one in from outside the box. Thank the Lord!! 1–0!! I can't remember being so relieved at scoring. It's not ecstasy, this, not even pleasure. It's pure relief. Thank you, Jamie Redknapp, thank you! I didn't mean any of those terrible, disloyal things I thought about you. I now realise that maybe, amazingly for one so blessed, you suffer from a slight lack of self-belief. So here we are, then. You've just proved what a fucking fantastic talent you have. You can be the greatest midfielder in the world. Believe it yourself and there's nothing to stop you. I think all of that in about six seconds flat.

We score another before the end and everyone stays back to applaud the team off as though we've just outclassed Boca Juniors. I give my little pal a pat on the back as he makes his way out with his family. Great stuff. We've really laid that Man. United game to rest, now. That's five League wins on the trot and, while no game is easy, we've got a comfortable enough schedule in the games immediately ahead. If we can get a good head of steam up here, keep the pressure up on United until they're back in Europe in March, they might just find it's all a bit much for them. We need to get Robbie Fowler back in the groove, though, and this sudden turn in the mood of the crowd towards him is not going to help that process. It's time for my first Dear Smithy of the year.

The ground empties quickly. The corner between the Anfield Road and the Main Stand has now been covered. It just needs the seats to be installed and the ground will be up to a capacity of 46,000. I can no longer see the trees of Anfield

Road through the gap in the corner, there. I've watched those trees, abstractly, from this stand for decades. I've seen the leaves turn colour in silence, immune to the passion play over the other side of the street. They've seen some sights, the trees of Anfield Road. Now I can't see them at all. It's all change.

17 JANUARY 1998

Leicester, away

Just Danny and myself, today, hurtling down the motorway to catch up with Jimmy Flowers' coach, which left at 9 o'clock this morning. They're heading for a pub in Beaumont Leys on the outskirts of Leicester which is run by a mate of Mono's. Danny keeps me supplied with cheese and ham butties all the way there and, after a slight overshoot coming off the ring road we're crawling through the elegantly – misleadingly elegantly – named Beaumont Leys. Beaumont Leys is like any other jaded outer-city quarter. It has big, peeling pubs, a busy dual carriageway, fat blokes in tracksuits being walked by muscular dogs, a printers which closes at 12 on a Saturday and a carbreaking yard.

In a sidestreet of modern semis off the main dual carriageway we spot Jimmy's coach and, hidden behind it, the pub. It's a 1960s bungalow-style affair, with a smoky bar and a bigger, smokier lounge. There's about 60 Liverpool fans in there and about half that many Leicester supporters. They all seem to be getting along okay, though the Leicester contingent are all down by the door at one end of the lounge while the Liverpool faction take up the rest of the floorspace.

There's been some drinking going on. Even at one o'clock, everyone looks pie-eyed. John Martin, a well-known Koppite, is singing *The Big West End*, an old song about a Liverpool boy who goes down to London to get a job as a bouncer. Everyone joins in with the chorus, the only bit we all know:

> '*Gonna get a job as a bouncer*
> *Down in the big West End*
> *When they hear my Liverpool accent*
> *It'll drive them round the bend . . .*'

Jeff, John Garner and Davey from Halewood are in the corner, arguing about driving duties, when to leave for the match, the correct cuff length of a Parisian blouson and the true source of the River Mersey. They're arguing about everything. Spen and Gram, two more Halewood braves, fill us in on the bickering. Garner is upset because Jeff wouldn't drive to Leicester today. Jeff wanted to come on the coach and have a drink like everyone else. This meant leaving at what Garner thinks was an unreasonable hour and, the drunker he gets, the more he's feeling hard done by.

I give Spen, Gram and Jeff a lift to Filbert Street. At least, I give them a lift to where Filbert Street usually is, but with four tipsy co-pilots on board, all barking instructions, I end up driving round in circles. Eventually I ignore them, go my own way, let Danny, Gram and Spen out within sight of the ground and park up in a twee housing development next to the hospital. I insist to Jeff, who insisted on sitting tight with a fellow driver-victim, that I know a short-cut across the hospital car-park. He's not convinced. I point to the floodlights, over there, within touching distance. We jog for 15 metres then collapse, exhausted.

We get to the ground. It's spookily quiet. There's only a smattering of stragglers racing around outside, trying to make kick-off, but something's wrong. We must be right on kick-off time and there's hardly any noise from inside the ground. It sounds like a reserve game. You can hear the thud of boot on leather inside, the aggressive cries of the players and the helpless applause of groups of individuals.

'Er, Jeff . . .' I start. It's dawned on me.

'This way!' he shouts, darting off down the side of one stand. I wait patiently while he shows his ticket to an amused policewoman. She calls over a colleague to share in the fun. Another square-jawed medical student in one of those stripy rugby tops runs past. Jeff shuffles back, ears burning. I know exactly what he's going to tell me. We're outside Leicester Rugby Club. We run back to Filbert Street, which is three minutes the other way.

'Listen. Don't mention any of this to Garner and them. All right?'

Standing by a police cordon, looking agitated, crestfallen and then, when he spots me coming, mightily overjoyed, is Danny Giles.

'Good of you to wait, Dan, but there was no need. It's my own fault I'm late.'

'Oh, I know. I would've left you. Except you've got my ticket.'

I can't even be bothered pretending I haven't got it. We click through, buy two chicken and mushroom pies and head to our seats which, being in Row One, are situated below sea-level. The game is taking place around us at approximately eyebrow level. If this is the view of the game Roy Evans gets from his dugout, no wonder the team looks okay to him. All you can see is the grim determination on Stevie Harkness' face, and that's something to behold in this team. Leonhardsen's the same. He's busy. From this close range you can see the sweat and the effort, taking him nowhere.

The highlight of a dire first half is the pie. It's outstanding. Best of the season. Leicester Chicken and Mushroom Pie, you are nominated hereby for Pie of the Year Award. It's a big, thick, rich pie – a bit like Prince Andrew – full of chunky pieces of mushroom and, indeed, chicken. Very good.

Second half is more deadly yet than the first. I find myself gazing off into the distance, focusing on a tower block, miles away. That'll be like the Anfield Road trees to the Leicester fans who used to sit on this side of the ground. I wonder how many young Leicester fans have grown up sitting here, spent months in hours here, before it was the away section, staring out at that tower block as Alan Birchenall and Keith Weller try once again to get something going. These are moments of our life, ticking away.

They have a couple of half-chances courtesy of our profligate defence, but Liverpool seem incapable of penetrating a sedentary Leicester midfield. The usually combative Lennon is subdued while Robbie Savage is full of running and willing but only in a reactive sense. He's blocking, stopping, marking, chasing, harrying. He hasn't created a thing. If McManaman and Redknapp put their minds to it they can slice this lot open whenever they feel like it. In the very last minute McManaman gets behind the Leicester defence for the very first time in the game. He pulls it back for Fowler who might have shot, but plays in Leonhardsen, better placed and unmarked on the far post. A first-time poke and it's in but Leo wants another steadying touch, which only takes the ball away from him. As the best chance of the game rolls agonisingly away from him, Leonhardsen lunges a boot out after it and gets a contact, but it's not enough to beat Keller.

We locate the car without too much bother and join a murderous hour-long queue out of Leicester. Mellor has already taken two 'Evans Out' calls – from fans in Cornwall and Humberside respectively – before we reach the motorway. It's the usual cat-call from the cheap seats. He's a Nice Bloke. Too nice to make tough decisions. Balderdash. Which particular Nasty Bloke do they want? Souness?

This gets Danny and I into a ruckus. Danny thinks Roy has had long enough, too. He points towards inept displays against Everton. Poor judgement in allowing Scales to leave while

Ruddock stayed. Blind faith in David James. I put the contrary point of view to him until we're motoring past the other-worldly oil refineries of Stanlow and, before you can say Istvan Kozma, I've dropped Danny at The Cross, he's given me two raps on the roof and there's only me in the car. I head off in search of a *Football Echo*, still turning over the debate in my mind. Evans out? Is it his fault? Not entirely. I think he'll win the League for us this season. We'll win it jammily, without playing well, and we'll turn into a side of true class over the next three or four seasons, as players like Owen and Matteo and Fowler come into their prime. If Roy Evans survives this season, he'll go on a roll. He'll become one of the most successful managers of our time.

I pick up a pink *Football Echo* and turn straight to Tommy Smith's letters page. It's not in. My letter about the fans' treatment of Robbie Fowler is not considered worthy of Smithy's comment. This is just as well. I signed it Tommy Vialli, Birkenhead.

20 JANUARY 1998

Newcastle, home

There was a moment in the home game against Aston Villa back in September when Michael Owen, receiving the ball with his back to goal, turned Alan Wright and manoeuvred through a scrap of space so small that you started to take Glenn Hoddle's point. Surely this boy is the Son of Satan. I turned to the astute Scottish man behind me and said:

'Have you ever seen anything like him?'

'Not since Dalglish,' he said.

If that was a key moment in the gradual dawning that Owen

is actually better, so much more brilliant than even he has been given credit for, then his goal in the fourteenth minute tonight against Newcastle is the final acclamation that he's here. He's no fluke. He's real. He's unbelievably good. And he's ours.

This is the game which was postponed due to the death of Princess Diana. The game where Roy and Geordie John conspired to snaffle my ticket. Well, they were at it again tonight, and this time he got his come-uppance.

Roy has already asked me if I'd mind swapping tickets with John, so that he can sit next to him. No problem. I don't mind swapping my comfy, familiar, convenient, regular seat for a restricted-view boneshaker in the frozen steppes. In the bar before the game, John makes transparently insincere offers to take up the crap seat but I won't hear of it. The more martyred I feel, the more certain I am that we'll win.

Owen's goal – the one where he gives his foot a quick shake before shaping it sideways and downwards to slant the ball in off the bar – is spectacular, even from the shitseats. I'm about five pews from the Anfield Road end and Owen scores at the other end of the ground, but you could see the brilliance of the strike from Mars. It's another of those which, if scored by Denilson or Batistuta would have David Lacey and Brian Glanville reaching for their Oxford Dictionaries of New Footballing Similes (ed. D. Lacey/B. Glanville). Glenn Hoddle, meanwhile, will be preparing a fresh speech telling us not to be deceived by this latest flash in the pan.

Apart from Owen's goal the match is memorable for a thumping Paul Ince tackle on the fit-again Alan Shearer. Shearer's a tough lad. He doesn't ask for any favours from defenders and he doesn't give them any back. He's been out for six months with an ankle injury. England and Newcastle have missed him. You might have expected his England colleague Ince to have gone a little easy on him in his first game back, but neither of them holds back. It's a 50–50 ball which just about marginally favours Shearer, but Ince considers it fair game, flies into the tackle at 70 mph and sends Shearer flying into the Kemlyn Road hoarding. The two England players give each other a brusque, macho slap on the back as they trot away, shaken but not disturbed. Liverpool hold on to win 1–0.

We console Geordie John with trite suggestions that the FA Cup has their name on it, but he's not too dispirited. He expected Liverpool to win. He hates Dalglish. He just wishes the two of them would get back together sooner, rather than later.

Next day, Wednesday, I'm perusing the *Echo* to see how this latest win really affects our title prospects. Since Man. U we've played seven, won six, drawn one, scored twelve and conceded only two. Both from set-pieces which any old Scottish colossus would've cut out with ease. But I don't get as far as the League tables. Because it's Wednesday. The Midweek Match, Tommy Smith's weekday football letters page. And there it is. My letter.

It says, basically, how can Liverpool fans tolerate two years of mischief by Collymore, chanting his name, helping him through his almost constant crises of confidence while Fowler just got on with it and scored 30 a season, when, now that Fowler's hit a bit of a rough patch and needs the support of the fans, they see fit to turn against him? Does a player have to come in on an inflated fee to guarantee the devotion of the hordes?

The letter is from Tommy Vale, Birkenhead. Clearly Smithy couldn't decipher that illiterate twit Vialli's handwriting. But he gave me a Fair Tackle. My blushing from the privacy of my own front room is enough to boil the River Mersey, two miles away.

31 JANUARY 1998

Blackburn, home

And if I'm not drastically mistaken, there's a difference, you know. Not that one poxy letter in Tommy Smith's column can change things at a stroke, but there's a tangible ground-swell of support for little Fowler. His name is the first to be chanted by The Kop, as it should be, always, and when things, once again, don't go instantly right for him, there's encouragement and applause and shouts of 'unlucky' instead of the bleat of disapproval that's been rattling round the stadium in the recent past.

The game takes on the exact shape and pace of last year's tussle with Blackburn. I'm glad to see that Damien Duff isn't playing for Blackburn. He's one young player who is going to become a world superstar – I'd love to see him bedded into a Liverpool team of the future with Redknapp, Owen, Fowler, McAteer, Matteo, Danny Murphy, Robbie Keane from Wolves and little David Thompson from our youth supply-line. And David James, as well. People forget he's still only 24. He's an absolutely brilliant goalie at 24, and at 34, a goalkeeper's peak, he'll be the best in the world. But anyway, Damien Duff. On the bench, today. Let's hope he stays there.

We hammer Blackburn for 90 minutes, they don't make one chance and it ends 0–0. During one desperate attack in the final quarter of an hour, McAteer finds himself in a promising position out on the right-hand edge of their penalty box. McKinlay comes across to narrow his options, but Redknapp is still there in a good position for the angled ball if McAteer can just look up and spot him. He knocks the ball past Billy McKinlay instead and stretches to swing a right-footed cross in. His standing leg seems to get stuck as he whips his crossing foot back. He goes over and immediately waves to the bench, slapping the grass in agony. Mark Leather is with him in a jiffy, but it looks bad. They call for a stretcher and Jason's off. He's been superb since he came back in the autumn, and has probably been playing the best football of his career in the last couple of months. It's no coincidence that we've managed so many 0–0 shutouts with McAteer, Babb and Matteo playing so well together. They're far from being the final solution, these three, but they have been doing well. It's crushingly disappointing to see a player like Jason wiped out like this. He's in pain down there. He could be out for a year.

On Radio Merseyside or City, one of them, after the game, the commentator describes McAteer's plight as an 'unnecessary injury'. So what's a *necessary* bloody injury, then!? And, while we're at it, is there a bag to put the points in? And do wantaway strikers actually *slap* their transfer requests on the table? Is there a table, indeed? These important points of protocol occupy my thoughts as I queue for the tunnel lane on Scotland Road. We played well, today. McAteer's totally unnecessary injury has selfishly overshadowed a satisfactory performance, but we were good, today. We did everything but score. It's 20 points out of the last 24 and Southampton, home, coming up next. Things are looking up.

4 FEBRUARY 1998

Middlesbrough, home
(Coca Cola Cup Semi-Final, 1st Leg)

But first, there's the small matter of a Coca Cola Cup semi-final, 1st Leg against Bryan Robson's resurgent Middlesbrough. They won't be easy. Since getting rid of his exotic but troublesome triumvirate of Emerson, Ravanelli and Juninho, Middlesbrough have been playing like a team again. It'd be unfair to mention the hardworking and influential Juninho in the same category as Ravanelli, but he nonetheless disrupted Middlesbrough's team pattern. Everything went through him. His colleagues came to over-rely on the little Brazilian, shipping every ball to his feet in the hope that they could stand back and watch him work his magic.

Now, Paul Merson is as close as Boro come to a bigtime Charlie and players like Craig Hignett and Steve Vickers are really proving their worth. Hignett, remember, had to take a pay cut at the start of the '96–7 season to prove to Robson that he genuinely 'wanted it'. What Ravanelli proved to him by insisting upon £42,000 a week plus his gas bills is open to speculation. That he intended blowing a little glass in his spare time? Having a few of the lads round for a bout of spot-welding? Why *did* he insist upon that gas bill clause? His agent must've earned a few points for that bit of negotiation:

'Hey, Rava, 42 Gs is not bad poppy but you can spend that in a *day* up there on your *heating* bill . . . so tell me I don't look after my boys!'

Liverpool city centre is aswim with drunken Middlesbrough fans treating this game like a Cup Final. It's understandable that visits to footballing shrines like Anfield should be a treat to the likes of Boro – it's not so long since they were staring the old Division Three in the face – but I think they're selling themselves short. We are not playing brilliantly just now. With Boro's new tenacity, and with Andy Townsend turning out to be a very good acquisition for them, Liverpool are going to have to work hard to break them down. I reckon we'll win this one 3–0, but I don't see goals coming until the final 20 minutes.

And I'd be right, too – if I wasn't so completely wrong. Paul Merson scores a goal of supreme simplicity – but still superbly executed – after only eight minutes. Boro then pack the midfield, an effective tactic which tries Liverpool's patience to the limit. Just as it seems as though we'll never break them down, Redknapp slams in a screecher from the edge of the box. He's going through a useful phase, Jamie, of popping up with crucial goals just exactly when we need them. He's got a fantastic, arrowing drive on him – he should be ordered to shoot on sight at least three times per half or have his pay docked. As it is, 1–1 at half time makes for an interesting second half.

And interesting it definitely is. It's a classic Liverpool siege from the good old days, with chance after chance going begging. Unfortunately, arch predator R. Fowler misses most of them. You couldn't complain about a couple of them – it's a miracle he gets any kind of touch on one particular volley which he sends narrowly wide – but he blows a glorious chance for a header with about 15 minutes left. Just as the Middlesbrough supporters are celebrating and just as we're wondering when Robbie is going to come through his tricky patch, Owen squirms through the jungle of lunging tackles on the right of Boro's box and, rather than taking an easy tumble – which he could have easily – he squares a nice ball back for Fowler who snaffles the chance ecstatically. 2–1. Far from magnificent, but it should be enough to put us through to a juicy final against Arsenal or Chelsea. Somehow I can't get too excited about it. It'll be a grin, no more – a good day out. But if we beat Southampton here on Saturday . . . now that's another story. That'll be the makings of a proper run of form in the League. That'll be Championship form.

7 FEBRUARY 1998

Southampton, home

A game which, if we were considering taking lightly, we might now reconsider in light of The Saints' convincing win over The Manchester United Football Club PLC the other night. Kevin Davies scored a beautiful header in only the sixth minute, but Southampton dominated the first half, weathered the storm in the second and could have had two more in the last five minutes. Hirst blasted over from just on the penalty spot and Palmer wriggled through to set up Ostenstaad for a far-post header which he directed into the side-netting. Southampton were worthy winners.

Alex Ferguson is a canny and hugely intelligent guy and, underneath all the bluster, a very decent man. He was the only manager to publicly support the players' strike in the late '80s. But he still hasn't learnt his lesson about public utterances. He dwells too much upon, and fatally over-estimates, the impact his remarks have on other teams and their managers. It seems he can't stop himself of late, but sooner or later he must learn the ultimate lesson: things come back to haunt you. He should also know that nobody, not even the dullest of the general public dull, is taken in by his pronouncements. His real meaning, the agenda he thinks he's keeping so cleverly hidden, is translucently clear from the moment he says it. Tonight he suggests that it's only sporting of United to give the pursuing pack a glimmer of hope.

'It's only Christian,' he smirks, chewing and shitting himself simultaneously. He shouldn't say silly things like that. It's a flaw which is preventing him from becoming a truly great manager.

And he didn't mention how well Southampton played. It's to be hoped that Liverpool's entire squad watched the game, because Simpleton are no longer an easy ride – as they prove almost immediately. It's like watching a slow motion replay live, as Liverpool react too late to each stage of the attack as it moves closer to our goalmouth. We don't close down the throw-in down at The Kop end which leads to the big boot which leads to the flick-on which leads to Hirst running with the ball in the penalty area, going slightly away from goal. Matteo tries to nick the ball away from him as he goes past, but brings him down in the process. Hirst bags the penalty himself in the absence of Le Tissier.

It's nothing more than a false start, though. On 20 minutes Owen notches a cool equaliser and for the remainder of the half Southampton are cowering.

Second half and, as news filters through from Old Trafford that Leicester are winning, Liverpool step up their pressure to breaking point. Southampton are going to crack any minute. You can sense it. Matteo runs upfield for a corner, leaving Harkness on the halfway line and only Jones back. The ball breaks for Matteo who, for a split second, has a clear sight of goal. He draws his foot back and, as he shoots, Southampton feet and bodies arrive from everywhere. The ball cannons away and Southampton, relieved, give chase. Matteo, too, limping badly from the challenge, goes after Ostenstaad who manages to cut back inside him and drill the ball under James. 2–1. It's completely undeserved, but there's more. As Liverpool push forward again in search of at least an equaliser, Southampton break the length of the pitch virtually unchallenged, for Hirst to tap in his second. With the score 3–1 and an irate Ince urging his team not to give up, Owen finally heads home a ricocheting ball which both Fowler and Murphy have been unlucky not to convert. 3–2. But it's too little, too late. A sickening defeat in light of Man. United's latest slip-up, and a game which we should only ever have won.

Luck has not been with us, this year. Whenever the Luck Factor has come into the destiny of a game this season, it has gone against us. Murphy at Wimbledon. Unlucky, son. McManaman at Blackburn. Unlucky. Fowler at Southampton. Riedle at Upton Park. Ince at Everton. Fowler at Strasbourg. Fowler at Bolton. If fate evens these things out over a season, then it's time to start blowing some fortune in our direction.

Smithy's letters column in the *Football Echo* provides a brief moment of light relief. There's a letter, presumably written by Mick Potter or Gag, suggesting that Liverpool should introduce specially themed cuisine to complement our opposition. For example, if we're playing Blackburn we could serve Lancashire Hot Pot. If it's West Ham we could offer jellied eels and wallies. And if Liverpool were ever to revisit those glorious European nights again, argues the letter, the pie could, quite feasibly, be in the sky. Goulash for the visit of crack military side Honved. Paella when Deportivo La Coruña come . . .

The list goes on. The letter is from K. Sampson, Birkenhead. I didn't write it, but it keeps me chuckling all the way back to Hamilton Square.

14 FEBRUARY 1998

Sheffield Wednesday, away

A change in the squad, today. Danny, under supreme pressure to work around the clock to have Conway Park underground station completed by its Easter deadline, has given his ticket to Jegsy. He also mentioned, during a Guinness and Jameson's swalleeoke evening – that's the gargle and a bit of warbling – that things didn't quite work out with 'the fraulein'. That's a pity. I hope he's not working off the disappointment, though, at the expense of the good things in life. L.F.C. and intoxicating liquor. That's what it's all about.

Jegsy's mate Clowy, who came to Amsterdam and is a good egg, is also on board. Jegs is driving and we're already in dispute about the best route to Sheffield. I would've turned right on the M53 and headed for the M56. Clowy and Jegs reckon the M62 is more direct. I hate people telling me which way to go when I'm driving, so I lie down in the back and SHUT IT!

We talk about Michael Owen's brilliant debut for England against Chile, and we talk about Salas' wonder goal. There's only one player in England who could've scored that goal, bringing the ball down on his thigh and volleying instinctively into the bottom corner. Robbie Fowler. Robbie Fowler who wasn't even in the squad. But Owen was dynamite. With a little more ruthless selfishness he might have capped a Man of the Match performance with a goal, especially in the first half when he was roasting the Chile defence, cutting past them at will, but looking then for a target man instead of shooting himself. He's got to go to France, though. Him and Fowler. It's stunning to think that Owen started this season as an almost complete unknown. May he and Fowler stay together for many, many, many years. It makes you shiver to think of the goals they're going to score over the coming years, those two.

Tranmere are playing Newcastle in the Cup today, a fixture which might throw Ian Rush against lookalike and ex-colleague John Aldridge. In a pre-match *Football Focus* interview, Rush recalls his memories of Aldridge with fondness.

'He was a good drinker,' says Rushie with a grin, going on to marvel that, from after a Saturday match until training on Monday morning, Aldridge was capable of almost miraculous feats of consumption. Today, Robbie Fowler will try, once again, to pick up the pieces of his temporarily shattered career. Last weekend the *Sunday Mirror* alleged that Fowler was being blackmailed by ne'er-do-wells who had photographs of him carousing with booze and cocaine. After a season of almost relentless sniping and gossip aimed at him, Fowler has felt compelled to make a public denial of these allegations. Driving to Sheffield (the long way), we reflect that, in so many ways, the game has changed beyond redemption. Whether or not John Aldridge was a famous imbiber, he scored some marvellous goals for Liverpool and never gave us less than his best. Ian Rush, too, wore his heart on his sleeve as he grafted to beat every goalscoring record he hadn't already broken. It didn't matter to us what went on their private lives, as we never heard or read anything about them to give us pause. Newspapers were not interested in following soccer stars around, waiting for them to fall over, any more than the public was interested in reading this tosh. It's boring. Whether it's Merson, Rio Ferdinand, Keith Gillespie, whoever, nothing is more boring than another footballer-losing-the-plot story. If anyone is going to rival Rush and Aldridge's records, it's Robbie Fowler and Michael Owen. But will they survive the pressure cooker of modern Association football? Will the voracious tabloids allow them to get on with their job? Will their adoring public give them the unconditional love and support they will undoubtedly need, time and time again over the years to help them through their troubles?

Heading on stubbornly past Tintwhistle and over the Woodhead Pass instead of turning right at Glossop and taking The Snake, Jegsy demands that we keep a lookout for a pub. It's about 12.40. A pint of shandy and a quick egg and chips is in order before we head on into Sheffield.

I spot a place, The Waggon and Horses, near Langsett. There are a few Reds in there but mainly it's couples enjoying the first of the early spring sunshine, out for a drive and a gammon and pineapple. Except that they don't do that sort of food. None of your pub grub here – it's a limited but irresistible menu of tempting-sounding dishes prepared from fresh local produce. We should probably have skipped it, but the smell from the kitchen is bewitching. It's like that Bisto advert with a tantalising aroma drifting through the pub, hypnotising everyone. We decide to take another peek at the menu, and as we're looking through it a young woman appears from behind the bar to take our orders. Only a brave or callous heart would have been able to say 'Nope. I think I'll leave it, thank you' at that point, anyway, but we're not going anywhere. Not now. We're rooted to the spot, transfixed. Is someone playing a joke on us, here? Is this a crafty Sheffield University Department of Human Psychology experiment to plot out how the male of the species responds to certain situations? If it is, I can tell you here and now how we respond. Predictably. We respond with pathetic predictability.

The thing is, the woman behind the bar has . . . she's got . . . she's wearing this white T-shirt, right, and her . . . I mean to say . . . her nipples are *extraordinary*. I immediately look away, determined not to make her feel uncomfortable but, by Jiminy, her raspberries must be three inches long. When we were puerile colts at Thingwall Primary School we nicknamed one fast-developing girl 'Puma Studs'. Such a sobriquet would be an insult, here. This woman's are far, *far* more outstanding. We order various local delicacies – sausage and the like – and slump away to the nearest table. I'm biting down an attack of the sniggers like a pimply schoolboy. I don't even want to mention her. The others might not have noticed, or they might not think it's that big a deal. Maybe it's only me who notices things like that. Whatever, there's no way I'm going to be the first one to comment. No way. We sit down.

'Fuckinell!' says Clowy. 'Did you see 'em!!'

'See what?'

Suddenly she's at the table, laying out cutlery and condiments. I keep my eyes trained on Clowy. He's grinning at my attempts to make 'normal' conversation.

'So . . . yeah . . . Don Hutchison. He was probably the first, wasn't he?'

'First what?'

'You know. To get drummed out of the club by the press . . .'

Clowy just bursts out laughing. The concealed Sheffield University Department of Human Psychology closed-circuit cameras must be having a field-day. Jegs brings the drinks over and lays them down.

'Now then. Who asked for lager and who asked for nipple?'

The home-made sausage and fresh-laid free-range egg with chipped, fried local potatoes (bangers, egg and chips) was fine, but it took forever to arrive. It's nearly 2 o'clock. We were planning to park up and meet Tony, my brother-in-law, in The Blue Ball. Jegsy and Clowy are so certain of their route into Sheffield that, by 2.30, we're on the M18 heading for Doncaster. How this happened, I have utterly no idea as I was lying down on the back seat, thinking depraved thoughts.

We manage to turn off and get back onto the motorway heading into Sheffield. We're right over to the east of the city. Still, there's plenty of football traffic, judging by the Sheff. Wed. pennants and scarves in the cars around us, so we can't be too far from Hillsborough. An R-registration Mercedes keeps overtaking then pulling back, overtaking then pulling back. He's not being funny, especially, he's just anxious to get to the game and can't decide upon which lane is going fastest. In the passenger seat is his well-fed, annoying-looking son, aged about 11 or 12. He's a classic Hollywood Spoiled Kid and, now that he's spotted Jegsy's Liverpool sticker in the back window, he's no longer just annoying-looking. He's annoying. He's a full-blown brat, sticking one finger up, Bronx-style (there's no place for that sort of thing in decent society) and shouting 'The Wednesday' each time his dad motors past us. We can see his dad, also well-fed and dressed like Bernhard Langer, telling him to put the window up, but the brat continues.

'The Whenz-deeah!!'

Then he does that Sheffield Wednesday New Football brass band tune, now beloved of England fans, too, waving his hands around like he's conducting his own orchestra. Jegsy shakes his head.

'Open that glove compartment, Clowy,' he orders. Clowy does.

'Give us that tangerine.'

He passes it to him. Jegsy veers the car across two lanes of medium-fast motorway, until we're parallel with the Mercedes. He winks at the little fat lad. Down comes his window again. Down goes Jegsy's. The kid's pink, tubby face opens up to give us another blast of the brass band tune. Jegsy holds the steering wheel with one hand and takes aim with the other, directing the tangerine with stunning ferocity into the kid's pudgy cakehole. For a split second he looks like a boar's head on a banquet table, a flabbergasted, fast-stuck Fat Lad, eyes wide open, with a tangerine stuck in his mouth. The tangerine bursts and rolls away down the motorway. The Mercedes takes off at great speed. We're still guffawing as we head down the hill to Hillsborough. But not for long.

Everyone is wearing the *Sun* paper bowler hats. When I say everyone, I mean we've parked on the other side of the ground with mainly Wednesday supporters and it's they who are wearing the *Sun* hats. Is this a very sick joke? Hillsborough, scene of the deaths of 96 football supporters in 1989, later castigated as drunken hooligans by the *Sun*, playing comely host to that same rapacious rag? Fuck off, Sheffield!!

It gets worse. With the sensitivity and tact we've come to expect from South Yorkshire police, they've erected a system of barriers from outside the uncovered North West Terrace right past the old Leppings Lane end, now called the West Stand. Every convenient route to the stand is closed off. You can see the West Stand there, in front of you, you can almost reach out and touch it, but you can't walk over to it. It gets further and further away as you're directed towards a speck of yellow in the distance by, admittedly, an embarrassed selection of police personnel.

'See that down there. Steward in yellow. Turn left by him and keep going.'

It's a minute to three. We leg it, and the yellow speck gradually gets bigger. After another five minutes of hiking, we're outside the West Stand. More confusion awaits. The ticket says Gangway Z. I spot ZZ, so we go and join a short queue. When we get to the turnstile, the ticket collector points to the bit on the ticket that says Entrance D. We have to turn back and run to the other side of the stand before we finally get inside. We're far from being the only latecomers. All over the stand, angry supporters are trying to find their seats. There was probably a very good reason for blocking off the little feeder roads that would've got everyone inside the ground on time. It's just that no one told us what that reason was. All the coppers did was point and blush, point and blush.

Matteo's out, still feeling the effects of his attempted heroics against Southampton. Kvarme's back. The first piece of action we see as we finally sit down is Carbone lobbing James. 1–0 to Wednesday. We come back ferociously and Owen has us on level terms smartish, after McManaman plays him in with a lovely through ball, bisecting the Wednesday defence. They repeat the move a couple of minutes later, but this time Owen fires against Pressman's legs. He's showing no signs of fatigue from his midweek exertions with England. As he keeps saying in interviews, at the age of 18, why should he? Every time we go forward we look like scoring. McManaman and Fowler have chances, although our defence looks like rice paper whenever Wednesday attack us. At half time, it could easily be 5–3 to us.

Second half is all Liverpool for 15 minutes. Fowler is working like a mad dog, tracking back, showing for throw-ins, trying to beat Pressman from every part of the pitch. At one point he's our last line of defence, sliding in on Di Canio and forcing him to miscue his shot. It's great to see Fowler like this, getting his head and his game together. He's sure to score before long.

But he doesn't. Our defence commits hara-kiri twice in

three minutes. First, we fail to mark up – HOW MANY MORE BLOODY TIMES?! – from a corner, allowing Wednesday to take it short to the apex of our box from where, wouldn't you know it, new recruit from Everton Andy Hinchcliffe fires in off the underside of the bar. You can't blame James. He might have made a better fist of blocking the initial shot, but he shouldn't have been placed in that situation, or anywhere near it, by his defence. What's going on with them? Then, just as the collective pulse of the West Stand (Upper) is approaching normality, there's old Harkness doing his dog-running-backwards-chasing-tail routine. He fails to get a telling challenge in and Di Canio gleefully nods home at James' near post. We've turned certain victory into a 3–1 deficit. The Wednesday fans can't believe their good fortune.

Roy Evans, sensing that the game is far from over and *knowing* that another defeat might end our season – in February, for fuck's sake – sends on Berger and Murphy, taking off Kvarme and Leonhardsen. Leo is now regularly being taken off as Evans tries to save games which might not have needed saving if he didn't still persist with Leonhardsen as a left-sider.

Berger makes an instant contribution, putting Fowler through on goal. Fowler's shot hits the post and rebounds to Owen, who nets it. 3–2. We come at them again. Ince plays a glorious ball inside the Wednesday backline. Owen flays Nolan for pace, draws Pressman and slams it past him. 3–3, and there's still another eight minutes to go. We have good chances to win the game, and Fowler bends Pressman's hands back with a thumping volley on the final whistle. I suppose we should be glad we managed to rescue the game but really, Wednesday are so poor. We should've hammered them. It's a muted crowd from both sides which makes its way out of the ground. I'm glad I don't have to come here for another year.

Driving back over the Pennines, the radio news is breaking a leaked story from tomorrow's *Telegraph* that Jack Straw intends to take no further action regarding Hillsborough. He's looked at all the evidence and decided that there is no new video footage which will persuade him that justice has not already been properly served. He wants this to be an end of it. He wants to put a lid on the whole thing, now. He obviously has no idea what, or who he's dealing with here. This is Liverpool he's taking on and Jack Straw is going to have to think again.

18 FEBRUARY 1998

Middlesbrough, away
(Coca Cola Cup, Semi-Final, 2nd Leg)

A glorious day. Too nice by far. There's me, Danny, Roy and Jegsy cutting through Newsham Park to join Jimmy Flowers' coach outside The Oakfield, Breck Road.

'Reminds me of the day we played PSG last year,' says Danny.

'Remember the last time we walked through this park on the way to a match, Roy?'

He grimaces.

'Everton. Same weather.'

Having been in good time for our debut trip on the Flowers Special, we're now suddenly running late. It won't do for the new boys to keep the coach waiting, so we jog the last half-mile, feeling every inch in stomach acids.

There's nothing else for it. It's a long haul to Boro, and crosswords are the only proven method of eating up the distance. By Tebay West, our refuelling stop, we've hacked our way through both *Mirror* tests, the *Guardian* and, erm, the *Star*. It just found its way onto the bus. No one knows whose it is. If I were to say that Keith from Doncaster was seen drooling over some nameless story in *the very same newspaper* only minutes earlier, I'd already be saying too much.

Keith from Donny is one of Liverpool's most dedicated fans. I feel a bit responsible for him. When he was actually Keith from Doncaster as opposed to Keith from South Liverpool, formerly of Donny, he used to write to *The End* asking for tips on how to become Doncaster's No. 1 Dresser. The evil Mick Potter used to think up the most outlandish fashion items – tweed Norfolk jackets and green wellingtons, for example – and write fashion pieces in *The End* suggesting that this was what Scotland Road's finest pickpockets were wearing. To our amazement, people would start turning up at *The End*'s party nights dressed in Norfolk jackets and plus-fours. We started printing that Dunn and Co. was the only place to shop, full-length Barbour jackets should be worn tucked into brogues and monocles should only be worn to away games. Keith from Donny wrote back that he'd tried Dunn and Co. in Doncaster, Rotherham and Sheffield but they weren't certain what a Norfolk jacket was. Could our resident artist, Mr John Potter, whip up a sketch for him to take in next time?

Keith and his mate Irelo turned up at all *The End* Christmas parties and The Farm's first gigs, fanatically dressed like Scousers, right down to the last detail. They were our honorary wools, lads we were proud to call our associates. It was no surprise when Keith moved to Liverpool in the mid-'80s to facilitate his obsession with L.F.C. He goes, literally, everywhere. He's one of the ones who makes the rest of us into part-time supporters. I still have to hang my head in shame when I think of that Norfolk jacket, though.

We kill time lamenting the sad departure of Ruud Gullit, surprisingly sacked a few days ago. Unwilling to let an opportunity to expound my Gullit conspiracy theories pass by, I wonder whether Ken Bates just simply got fed up with his team manager's blatant xenophobia – or Anglophobia, at least.

Right up to the end, he was quivering and quibbling about the terrible backwardness of poor old Britain. In the game at Highbury he felt that Steve Bould tripped Vialli in the penalty box. He got a free-kick outside the box, and Bould was merely cautioned. Seething with the churlish injustice of it all, this country with its redneck amateur refs and its guileless journeymen, Gullit stuck out his bottom lip and shook his beads:

'In any other country . . . anywhere in the world . . . he's (Bould) got to go . . .'

Didn't feel quite that way when Lambourde was sent off at Anfield, though, did he? What did he say?

'With eleven men it's a different game . . .'

Sorry, Ruud, it's you who needs to catch up with the modern game. The game that plays, every day, in your mind takes place in 1988 and has you as its central star. That was a very, very long time ago. Even Liverpool could play in those days.

We pitch up at Newton Aycliffe, about ten miles from The Riverside, to get down to the serious business of gargling and singing. The Sam Dodd's flag is hung from the wall, bets are placed with the bookies next door and all is set fair for a grand semi-final night out.

At some point we get split into two factions. It's like a church hall disco. Jimmy Flowers, Lenny Woods and the over 50s are sat on one side of the pub, singing long, complicated songs they think us young pups won't know. On our side of the pub there's Bucko, Jegs and Danny leading the resistance. The drunker we get, the bolder we feel. I've got a little verse on *The Famous Man. United Went to Rome to See the Pope* theme, but I've never tried it out in public. Emboldened by poisonous Middlesbrough ale, I stagger over to Jimmy's table and shout:

'What did the Pope say to the famous Man. United?'

They look genuinely shocked and confused, but I bluster on:

'This is what he said –

> *The famous Liverpool have already been here before*
> *Liverpool were here in '77 and '84*
> *If you think you're Kings of Europe*
> *They've already clocked up four*
> *So politely I must ask you once again*
> *WHO ARE YOU . . .'*

Jimmy looks at Lenny. Lenny looks at Jimmy.

'Cracker', grins Mr Flowers. 'You'll have to write it down for us.'

I hobble back to our side of the room, shoulders hunched, to sustained applause from the Young Boys (average age 36). Surely it's going to be one of those great nights. We're going to win 4–0, here.

Nobody who was with us can remember the coach ride from Newton Aycliffe to The Riverside. There was definitely poison in that ale. What we can remember about the match is that it was marked by more in-fighting among fellow Liverpool fans than you'd think possible. It was going off everywhere. Liverpool's own fans were battering each other. They were fighting with each other, because Middlesbrough were 2–0 up, we never looked like scoring and yet another C-list prize was disappearing over the horizon. Robbie Fowler, again, ran his feet raw to no avail. We were well and truly on our way out. It was all too much for some people. All the simmering resentment against the team, individual players, supporters who boo, all this, and the gradual erosion of our once-almighty team as a name to be feared, suddenly blew up into open warfare. There were 8,000 Liverpool supporters there at The Riverside, trying their hardest to roar the team on to something better. It never looked likely for one moment.

We were wretched. We accepted the beating meekly. Once upon a time, it'd be a shock if the likes of Watford or Brighton knocked us out of a prestigious cup competition. It'd be a real shock, followed by key changes in team personnel. Barry Endean's goal for Watford in 1970 led to the break-up of the great Liverpool side of the '60s. But this defeat at Middlesbrough – we'll probably just take it, dress it up as a blessing in disguise and do absolutely nothing about it. Until next time. Next time is Everton, home, on Monday night. Something better change.

23 FEBRUARY 1998

Everton, home

This is surreal. It's 6.29 on the evening of Liverpool versus Everton, a game of supreme importance to both clubs and by far the biggest news on Merseyside, today. But I'm queueing my way along Scotland Road, listening to Radio Merseyside, hoping for team news, pre-match scene-setting, anything to do with the Big Match and all I can get is . . . organ music. Church organ music. And it isn't even playing a tune, not even a churchy, ecclesiastical sort of tune. It's like a Monty Python piss-take of a seaside community cinema organ. It sounds like Star Turn on 45 Pints and it's on, now, live on BBC Radio Merseyside.

We'll forget the Derby, then. We won't worry about the frantic tens of thousands, desperate for any sliver of team information, speculation, Expert Opinion, anything. I've been jamming on the Teletext all day, waiting for that newsflash – Matt Elliott has signed and passed his medical in time for inclusion in tonight's squad. Georgi Kinkladze has joined him at the eleventh hour, ready to make up a devastating roving winger-with-portfolio role, alternating with McManaman, switching from flank to flank, tying defences in knots. I've hit on every Teletext supplier and called up every clubcall number. All they can tell me is that we're still interested some geezer called Staap Jam from PSV Eindhoven and that Rob Jones is likely to play at left-back tonight, in the absence of Harkness.

Still the seaside organ blares. Maybe this is a weird Evertonian takeover of the airwaves, intended to psyche Liverpool fans into a trance. There isn't even any 6.30 news. This terrible caterwauling organ just plays on and on and on. The match IS tonight, isn't it? A sickening shudder of realisation shoots from temple to toe, just like at Leicester when we were scrambling around outside the rugby ground and it suddenly dawned on me . . . But no, the shock passes. Why else would thousands of other cars all be jostling up Scotland Road, all their drivers scratching their heads as that amusement pier organ whines on? After an eternity, a Pathe News-style voice announces:

'That was a repeat of last month's popular recital of Bill Dixon playing The Blackpool Tower organ . . .'

Honestly! That's exactly what the voice said. I mean, strikealight, but am I missing something here!? Are we in Liverpool? Is there a match on tonight? A match of some small significance to the citizens of this Liverpool? I don't want to demean the cultural significance of Bill Dixon's organ recitals but WHAT'S THE BLOODY TEAM NEWS!!!? That, and only that, is the purpose of a local radio station on Derby Day. To tell you who's playing, who's injured and who the two managers currently consider to be shit. Bill Dixon can wait, thank you very much.

Channel 5's Teletext steals the pre-match exclusive. No Mark Fish, no Matt Elliott, no Robbie Keane – but there is News. Rob Jones is indeed playing on the left of defence, with

Kvarme playing at right-back. That's fine. That's very good, in fact. As previously stated, there's no doubting Kvarme's tackling ability, his speed, his reading of certain situations. At right-back he's less likely to find himself alone and in space without a team-mate close by. He can come inside and give the ball to Matteo, or he can push on a few yards and give it to McManaman, Redknapp, Ince, Owen – whoever is making themselves available in that deep right channel. I reckon he'll do fine tonight, young Bjorn.

The usual poisonous atmosphere hangs in the air as the match kicks off. Liverpool, again, are overwhelming favourites and this time we start about them as though we mean business. Fowler is immediately into the fray, working his socks off up front. Michael Owen drifts wide, looking for a bit of space, and it's from this position that our first sniff of a chance comes. Ince runs the ball over the top of Everton's back-line, with enough spin on the ball to kick it back into Owen's path. Owen's through, with Fowler and Leonhardsen both in the box screaming for the pull-back. Owen glances up at them, has a look at Myrhe's positioning then sets himself up for the shot. It skids across Myrhe, but beats the far post as well. The move is repeated two minutes later. This time, with no one to square the ball to, Owen slams the ball at the gap to Myrhe's left at his near post. If he'd squirted it along the deck, it's a goal but, although the shot is vicious, it's at a comfortable height for Myrhe to parry for a corner. As Everton try to break from the corner, McManaman rolls the ball into Robbie Fowler's path. With barely any backlift he cracks the ball left-footed at the angle of post and crossbar. Over on Sky the shot must be off the speedometer – it must be travelling at 150 mph. It's a screamer and it's going in. We're out of our seats, just waiting for the confirming bulge of the net, half-glancing down at the linesman to check that he's not offside, when the ball takes a devious outswing, allowing Myrhe to get three fingertips to it.

What a goal that would've been! There's barely a quarter of an hour gone, and we could've been 3–0 up.

Before Everton have even crept into our half, Owen's away again. This time Fowler dummies a McManaman pass and Owen's in a one-to-one chase with Dave Watson. Watson tugs desperately on Owen's shirt as the teenager threatens to sprint away from him. If he can get past Watson there's only the goalkeeper to beat. Owen ducks forward, ready to race away with it when Watson, a savvy old dog, glances up to check the ref's line of vision and, using the piston-motion of his arms, elbows little Owen smack in the chin. Owen goes down holding his face. The ref couldn't have seen what happened, and only awards a free-kick, which Liverpool waste.

It's still 0–0 at half time. The Everton fans, who've been muted throughout the first half, start the second in good voice. It doesn't take long for their reward to come. Our defence, which has looked resolute so far, suffers a momentary lapse of concentration in dealing with a looping cross from the right. The ball bobbles around the six-yard box and Ferguson, leaning into a half-volley, smashes the ball high past James. It's a totally undeserved but not unexpected 1–0 lead for Everton.

Something catches my eye. It can't be. I crane to my left for a better view. Weird! The Bon Viveur is jumping up and down the steps like a kid, fists clenched in triumph, round face even more flushed than usual, eyes alight. He must have £1,000 on Ferguson for the first goal. But no, what's this!? He's running – well not running, strictly – he's waddling, and gasping quite a lot, but he's moving in a forwards direction – back up the steps towards his two lads, pointing gleefully. His moist mouth, which probably still harbours chateaubriand and strands of asparagus, is opening in slow motion and he's shouting and pointing:

'Fuck off yah red bastards!! One nil to the blue boys!! Ah-hah!!'

This takes time to sink in. I look away to the centre and look back, just in case I've imagined it all. But no. The Bon Viveur is a Toff.

I nudge Roy.

'D'you see that.'

Roy nods.

'Weird.'

'Weirdest thing I've ever seen.'

But it isn't. Something yet weirder happens. Sensing that a home defeat against Everton might be just the straw that ends his long, unbroken sequence as Liverpool's Number One, David James comes out, ill-advisedly, right to the edge of his box to jump for a ball which was never there to be claimed. He collides with Rob Jones and fluffs the catch. The ball squirms free to Mickael Madar, Everton's new loan-deal signing from France. This is the weird part. Rather than hurl himself at Madar's feet or race back into his goal or even push Madar over, David James just stands there. He stands at the edge of his penalty box hugging Rob Jones as though to say, never mind, it wasn't your fault, these things can happen in football. This is the moment, I think, that most of us know Brad Friedel will be in goal for Liverpool's next game. James, grinning ruefully, seems to know it, too. Madar merely has to choose whether to walk the ball into the net or whether to sidefoot it. Mercifully for Liverpool he does both – that is, he does neither. He sort of putts it slowly along the ground, going for accuracy and no power, allowing Babb to race in and clear off the line. James is still nowhere near his goal-line. It's a truly bizarre moment in Liverpool's bizarre modern history of goalkeeping eccentricities and only when the ball is back in Everton's half, fully 15 seconds after he first came for the ball, does David James retrieve his position. This is all getting a bit too much for me. All I want is for us to be great again. It's not much to ask, is it?

Paul Ince rattles in a spawny equaliser straight from the

clearance, Redknapp almost squeezes a daisycutter inside the far post and Robbie Fowler injures himself challenging for a half-chance with Everton's new hero goalkeeper Myrhe. He manages to hobble off, come back on for another couple of minutes then walk off with a bit of support from our physio, so the injury can't be too bad. None of this registers, though. Ince's goal, our late rally, Fowler's injury – it all seems to drift past me as if it were taking place elsewhere. I'm staring straight ahead watching The Bon Viveur waltzing with David James to the soothing strains of Bill Dixon playing the Blackpool Tower organ. It's all got too weird for me, this weirdest of seasons. First home game of the year against Wimbledon and things were looking good. Since then we've drawn with Leicester, Blackburn, Sheffield and Everton and managed a home defeat against Southampton. We're not going to win the League this year, are we?

Ten of us show up in The Albert for a funereal singsong, but it's one of those nights when people go to make a phone call and never return. Danny and I walk down to The Cunard on Boundary Street with Mick Potter. Mick used to live in the flats opposite until they were bulldozed by the council a few years ago. Mick's bedroom used to have a small round window, 'Potter's Porthole' as it was known. Many an epic day started with a tap on the porthole and a barked reminder to the slumbering Potter:

'Watford! Carlisle! Arsenal!'

Even our visit to Walsall in the League Cup started with a drink at The Cunard. Balmy days which ended in victory. It seems a long, long time ago. These days we're grateful for a point at home against Everton.

28 FEBRUARY 1998

Aston Villa, away

Nothing has happened since Monday night – nothing at all. In spite of my unstinting day and night watch on the Teletext pages, transfer deadline day is approaching without any seeming activity from Liverpool. It's as simple as this. We play Man. U at Old Trafford in a few weeks' time. If we don't buy a commanding centre-back, United will score from a header. Probably from a set-piece. I don't know how many warnings we need. Everyone scores free headers against us, but Man. U more than anybody have found this a particularly rewarding source of easy points. They've found that they don't really need to try against us any more. Just knock a few high balls in and the goals will surely follow. So I've been studying Teletext, knowing that *any moment* the news will flow through that we've bought Matt Elliott or Jaap Stam (real identity now revealed as opposed to previous confusing alias). But there's nothing. We're determined, it would seem, to go into battle against United, and everybody else, with what we've already got.

And we have to beat United, this time. We have to. Because the other thing that's happened this week is the flaring up of yet more pitiful symptoms from Old Trafford. Everyone knows they suffer from delusions of grandeur in which having a great big stadium full of European day-trippers equates to success. Of course any fat businessman can buy an Aston Martin. It doesn't get rid of his fat gut and turn him into Simon Templar, though. And what is a Theatre of Dreams for, if not for dreaming in? Dream on, fatties.

The other, less well-documented malady emanating from Manchester, though, is a serious form of penis-envy directed towards their well-endowed neighbours from Liverpool. In this case, the European Cup can be clearly seen as a penis substitute. The more Manchester United are deprived of one, the more desperately they want one. So much so, that at their FA Cup replay against Barnsley on Wednesday – which Barnsley won at a canter – the United fans blew a smokescreen over their own failings by unfurling a banner which said:

'Fourth place in a two-horse race.'

It had a bold, throbbing Liver Bird at its centre.

A more experienced group of supporters would have known not to crow too soon, but, following the lead of their inexperienced manager they were effectively sticking their chin out at the nation and saying, come on, have a crack – we deserve it.

At our most successful – which is considerably more successful than *yao* – Liverpool fans had a sense of decorum. We didn't crow until we had something to crow about. This United lot have got a long, long road ahead and a lot to learn on the way. They're upstarts. It'd be lovely to stuff them at Old Trafford, to ram their obsessive, paranoid jealousy of all that we've achieved back down their bloated PLC. But without a centre-half, it seems unlikely.

As does the prospect of giving them any sort of fight for the title. As Danny and I drive through the drizzle on the M6, Manchester United are holding firm against Chelsea in the morning game at Stamford Bridge. It sounds as though Chelsea aren't even troubling them. There's five minutes left and Man. U are sitting pretty on a 1–0 lead. Before this morning's match they were nine points clear of us. If Chelsea beat them and we beat Villa, we could claw it back to six points, with us still to go to Old Trafford. The way it looks now, we'll be kicking off at Villa knowing that United are already 12 points ahead and disappearing over the horizon.

Villa is a tough place to pick up points in any event, but today is going to be extra tough.

Factor 1: they have a new manager. Brian Little parted company with his beloved Villa during the week, and John

Gregory has been called back to try and stabilise things. Teams with new managers always win their first game or two before slipping back into their bad old ways, so we're going to have to be on top form just to get a draw.

Factor 2: Robbie Fowler is out. The injury he picked up against Everton is much, much worse than first thought. It's a bad cruciate ligament injury, similar to the problem which kept Alan Shearer out for so long. Fowler, who's had a wretched time of it virtually all season, won't kick a ball again until well into next year's campaign. He can forget the World Cup. At his age, he was ready to take his reputation global. Now he'll be watching as, perhaps, his young partner Michael Owen gathers the plaudits. Whoever said this is a funny old game was a comedian.

Factor 3: and saving the worst until last, we're up against old Collywobbles today. In Collymore's feverish imagination he was badly treated by Liverpool F.C. and its callous supporters. He wants his revenge. He wants to show everyone just what they're missing. And he'll do it. So inflated is the man's ego, so unhinged is his temperament that he will go and score today. Not for Villa. Not for their supporters. He'll do it for himself. He'll score today, because he wants to, to stick it up Liverpool. And then he'll pick up a strain or a chill or a bruised finger and he'll go missing for the rest of the season.

So, by my reckoning, we have to score at least three today. One to cancel out Collymore's inevitable strike. Another to equalise the new manager effect. And one more to win the game. Actually, we'll probably need four, because our defence hand everybody a goal start, anyway.

We park up by Villa Leisure Centre and amble up to the ground in suddenly searing hot sunshine. I'm tempted to run back and stick my sturdy Bonneville windcheater in the boot, but we're already on top of the ground. Besides, we've been distracted. Everyone knows it's rude to stare but, blimey, this is a *specimen*. Standing by that strange, turreted building on the corner that looks like it was once a pub is a true freak of nature. This is an *outstanding* specimen. This must be what is meant by a Fashion Victim. In the good old days, Brummies wore extremely wide trousers and used to bleach their hair but in Tony Blair's Cool Britannia they've been given a new lease of life. This geezer, who must be six feet and six inches tall, is dressed from head to toe in black. That's not actually true. His head is clad in a claret and blue silk Hermes scarf. I can't be specific that it's a Hermes, but it's a woman's headscarf which he has tied into a rakish bandanna. When the occasional gust of wind lifts up the knot-tails at the back of his bandanna you can see he's bald as Yul Brynner. But everything else is black. Black Adam Ant blouse, black leather kecks, black over-designed boots with big mad buckles all over them. And sunglasses, of course, pushed up above his eyebrows. He looks bloomin' ridiculous.

The thought of him keeps me tickled all the way round the ground until we're in our seats. I can't help imagining Bandanna Man urging his team on from the Holt End:

'Come on, Collymore!! Kick the ball in the goals!!'

As we shuffle to our seats, the team is warming up. Friedel is indeed making his long-awaited Liverpool debut. Long awaited by him, that is. He must be mystified. Liverpool go to extreme lengths of pleading and courtship to get the Department of Employment to allow the boy a work permit and, knowing that he has to start playing immediately to fulfil his quota, we do the logical thing and banish him to the subs bench. I'm a huge James supporter, but I've got to admit to being stumped by the Brad Friedel saga.

Our seats are right behind the goal. As the teams are kicking in, four burly and acutely embarrassed Villa ground stewards shuffle across to the goalposts and drop to their knees. The youngest one's ears are burning up madly. After, presumably, a secret code from their chief steward, the four conscripts hoist themselves – and the entire set of goalposts, nets and all – up to a knee-high Precious McKenzie squat position. From there they juggle the goalposts up to a comfortable lifting height and drag them about two feet to the right, before setting them down again. They've moved the goalposts! Villa have, quite literally, moved the dashed goalposts!

Just before kick-off the occupants of the four seats to my left file in. It's the little Sikh kid from the Wimbledon game and his family. I say 'a'right' to him and give him a thumbs-up, and get a shy grin back. The game starts. It's so hot in that uncovered away end that the jacket has to come off. There's no room to jiggle my arms out of their sleeves and, trying to pull the thing over my shoulders instead, my head gets stuck. A big shout goes up from all around me. I disentangle myself from the jacket and emerge to find we've got a penalty. Remarkable! Owen slots it coolly and we're in the unusual position of being a goal ahead. I can't remember when we were last in the lead against anyone. This'll be a test for the lads, trying to dictate the pattern of a game we don't need to chase.

A test which is, of course, way beyond Liverpool's meagre defensive capabilities. As Villa are lining up for their first corner, McManaman and Ince effect a pincer movement on Collymore. Collymore has been invisible during the first encounters of the game, and seemed to duck out of his first challenge with Harkness. Something about this incident with Macca and Ince has got to him, though. He turns and sees McManaman pointing aggressively at him, as though he's saying:

'Don't let HIM out of your sight! Let's see who's a Spice Boy at a quarter to five . . .'

Collymore reacts angrily, throwing off their attentions and moving out on to the left wing.

The move pays off almost immediately, with Collymore finding room after two lucky deflections from Babb and Harkness fall his way. He sets his sights and fires from 20 yards.

A third lucky deflection takes the ball away from the diving Friedel and equalises for Villa.

With this, Collymore is transformed into a marauding demon for the next hour. He's unstoppable, by fair means and foul. When he's not causing panic in the Liverpool defence, he's stopping our own attacks. One clever break frees McManaman, who is simply hurled to the ground by Big Bad Stan. He's already been booked and should really go off for this second bookable offence. The ref seems to warn him that he's definitely on his last cigarette, which is no use at all to us. McManaman only had one man to beat, but all we've got from the attack is a free-kick on the halfway line, which Villa can defend at their ease.

Almost directly from this free-kick, Villa break away on goal. Taylor does well to hold the ball up, get himself in a shooting position and slip the ball past the onrushing Friedel. Agonisingly for him, the ball rolls against the far post and away. Agonisingly for us it goes as far as Collymore, who stabs it into the empty net. 2–1 to Villa. He celebrates as though he's scored the Midlands Cup winner. The Villa fans are riotous with joy. The sun disappears behind a big, black cloud. It rains. It snows. It hails. Nicky Holt storms out five minutes before the end shaking his head. This is somebody who's the definition of a true supporter, thick and thin, home and away. It's not just the weather that's got to him. Something's wrong in the state of Anfield.

We trudge back to the car, which I've perched on a traffic island right by the exit to the Leisure Centre for a sharp getaway. Small mercies, indeed, and short-lived small mercies, at that. As we go to turn onto our usual filter route to the M6, we're waved away by traffic cops. The whole roundabout is coned off. Diversion signs are everywhere. We have to join a seven-mile queue along the A34 to rejoin the motorway near Walsall. This is torture.

Mellor is swamped by Liverpool fans who reckon this is

Liverpool's best result of the year because it'll lead to Roy Evans' resignation. Danny and I have the usual debate about who would take over.

'Listen – if he dropped Leonhardsen and played Murphy, we'd be challenging for the title, still. Fowler's out. Wright's out. McAteer's out. You're talking about players who make a difference.'

'Who picks Leonhardsen? Who bought him?'

I'm bamboozled for a second.

'But who *wouldn't* have bought him? Everyone was after him! We were made up!'

Now Danny's struggling.

'He's got to go. He doesn't give a good interview.'

The argument gets surreal.

'*What!* A good interview! What's that got to do with anything?'

'All the things he could say . . . and all he ever says is "reasonably satisfied", "reasonable performance" . . . he's too fuckin' reasonable!!'

I know what he means. Roy could make a better fist of it with the media, especially in his jousts with Ferguson. It wouldn't take much to put him in his place. Like when Man. United wanted their game against us brought forward to help their European preparations. It was a chin begging to be hit. He could've said:

'With our unrivalled pedigree in Europe we fully sympathise with Alex. And if United want to achieve even half our success in that competition, they're going to need all the help they can get. We're happy to offer what little assistance we can . . .'

Instead we huffed and puffed and let the game be brought forward to 11.15 in the morning. But, whatever, you know. It'd be nice if Roy Evans was an inspirational wit and raconteur. I'll settle for a good manager, though – and I think he is. Maybe a little vote of confidence in the form of a letter to Smithy is called for.

I join Danny for a quick pint in the new John Laird pub in central Birkenhead, which means I don't get my two raps on the roof as I drive off, later. I miss that.

7 MARCH 1998

Bolton, home

The day starts promisingly. Alex Ferguson, determined to take every TV interview he's offered in order to try and hoodwink the country – and in particular the inhabitants of London N5 – that he's calm, confident and in control, has gone out on *Grandstand* and proved unequivocally that he's losing the plot. He's standing there prior to Man. U's game at Sheffield Wednesday, smiling a lot but still chewing, trying to give off this air of *savoir faire*. It's completely bogus. Even a jealous Scouser can see through it. Does he really believe that any one person in the world is fooled by these childlike and transparently panicky attempts at psychological warfare? His latest statement, again in the general context of the unknown twists and turns this year's Premiership may still have in store for us, is to state that Arsenal have a woeful record at Old Trafford. Is this not tantamount to inviting certain defeat when the Gooners visit them next week? Isn't he *skipping* to the nearest birch tree, plucking a firm branch, whittling it to a supple cane with his own teeth by saying this and asking to be thrashed until his hide seeps?

The match is so stultifying that I spend the first half debating whether to ask The Bon Viveur what the heck he's playing at.

What's it all about, fat, bearded chappie? You a Blue or what?
And what did you have for pudding today?

Thompson scores with a rasper. So what? Everyone scores
against us. Thompson rattles the crossbar. Yawn. Perhaps
that'll wake us up. The Bolton fans shout '*Fiiiiiiiiish*'
whenever, er, Mark Fish touches the ball. This, along with
West Ham's '*Abooooooo*', is one of the best drug-addled chants
in the division. I still laugh out loud every time I hear it. It's
ace. '*Fiiiiiiiiiiish*', like a collective disappointed sigh. Know the
feeling. We go in at half time 1–0 down, but I just know we're
going to sneak a turgid 2–1 win.

It's a pleasant surprise to find that the second half isn't so
bad. We step up several gears and tear poor Bolton apart. Ince
and Owen score, Redknapp nearly gets a third and there's
something other than possible new signings and new managers
to debate in The Albert. Sheffield Wednesday have beaten
Man. United. At last we've made up some ground on them.
Can we still think about the Premiership? Is there any chance
at all? Not really. We certainly don't deserve it. But then,
neither have Man. U for the past two years. So long as we're
still in it, I suppose, we're still in it.

8 MARCH 1998

My house

Reading through the report of Everton's comprehensive defeat
at Southampton yesterday, a thought occurs to me:

'Joe. Tom hasn't been to play for a while. D'you want to
give him a ring?'

14 MARCH 1998

Tottenham, away

This is another of those used-to-be-lairy grounds that you
can't get used to in its new, friendly guise. To a shameless
coward like me, the walk up from Seven Sisters Tube used to
be the longest, most nerve-racking hike to any League ground,
anywhere. Mobs of slobbering hooligans would appear from
sidestreets, bouncing up and down, dying for a row. To me,
these blokes always looked at least 45 years old. I suppose they
could've been. Jegsy's 59.

Today, striding up the Seven Sisters against a perky March
wind, an old lady dropping her pint of milk still induces a
heart-attack in me, but the sidestreets are full of BMWs and
merchandise sellers while the hooligans are selling match
tickets for £120 a pair. The pubs are still crowded with punters
watching the replays and interviews from this morning's Man.
United versus Arsenal game. Speaking after the game, the
crumbling Manchester United boss makes a series of fantastic
utterances. He says:

'We're good to Sky viewers', meaning that he wants to give
an impression of relaxed, detached amusement at the way his
team seem to be conspiring to shoot themselves in the foot and
turn this one-horse race into the St Leger. He looks haunted.

He also says:

'We don't count on winning it (the Premiership) any earlier
than we normally do.'

He did! He said that! He's such a cunning old fox, Fergie,
isn't he? Such a head-wrecker. Arsene Wenger must be tearing
himself apart with anxiety.

Danny has made his own way to this one, travelling down
yesterday for a weekend on the swallee with his old
bricklaying pal Richie. I promised the two of them last week
that I'd meet them for a drink before the game, but these are

two men who consider anything less than ten pre-match pints with attendant Jameson's chasers to be a basic admission of cross-dressing. I ducked out on Wednesday with pathetic claims to having a bit of a cold and caught the 10.45 this morning, taking the Victoria Line direct from Euston to Seven Sisters. I'm cutting everything a bit fine, but that's the way I fancy doing it today. No messing about. Three points, in and out.

As the train rattles through the Nuneaton area, we pass a big playing field divided up into four separate pitches, with a junior game taking place on each. I follow the action on the nearest pitch, amused by the massive effort put into the game by such tiny competitors. The kids must be about 8 or 9, and they look minuscule in their billowing shorts, little mouths squeaking out instructions from tightly cropped heads. A motley collection of dads and mums gathers on the sidelines, flapping their arms self-consciously and shouting unhelpful remarks to their issue. A titchy, half-pint skinhead nicks the ball off a wannabe Rio Ferdinand who's dwelling too long in possession, and races in on goal. His little legs are jerking as fast as they can take him. It looks as though he's overrun the ball. I crane my head as the train takes us away from this piece of footballing history – who knows what may become of any of those kids out there – trying to see who gets to the ball first. At my last sight of them it was a close call between the nippy little skin, the loping Rio lookalike and the hefty goalkeeper. I hope he scored.

I find my seat behind the goal and look around for faces I know. With Arsenal continuing their woeful record at Old Trafford by beating Man. U this morning, this game has taken on an extra piquancy. United's desperate run of form means that, in spite of our own moody results, we're not far off making a dash for the finishing line ourselves. Three points today and we're right back in the fray – I'm looking forward to it tremendously. Liverpool and Tottenham games are always easy on the eye, and this one has all the symptoms of another classic. Tottenham are guaranteed to let at least two in, but then so are we. With Ginola in such sparkling form and McManaman and Owen playing so well, we should be in for a corker.

We get a corker. Liverpool start well, with McManaman seemingly afforded as much space as he wants. Twice he bamboozles Campbell and sends in nasty, bending crosses but the first is blocked by Vega while the second is disarmed equally effectively by Leonhardsen. Tottenham look threatening, too. Ginola makes one wonderful if aimless run from the right touchline to the left before he simply runs out of ideas, then, just on the quarter-hour, Tottenham score. Ginola, again, drifts through the Liverpool defence and digs out a perfect cross for Klinsmann to head home. Klinsmann. He's been awful since his return to White Hart Lane, so it's odds-on that he'd have to score against us, innit?

We don't seem too deterred. After riding out a sustained period of Tottenham pressure, McManaman and Ince start to take over in midfield. McManaman, in particular, is roaming past Vega and Campbell as though they're not there. The ease with which he takes the ball round Sol Campbell does not bode well for England. Hoddle's bound to pick him. He plays for Spurs. But today – and let's hope it's an off day – Steve McManaman can do whatever he wants with him. He plays Owen in for a half-chance, which Baardsen saves well, before Owen returns the favour and Macca steers the ball home. 1–1. The remainder of the half is all Liverpool pressure. Ince is snaffling up everything in midfield and starting up attack after attack but Baardsen, looking like a very able deputy for Ian Walker, makes two excellent saves from Owen before the break.

At half time I find myself playing Scruples. I'm queuing for the toilets when up ahead I hear the unmistakable tones of Mr Danny Giles. No doubting it. It's him. What do I do! I can't blank him. But on the other hand, if he spots me I'm done for. There is no excuse in the world which is strong enough to deter Danny from press-ganging me into a night on the swallee with him and Richie. I can't do it. I'm booked onto the 18.55 from Euston and that's that. If I miss that train I have to pay full whack, but the main thing is . . . I don't *want* to go on the ale with them. There's nothing for it – I shuffle around and head back to my seat.

Second half kicks off. Miraculously, a vague urge to go to the bog has transformed itself, now, into an unbearable downward weight on my bladder. I'm done for. If I'd have gone ahead at half time and just kept my head down in the crowd, I could probably have brushed through without Gilesy spotting me. And even if he had I could just have thrown myself at his feet and sobbed:

'Please, please, *please*!! Don't make me go out on the gargle with you and Richie! I'm not thirsty!'

But I didn't. And now, at 30-second intervals, I feel this excruciating bloated tug from my lower belly.

'Pisssssssss!! Pisssssssss!!' it's saying. 'Let me out!! Do it right here!! Piss your kecks!!'

I can't concentrate on the game. Ginola seems to be dancing past outstretched legs at the other end and . . . he's scored! 2–1 to them! Great bloody goal! That's it – I'm off to the lavvy . . .

The nearer I get to the urinal the more convinced I am that I'm going to burst all over myself before I manage to get the thing out. It's a close-run thing. The sharp sequence of zip down, knob out and waste expelled is a blur of feverish relief. Aaaaaaaagh!

I don't care, now, if I'm spotted. I do that self-conscious half-jog back to my seat, head bowed, and get there unannounced. Everyone's still talking about Ginola's goal. Not the extravagant curl on it from over 25 yards, but the amount of space he was allowed to stroll through, to look up, pick his spot and let fire.

Let's face it, here and now. This team ain't right. We're not going to win a thing this year. We're incapable of coming down to a place like Tottenham, knowing that Man. U have lost again, and squeezing the life out them. That's what we need to do to teams like this. Strangle them. Suffocate them. Then go down the other end and kill them off. But we still think we're too good for that. I don't think it's the manager who needs to go. It's half of this team. They've got their own agenda, and good luck to them. But not here at Liverpool. With Tottenham 2–1 up, I'm starting to think about next season.

Poor old Leonhardsen, a trier if ever there was one, goes off injured. The terrier-like David Thompson replaces him, and we start to look a little more direct. Thompson, who combines great skill with speed and aggression – a bit like Martin Bullock at Barnsley – gets behind the Spurs defence and hangs a lovely cross in mid-air for Ince to spin and volley the most spectacular overhead kick hard into the net. It's right in front of my forehead. What a goal! Come on Liverpool! We can win this League! Course we can!

But it's Tottenham who show all the fight. Ince is doing a superb job in the centre of midfield, winning everything and driving the team forward, but the defence has no answer to David Ginola. On 80 minutes he crosses for Nielsen to smack a header onto the crossbar. It's scrambled away, but the respite is brief. From the resulting corner, Vega powers in unchallenged – what? against Liverpool? unmarked from a corner! seconds after warning was served with a near-miss? – and gleefully heads Tottenham into a 3–2 lead.

They're not done, either. Nielsen hits the post when scoring would've been way, way easier and Campbell heads wide from a promising position. With a couple of minutes to go, Ginola is substituted to a standing ovation, many Liverpool supporters getting out of their seats to give the maestro a hand, too.

Ginola stands anxiously by the touchline, too worried to fully get his tracksuit top on, willing his team-mates to hang on for this final minute.

But they can't do it, poor old Tottenham. Ince, just pipping McManaman as Liverpool's Man of the Match, wins another crunching midfield challenge and sets Owen scampering in on goal. We're all up on our feet. The kid is supersonically fast. He's in on Baardsen who tries to stand up and make his goal narrow, but Owen holds his nerve and takes another step before sliding the ball past him. The Liverpool fans are jumping up and down in frenzied celebration, but the ball beats the keeper and hits the post. No matter. Steve McManaman, looking almost embarrassed, taps home the rebound and turns to give the crowd a relieved salute.

A draw. A point. Not a defeat. And a fucking great game. That'll do me. I barge out through the gangways, grinning, and jog down the Seven Sisters. A No. 73 with an open back trundles past invitingly, so I hop on for the last half-mile.

Sunk into my seat at Euston, though, waiting for the train to pull off, I'm struck again with the depressing reality that this team of ours is not going to win anything. The symptoms have been there all season. The failure to beat Everton, for one thing – everyone else can, and until we do, we won't win the League, plain and simple. Other signs that we are far from being Championship material – the capitulation against Strasbourg. The regular dropping of points at home to teams like Leicester, Southampton and Barnsley. The ease with which other teams score against us. Today, and at Sheffield, we've scored three and failed to win. At Bolton and Blackburn we were five minutes from victory but couldn't hold on. We're too easy, too often. We're not Champions.

I slump back as the train rattles through Watford and try to pinpoint who should be sold and who should be bought, and find myself thinking that Roy Evans should, against his credo, 'rip the whole thing up'. It hasn't worked so far, why should it work next season? If this team has proved anything, it's that, for whatever reasons, the blend just isn't right. Roy can raise £25–£30 million just by selling off his fringe players and failed signings. I don't think we have a choice.

28 MARCH 1998

Barnsley, away

A bright, bright, sunshiny day. The squad's received a boost today with gritty midfield general Mick Potter making the travelling party alongside playmaker Danny Giles. We've exhausted the latest baffling outburst from Glenn Hoddle in the wake of England's midweek draw in Switzerland. Apparently Michael Owen, having previously been tarnished by his national coach as a Bad Penny, is from now on not to be classed as a 'natural goalscorer'. It's difficult to try and second-guess what sort of motivational machinations Goddle's up to now, but if I were Michael Owen I'd do a Chris Sutton. I'd tell Hoddle to fuck off and win the World Cup with Teddy Sheringham and Darren Anderton (out all season but BOUND to make the final squad. Just watch. Probably at the expense of McManaman.) Owen's only 18. He doesn't need some Harlow crank messing with his head. He can come back with Robbie Fowler in a few years' time when Hoddle's spoonbending years are just a grim memory and reap the glory he already deserves.

We pass the soon-to-be-complete Trafford Centre on the outskirts of Manchester. Whenever Manchester starts puffing its chest out and making outlandish bids for the Olympics (in *Manchester*! Stop it!) and the Home Shopping Convention and all that, we start to get the usual shake-down about how Liverpool is getting left behind. In demonstrating just how far Liverpool's falling back, economists and sages always point to our lack of a suitable convention centre such as G-Mex or the Sheffield Arena, and the lack of a prestigious shopping complex like the Metro Centre in Newcastle, Twin Peaks in Sheffield and now the Trafford Centre. Excuse me, folks. Am I missing something here? Are we saying that Liverpool is not a great city because we don't have a big, antiseptic, Anytown shopping arcade? A *mall*? Loveaduck! I don't know how we'll cope without a handy supply of Grandma Lee's Muffins! And if I don't get me an engraved car windscreen soon, my motor will probably take off and steal itself! The Trafford Centre my arse. This is nothing to do with all the usual Liverpool–Manchester malarkey, right, this is a simple truth. If Liverpool built a place like that I'd be embarrassed. I'd be ashamed. It's because Liverpool *isn't* blighted with hideous megadromes and supacentres that the city is unique. Liverpool is a real city. Dangerous and angelic, passionate, evil, generous and honest. Manchester is a big, anonymous northern town. End of story.

Danny coos at all those bricks which must've gone into the place and throws out a question:

'Give me a Liverpool team with each player appearing in his regular position, whose players' first name and surname begin with the same letter.'

'Eh?'

'Example. Centre back. Gary Gillespie. See what I'm getting at?'

We get it. Not a bad one. It keeps us going way past Tintwhistle, where an army of bevvied-up Manchester City fans are waiting for their coach. Possibly the most loyal supporters in the world, City. I remember them coming to Anfield twice in a few weeks during that fateful season with Alan Ball. We beat them 4–0 in the League and 6–0 in the

League Cup and all the way through both games the City fans kept up a noisy barrage of gallows humour:

'Alan Ball is a football genius', is one chant that stays in the memory. If a hamlet like Tintwhistle can throw up 100 devoted Blues, imagine what they'd be like if they won something. I hope they do, one day.

By the time we reach Barnsley, I've come up with Joey Jones, Steve Staunton, Mike Marsh, Kevin Keegan, Alan A'Court and Tommy Tynan. Mick has chipped in with Ronnie Rosenthal, Alf Arrowsmith and Larry Lloyd. We already know Gary Gillespie, but we're pooped for a goalkeeper. Danny gives us a clue so obscure as to make the question even more difficult.

'His first name could be constructed as a nickname.'

'Constructed?'

'Yes,' he says, definitively.

'Construed?'

'Constructed.'

We run through the names and nicknames of every Liverpool keeper we can think of.

'Lardarse Lawrence?'

'Nope.'

'Jessie James?'

'Wrong.'

Suddenly it comes to me. I cackle to myself, knowing it must be right.

'Who?'

'Bob Boulder.'

'Is right.'

Bob Boulder. Shouldn't be allowed. Where d'you draw the line. Razor Ruddock? It gets us to Barnsley, anyway.

We park up in a supermarket just down the hill from Oakwell, which we can distantly remember from the FA Cup in about 1985. That was the day of the famous 'Ron Atkinson's Long Leather' banner. Dear old Ron. Weird to think of such a maverick inspiring such hatred that Jegsy Dodd felt compelled to write a poem about him. I quite like Big Ron, now.

Terry Miles and Frank Banner are just up ahead, trying to tell the stewards they're on the guest list. The Barnsley stewards look at them like they've escaped from a secure unit, and, shaking their heads in bafflement, let them in. We make it into the ground just on kick-off time. What an atmosphere, though! Barnsley hate us! Every wild-eyed Yorkie in the stand to our left is standing up, ignoring the game, pointing over and making menacing gestures. It's quite a hoot. They're ordinary enough blokes, a few skins and scallies mixed in with them, but this lot think they're the Cosa Nostra. Apparently there was some trouble after the Barnsley game at Anfield back in November, and this is the Revenge Squad, intent on drinking a great deal of beer and shaking their fists at us all afternoon.

If only it were that simple. Possibly my most unusual two hours inside a football stadium unfolds. It starts in the most orthodox way, with Liverpool conceding a soft goal to Neil Redfearn through poor marking. Just on half time Riedle equalises, and we spend the break nattering with Keith from Donny about the possibilities of him defecting back to Yorkshire now that he can smell the air and feel the width of those kecks.

The game recommences with Liverpool looking unusually lively. A neat through ball sends Owen skeetering in on goal with Barnard hopelessly trying to make up ground on him. As Owen bears down on Watson, Barnard brings him down. As their last man back, he has to go. Red card. He's off.

With only ten men to play against, the game suddenly opens up for Liverpool. We keep the ball and use it intelligently. It's only a matter time before we score, but Riedle makes it a treat, thrashing the ball home from outside the box on the hour. 2–1. We should be home and dry as it is, but five minutes later Barnsley conspire to hand the points to Liverpool. Once again

Owen is set free down the left. Barnsley have pushed too many men forward in search of the equaliser which may yet preserve their Premier League status, and only Morgan stands in the way of Owen and goalkeeper Watson. Owen tears him apart for pace and, as he passes him, Morgan appears to bring his forearm across Owen's windpipe, smashing him to the floor. Owen lies there, stunned. The ref runs across, already reaching for his red card. He's off! Barnsley are down to nine men!

This is all too much for some of the Barnsley fans to take. Ones and twos spill onto the pitch, mainly from the paddock to our left. Some make a run for the referee, others charge towards the jubilant Liverpool support. The police are on the field and the players are scratching their heads. But where's the ref? The ref is nowhere to be seen! For fully five minutes the players and their managers mill around while the police restore control to Oakwell, and only then does the ref restart the game.

Liverpool being Liverpool, we find it impossible to make any kind of impression against nine men. Instead, Barnsley find their rhythm and start to pummel our quivering defence. They have a good shout for a penalty which is waved away. McManaman carries the ball clear of the danger area and slips the ball inside the backtracking defence for Owen to run onto. He's one on one with Watson who shuffles out to narrow the angle. Owen blasts the ball across him. It looks a certain goal but Watson, who's a terrific young goalie, manages to throw his right leg up at an impossible angle and the ball goes out for a corner. Redfearn is completely losing his rag out there, with McManaman his main target. Macca is giving as good as he gets, and for a moment the pair of them are head to head, pushing each other round the penalty box like a couple of billy goats.

Barnsley clear the corner. There's about a minute left. They hoof the ball down the other end and Hristov manages to trap it and turn in one movement, which takes him away from the danger area. Babb seems to be shepherding him out of the box when, for reasons best known only to Philip Babb of Old London Town, he attempts a slashing slide tackle. Hristov is not a player who takes much persuasion to go to ground. He writhes in agony until the referee, possibly out of the sheer embarrassment of having to watch a grown man throwing himself around like that, points to the penalty spot. This is about to become our most embarrassing moment of the season. Barnsley, a team who have been routinely thrashed by unfathomable margins by everyone from Chelsea to Man. U, are about to outpoint Liverpool. Three points at Anfield and another here at Oakwell – four–one to the Barn-za-lee. Redfearn wellies the penalty home with relish and makes some sort of a remark to McManaman as he runs past him to restart the game.

There can't be more than 30 seconds left. Liverpool pile everyone forward. Owen is kicked horribly on the right-angle of the Barnsley box. As Redknapp goes over to take the kick, Redfearn rakes McManaman down the back of his calf. McManaman turns angrily and the two of them are at each other again. Ince becomes involved, and Sheridan runs over and throws his head into Ince's face. It's not a clean contact, otherwise Ince would be down and out with a bleeding nose. In the mêlée, the free-kick is taken. The ball squiggles through a forest of legs and bodies to McManaman. Redfearn makes a lunging tackle which would have put McManaman into the dugouts – if he hadn't danced around him and chipped over the sprawling Watson into the net. 3–2. Delirium. Everyone's on the pitch, mobbing a delighted McManaman. I let out a scream made up of joy, relief, anger that the team could come so close to letting it slip against a nine-man Barnsley side and pride that Macca has won his personal battle with Redfearn. It was a beautifully executed goal. Over on the touchline I see an overjoyed Robbie Fowler hobbling up and down with his crutches in the air.

It's all too much for the desperate Barnsley public. It's about to get worse. The linesman waves the referee over. After consulting with him he jogs back onto the pitch and, ashen faced, shows Sheridan the red card – presumably for his head-butt on Ince. That's it. All hell breaks loose. Fans invade the pitch from all sides. Police, stewards and players apprehend individuals. Paul Ince rugby tackles a bloke with a combination of power and technique which'd do Twickenham proud. The game restarts in an atmosphere of anarchy. We know it's going to be a tasty little walk back to the car.

Right outside our end all the young Liverpool urchins, about 60 of them who've come by train, are mobbing up, ready to run the gauntlet back to the station. As we get to the intersection, a stretch of about ten yards which brings the away supporters into contact with the Barnsley crowd before tapering away again into the away parking area, irate Yorkies are spilling out onto the street, fists up. Again, it's just ordinary fellas who've taken more than they can handle and are now looking to get it out of their systems. They're actually rolling up their sleeves and marching over for a few rounds of Queensbury Rules. Their anger has not made them any more lucid than usual:

'You Northern Ireland rejects!'

'Cheating scum!'

'Fucking Scousey scroungers!'

One bloke, who looks like Peter Stringfellow fallen on hard times, comes bouncing towards me, tugging off his weird tweed zipper jacket. I can't help it. I start laughing. Before he can take a swipe at me, two buxom lasses push him aside, ready to get stuck in. One of them, with badly peroxided roots, her sunbed-orange beergut resplendent in a black bra top, takes a swing over the ticker tape which is standing firm between the fans. She's not mincing her words, this one:

'You fuckin' Scouse cunt! Come on!'

Again I laugh out loud, but turn to check that tough Mick Potter from Scottie Road is there in case she gets any closer. Her mate, dressed identically in a tight black bra top, milky breasts wobbling in all directions as she jumps up and down, aims a kick under the rope. She then jumps as high as she can and, as she's coming back down to earth, tries to send a volley of spit over the divide. Unfortunately her sudden crash-landing sends the yock not into the faces of her new enemies, but dribbling feebly onto her own bust. It has a pathetic but powerful resonance with Barnsley's fight against relegation.

We're in the grassy car-park, joking about the incident with Mono, Jeff and John Garner, when bottles and bricks come flying over the dividing wall. A roar goes up as dozens of Liverpool fans go running round the corner to find the mystery bottle-throwers. There's only a handful of them, who run back in the direction of the ground. We walk back towards the car. Behind us, this time a long way back, is the sort of roar you only hear when the ref has turned down a penalty. It's the noise of a mob who've broken through police lines. It's hard to know where they are, where the shouting's coming from. We're back at the car now, but we wait to see what's happening. The road is blocked with all the ordinary Barnsley fans trying to get away from whatever's happening back by the ground, so we won't be going anywhere for a while, anyway. A rumour goes around that a Liverpool fan has been stabbed. Mick goes back into the street to take a look. It's mainly Liverpool fans walking down now. There's an ambulance down at the bottom of the road, but it's attending to someone who's been hit by a car. One enormous Barnsley fan, drunk out of his mind, stands two yards from the police, challenging them to have a go. They ignore him. He turns his attention to the ambulancemen and asks them if they want a fight. He really, really wants a fight with someone – preferably an authority figure. Bizarrely, he staggers round and round, fists up, like a St Bernard chasing its tail, then slumps peacefully onto the pavement and goes to sleep. It's all been a bit too much for him. Cars, which have been waiting so long they've turned off their engines, suddenly crank into action and start to move. We leg it back to the car and nose out into the bitumen-slow traffic.

Mellor's lines are jammed with Barnsley fans flying conspiracy theories. I had a good view of each and every one of the sending-off offences by the three Barnsley players. They all, for differing reasons, had to go. The ref had no choice, and if he'd have seen half the stuff Neil Redfearn was up to, he would've been there in the bath with them, long before the game ended. You can understand the despair of the Barnsley fans, but the truth is that most Premiership fans want them to stay up. All this tosh about referees being instructed to protect the status of Tottenham and Everton, while Barnsley and Bolton burn is . . . tosh. Isn't it?

By 7 o'clock we're back on the Woodhead Pass. The sun is dropping down behind the Peaks. The events of the past couple of hours seem a world away. When we set out to Barnsley this fine spring morning, the last thing we expected was a riot. It's a funny old game, football.

11 APRIL 1998

Manchester United, away

Man. U, despondent at being knocked out of the Champions League by lowly Monaco, are now seeing the wheels fall off their Premiership wagon, one by one. On Monday night they scored an impressive win at Blackburn to keep their hopes flickering, but our aim today is to extinguish them for good.

One of our most enjoyable days in recent years was the day Leeds won the League in 1992. Round about the March of that year the Man. U fans had taken to singing:

'We won the League on Merseyside.'

It was the year of *Always Look on the Bright Side of Life* – you'd have to if you hadn't won the League for a quarter of a century, wouldn't you? Suddenly, the more they sang about winning the League by the Mersey, the more points they started to leak. They lost games they should have won with their bootlaces tied together. By the time they came to Anfield, they were neck and neck with Leeds, with only one more game to play. In the preceding week, Man. U had blown their chances – and their confidence, spectacularly, with a home defeat by Nottingham Forest and another defeat away at West Ham. Now they were left praying that Leeds would slip up – because Liverpool were going to make it three defeats in a week for Man. U. Leeds played Sheffield United in the morning, beating them 3–2. United now had to WIN at Anfield, just to stay in it. Of course we beat them, condemning them to another year without the Holy Grail. The sad thing for us is that stymieing United is about as close as we get to fulfilment these days. We haven't even come close to winning the League ourselves in all that time since. We can, for now, only pride ourselves on being a thorn in their sides. Nonetheless, it's a role we need to approach with suitable application.

Watching that game at Blackburn on Monday night, it sounded like all the Good Old Boys had come back to try and give the United team some courage. The noise out of them was relentless, with all the old songs coming out. It took a combination of 20 minutes of Blackburn drizzle and a clueless display by their own team to shut the Man. U hordes up. I thought then that today's game, with a 5 o'clock kick-off and ample time for city centre drinking, might be a bit dicey. There've been more and more reports of crowd trouble at grounds all over the country in recent weeks. I blame these awful hooligan books like *Awaydays*. If it's going to go off anywhere, it'll be at Old Trafford, today, if we beat them or if we taunt them too much about Monaco, or just because.

At the last minute, Mick has to pull out. It would've been good to have old Potter at Old Trafford, but we recruit a very able substitute in Ally, who I haven't seen since the home leg against Celtic.

We're in Manchester by 4 o'clock, parked up by the Virgin cinema and walking through the gentle spring rain towards Old Trafford. It's always a cheering sight as you head over the little penny bridge near the ground, when the Liverpool Company bonded warehouse looms up in front of you. An enormous anchor either side of the warehouse bears out the extent and the longevity of the rivalry between these two cities. Manchester wanted to be a port, just like Liverpool. So it built the Ship Canal. It's been spending freely ever since, trying to emulate the well-hung docker down the road.

The walk up to the ground is dotted with familiar faces, arriving in twos and threes, hoods up against the rain. There's an eerie atmosphere. Perhaps it's the dullness of the weather and the artificiality of the 5 p.m. kick-off, but there's no sense of a big occasion. It doesn't feel, at all, like a Liverpool v. Man. U event. Everyone stands around on the concourse outside the old souvenir shop, chatting and waiting. Over to our left, underneath the Munich Memorial Clock, Paddy Crerand is giving an interview to Sky's cameras. Everyone looks over as a ripple of laughter builds to a mass of cackling. People are laughing and pointing. They're pointing at John Garner, who has popped up behind Crerand's head with a cut-out replica of the European Cup. It takes a while for Angry Paddy to realise, by which time Garner's trademark grin – and his European Cup – has been transmitted into the homes of millions. 1–0 to Liverpool.

We go inside. Jegs and I are in the South Stand, alongside

but not among the majority of Liverpool supporters who are packed together in the corner of the East Stand. The atmosphere inside the ground is building, the nearer we get to kick-off time. The Liverpool fans are singing, the home supporters silent. To the tune of the Patrick Berger song, to which the United fans now sing:

'Oh Andy Cole, Andyandyandy Cole . . .'

etc., the Liverpool contingent are singing:

'Oh Monaco, Monamonamonaco . . .'

This sparks the Old Trafford millions into action. At exactly ten-to-five they crank out a couple of warm-up chants then get down to the business in hand – a thunderous chorus of:

'If you all hate Scousers clap your hands.'

This is more like it! A bit of atmosphere. As the teams come out to that ludicrous, pompous, vainglorious operatic bombast that Man. U have started playing as Theme To Old Trafford, the crowd's noise is, genuinely, uplifting – and, thankfully, drowns out that *stupid* classical music. The Red Action chaps, who've fought a spirited scrap all season to try and invoke a limited return to terraced areas inside the stadium, should turn their attentions to getting rid of that theme tune next season. It's embarrassing. It'd be embarrassing if it was introducing England back to Wembley as World Cup winners, but for Man. United with their modest achievements and their big dreams . . . it says it all, really. They're in denial. They think they're a grand European entity, up there with Real Madrid, Juventus, Bayern Munich, Ajax . . . Up there with Liverpool. But they're not. And that outstandingly inappropriate signature music doesn't foster the illusion of greatness – it only underscores the harsh reality. They've got a fuck of a long way to go, Man. U, before they can run out to theme music like that without a massive collective cherry-on.

The game starts. Danny Murphy's playing just behind Michael Owen. Great stuff. This is what we've been asking for all season, now let's see how it works. At first, it doesn't. Man.

U pour forward, cutting through our buttery defence with menace and playing Giggs through. He gets a lucky rebound from a well-timed Babb tackle and finds himself one-on-one with goalkeeper Friedel. Friedel spreads himself well, blocking Giggs' attempt on goal, but the rebound falls perfectly for Paul Scholes. He thrashes the ball back on goal, but Babb slides in to intercept on the goal-line. Eventually we clear it. Not for long. Another raid, this time down the right, sees the unmarked Sheringham head weakly on goal, but Friedel palms over for a corner. Do Liverpool take heed from Sheringham's freedom in the box? Have we had a little sit-down with the training staff and pointed out that, in the past three seasons, we've given away 37 goals directly from or as a result of set-pieces (including Cantona's spawny winner in the 1996 Cup Final)? Have we, in short, learnt anything about our defensive shortcomings over the recent past? Have we thump. Beckham floats over an admittedly gorgeous corner and Ronnie Johnsen bustles in and heads unchallenged into the roof of the net. 1–0 to them.

This, at least, has the desired effect on Liverpool. Redknapp starts to impose himself in midfield and, winning a lot of possession from Beckham, is spraying some terrific balls out towards Murphy and Owen. One such move leads to a vicious drive from the inrushing Ince which Schmeichel does well to palm around the post. It's encouraging to see him screaming at his defence. McManaman spoons over from a good position and Owen cuts a shot across Schmeichel and just wide of the far post. These are not just chances, they're great chances – we're going to have to stick one away sooner or later.

McManaman pops a little ball behind Pallister for Owen to run onto. It looks like a mirror repeat of the foul Dave Watson did on him in the Anfield derby, with Pallister getting his forearm across Owen then seemingly smashing something into his face or his windpipe to bring him down. We can't see it clearly from this spec. Both players have their backs to us and are on the other side at the other end of the ground. Something must've happened for Owen to go down like that. He got a lot of stick after the Barnsley game for hitting the deck too easily, but he is categorically not a cheat. He'd rather stay up and score. There've been half-a-dozen occasions this season when he's stayed on his feet in unworkable situations and set up Fowler or Riedle or gone on to score himself. Defenders like Tony Adams, who've seen it all, cheerfully tug Owen back, shrugging their shoulders at the ref in a 'what would YOU do' sort of way. What's more sinister is the other type of player, who'll bring him down with snidey kicks and punches then complain to the ref that Owen's dived. This is what happens here. Pallister stands over Owen and seems genuinely irate with him. Maybe Pallister thinks that if Owen wants to play out with the big boys he should be ready for a bit of rough stuff. But that's not written anywhere in the rules. The ref agrees and gives us a free-kick which Redknapp takes twice and bends into the defensive wall both times.

We're getting the upper hand, though, and the break-through is not long in coming. Murphy executes a neat lob over the cumbersome Pallister who hesitates, waiting for Schmeichel to come and claim. Owen darts between Pallister and Johnsen, takes the ball on a stride, drawing Schmeichel, committing him to a dive and clipping the ball over his spreadeagled body. He turns away in delight, having proved his point to Pallister in the best possible way. 1–1, and we're looking good.

United, the team and the crowd, are muted. There's still a quarter of an hour to half time and, with McManaman starting to roam and Giggs hobbling off, Liverpool look likeliest to score again. But just as everything's starting to look promising for us, Michael Owen goes potty. Only he and the Man. United defence know for certain what's going on out there, but Michael has already made a few aggressive challenges and been booked for going in hard on Schmeichel. This time, he chases down a pass-back to Johnsen. Johnsen, for a split second, miscontrols the ball which is all the encouragement Owen needs. He sets off at terrific speed, probably hoping to panic Johnsen into a hasty clearance which might concede possession. This is fine. This is the kind of hunger you want to see from your strikers, even when they're rattling in 30 goals a season. He has a lot of ground to make up on Johnsen and, halfway there, Johnsen regains control of the slippery ball and goes to make his clearance. To give Owen the benefit of the doubt you'd say that he still considered it might be worth throwing himself in front of the ball – perhaps he thought he could still block the clearance, put it out for a throw. But that'd be to give him a very hefty benefit – unemployed families of 13 in the West Midlands get less. His challenge, sliding in on wet turf with studs showing, is ill-conceived and ugly. Johnsen was always going to get the ball clear and, at best, Owen could only ever have got his body in the way. His studs should be nowhere on view, but in the event, his studs rake Johnsen badly, causing him to join his assailant in the bath moments after Owen is sent off. It's a shame. Michael Owen has been so transfused by the tumult of this game that he's prevented himself becoming its key performer. He's not a nasty player. He'll learn from all of this. But you just know that had he stayed on the pitch, he'd have learned so much more. Like how it feels to win at Old Trafford.

The second half sees chances go begging for both teams. Leonhardsen produces a fine low-down save from Schmeichel, but with ten men Liverpool are doing well to hang on. The Old Trafford crowd, sensing a shut-out from their detested rivals, start up a chant:

'Where's your famous Munich songs?'

Split pause. The Liverpool supporters sing back:

'Where's your European Cups?'

Then, to the tune of *Amazing Grace*, for fully five minutes:

> *'Four times, four times,*
> *Four times, four times,*
> *Four times, four times,*
> *FOUR TIMES!!'*

There follow some blasphemous and unprintable allegations about Posh Spice and the places she likes to receive gifts. If anything, it goads the pedestrian Beckham into action. He's been completely outplayed by Jamie Redknapp, today. If Jamie, Fowler, Owen, Ince, McManaman and McAteer were fit, available and in the mood every week, who could stop us? Make it happen, boys. Make it happen.

As Jegs and I have been seated towards the back of the South Stand, we're out of the ground quickly and shuffling with the crowds back towards the Munich Clock, where we're meeting Danny and Ally. Straight away you can sense the tension. The Liverpool fans, with one exit down a narrow set of steps, are just beginning to trickle out. A few voices from the Man. U fans start shouting:

'Come on then! Come on you Scouse twats!'

More and more of them take it up. Filtering in from the passageway under the South Stand, we're stuck in with the United fans. A bigger shout goes up. People are stopping to see what's up. Now, a few dozen United fans run across the concourse and wade into the handful of Liverpool fans who've so far made it out of the ground. One on one fights start all over the area outside the away end. Just then, an almighty roar and, from everywhere, from all directions, Man. U fans in their hundreds come swarming down the little slope, joining in with the fighting. I've lost Jegsy. From behind me, three or four Man. U lads run in, pushing me forward, thinking I'm one of their mob, urging me and each other and everyone else to pile in. There's nothing to stop them. There are half-a-dozen coppers with truncheons drawn, but by now there must be 500 United fans on the bounce, with 50-odd Liverpool fans backed against the wall, fighting wildly for their next step, just to be able to stand up, at this stage. The remainder of the police have thrown a line across the away exit, penning the bulk of the Liverpool fans in. This means it's 500 against 50 outside (some reports later suggest there were over 2,000 Man. United thugs involved, but most of the crowd out there just stood and watched).

I jump up and down, staying exactly where I am, looking keen. I can see the headlines now:

'Hooligan Author Arrested in Old Trafford Brawl.'

I'd settle for that, just now. The way this is shaping up, it could be a fate worse than mere arrest. I'm looking all around me for someone, just one face I know. Whatever happens, these are crucial moments. Police are arriving on horseback and I don't want to get chased back towards central Manchester with all their skins. At the same time, I don't want to commit myself to trying to get back to the Liverpool fans. The plod might just see it as a solo attack and club me to the floor or, worse, throw me back in with the hyperventilating Man. U multitudes who'll then know I'm not one of Them. I don't mind taking the kicking so much. I just don't want to do it on my own. I can't see anybody. The fighting is spilling all over the forecourt, making big spaces where onlookers have backed away, but there are still no familiar faces. Police vans are now joining the horses. The main body of United fans backs off towards the gates at the top of the slope but remain there, chanting up at the Liverpool fans on the exit steps and goading them to break through the escort. Hundreds more gather over by the old souvenir shop. It's a Sioux uprising with a cluster of wagons in the middle. It's going to be a long Good Friday.

Again, a few older lads start pushing everyone around them,

me included, trying to get us to run in. They rush down again, only about 20 of them this time, but the mob by the souvenir shop starts coming across, too. That's when I spot Jegsy. He's about 50 yards away. I start to walk, slowly, towards him. He's with about 20 Liverpool fans, isolated over by a big hot dog van, but not looking too concerned. As the souvenir shop mob advance on the little pocket of Liverpool fans, the Scousers run at them and this time it goes off properly. The police wade in and drive the whole crowd back. I'm now in a complete no-man's land. I head forward as slowly as possible, making certain this can't be mistaken for a violent sortie, towards the stairway where all the Liverpool fans are cordoned off. A copper comes for me with a truncheon. I raise the palms of my hands to him and point towards the away exit. He looks past me, crouched, eyes frightened but alert. I make it over to the steps and turn to see the lone policeman confronting five or six Man. U fans, all bouncing and mouthing off and challenging him on that very spot on the concourse I've just come from. One of the Man. U fans makes a lunge for the copper, who, impressively for a little bloke, pins him down on the floor with his face in the tarmac, a long truncheon stuck in his back. A White Maria appears from nowhere and the angry brawler, round stomach displayed now his shirt buttons are all over Old Trafford, is bundled into the back. His mates scamper back to the railings. Bodies are being headlocked and half-nelson'd away from the fighting by the dozens of police who are now pouring into the area.

I stand at the foot of the steps. In ones and twos, some out of breath, the Liverpool fans who've been out there begin to congregate. John Gaghan is there, laughing:

'That was great, wasn't it?'

Jegsy and his valiant 20 see it as a show of weakness to accept any kind of police protection. They stand in a huddle under one of the exits, looking over to the souvenir shop to see if anything else is going to happen. There's a show of bravado from the Liverpool fans outside the ground to the thousands still inside, most of whom don't even know there's been any trouble. Those who are backed up on the actual steps are shouting down to people they know. There's a strange atmosphere. I know it isn't over yet. Not by a long way. All the police have done is clear the area. We've got to get back over the penny bridge, yet. That'll be fun. Everyone else seems to be smiling and joking and looking forward to the chicken run back to their transport. Maybe it'll be all right once everyone's out of the ground. A voice shouts out from way above:

'Is it safe to come down yet!?'

Roy White from Speke. Out of a funny mob from Halewood, Speke and Garston, Roy is probably the funniest of all of them. He's about five foot three, nine stone and rapier sharp. He comes down the steps. He's in a car with Gaghan. We're about ready to move. Jegsy comes over and asks what I want to do.

'We'll have to wait for Danny and Ally, won't we?' I say.

'They'll be well gone. They'll've been the first out.'

'If they were first out they'd've been straight into all that, wouldn't they? They'd be here.'

We hover by the clock. There's a bit of an escort up ahead. No one else seems to be coming out of the ground. We jog along to catch up with the trail of Liverpool fans, none of whom we know. The escort turns left after exactly 500 yards, leading the fans to a parade of coaches. This leaves Jegsy, five or six others and me to head on, alone, to the traffic lights. It's half dark. Up ahead are little knots of people, some walking away from us, some walking towards us. The ones coming towards us are a motley collection of Liverpudlians, walking back from the Liverpool Company warehouse:

'Don't go that way! There's hundreds of the bastards kicking off . . .'

'Any Liverpool there?'

'Dunno. Didn't wait to find out.'

I look to Jegs.

'What d'you reckon?'

'Dunno. Just gonna have to go for it, aren't we?'

'What? Two of us!'

I know there's a mad detour we can take over the other bridge, around Salford Quays and back past that big Pier Bar. But I also know there's no point trying to talk Dodd into going that way. It'd be an admission of defeat to him. We get to the first big anchor. It's confusing in the near-dark. We're actually round the other side of the warehouse to the way we arrived at Old Trafford. This is the second anchor – the other anchor. There's a fenced-off building site to the side of the warehouse, right next to the little bridge. On the way to the ground we'd have walked straight past this building site without giving it a second glance, but now, stacked with bricks and poles and planks, it might just offer us something. On the other side of the warehouse there are blue flashing lights, angry mob noises, smashing glass. This is it. We've got to get past that lot to make it back to the car.

We pull back the fencing and wade across the site, trying, ridiculously, to keep our training-shoes clean. I stop to pull at a pallet of bricks.

'Here y'are!' hisses Jegs. He beckons me over. 'We're all right here. We're through.'

He's right. All the activity is taking place by the junction at the front of the warehouse, 100 yards back to the right of this building site. There are police vehicles and motorbikes blocking the road. If we continue across the site and turn left we're right onto the bridge and into the final straight. There's a little pub just below the bridge, but it seems quiet. The two of us amble past the pub, across the lights at the main junction with Ordsall Lane and we're there.

Danny and Ally are not. I hide in the car while Jegsy walks to the nearest pub to see if they're sheltering from the rain. No sign of them. With the car windows beginning to steam up and the traffic down to a trickle, we're starting to think they might have taken a lift with someone else. Out of the steaming foggy drizzle of a Manchester Good Friday, two bedraggled silhouettes appear, one the ludicrous caricature tough-guy walk of Danny Giles. Even with my eyesight I can see him furlongs away. I flash the lights at them, start the engine and within minutes we're haring down the M62, trying to get our tales out.

I drive and listen and let my mind wander. Is that what we want, then? All season we've been complaining about New Football and its antiseptic fans. As early on as the Leeds match at Elland Road we were almost tearful for the days of the fearsome Peacock and the long walk back to the station. Well today it was back to the '70s. In every sense, it was How It Used To Be. A partisan crowd of 55,000. A game of pride, passion and incident. And an almighty kick-off outside. Is that what we want? No. Not really. But at least it meant something, today. Too often, now, the football is a meaningless sideshow, just one element of a business portfolio which stimulates the overall growth of the parent company. You get the impression that, if they lose, it doesn't hurt the players too badly any more. They're cocooned, so many of them, by lucrative sponsorships and endorsements. Today's match and the events surrounding it showed that football is still capable of cutting through all that and providing a passion play. The players cared. Both sides fought to the bitter end. The fans cared. There was feeling. If that feeling ran out of control for a while at the end, there's still something good in the underlying reasons for that. May the day never come when we're, any of us, Liverpool or Manchester United, blasé about the outcome of a match between our sides.

A foul and overpowering stench pollutes the car, nearly forcing me off the road. We're nowhere near Widnes. That smell is unmistakable. That's a brickie's fart.

'Sorry boys,' says Danny. 'Bolted my breakfast a bit.'

The smell still lingers at 10 a.m. the next morning.

13 APRIL 1998

Crystal Palace, home

We're still clinging to the outside prospect that we can nick second place off Man. U. Arsenal are now equal with them on points with two games in hand. The title's theirs. But if Man. U slip up at home to Newcastle today, we can start to exert a bit of pressure on them for that second Champions League qualifying place. At the end of last season we conned each other that we were pleased not to have qualified. The team wasn't good enough. We'd embarrass ourselves. We'd have a year of consolidation with the new squad, win the Premier and take Europe by storm next season. Thing is, nothing much has changed. We're still not that great. Perhaps we need the lure of the Champions League to persuade the best of the best to come and join us.

The name of Jaap Stam has started to be mentioned again – but in the context of a move to Man. U. PSV Eindhoven want £15 million for him. United have offered £10 million. What's £5 million to them if they really want a player? Surely they must have learnt from the terrible pain of missing out on Glenn Hysen in 1989? I hope their penny-pinching kills the deal. I hope he goes to Arsenal, instead. No. I hope he comes to Man. U for £15 million and he's crap.

There's a full Easter Monday house, taking our season's

home attendances over a million, and a picnic-like atmosphere of quiet anticipation. Palace are down. They're the worst team to play in the top flight since Swindon in the early '90s. What we need today is to wallop them about 6–0 to get the goal difference ticking over again. Who knows? It may yet prove critical at the end of the season.

The game kicks off, though you'd barely notice. Everyone's still chattering about this and that, hardly watching the match at all. Even UCN seems calmer, these days. He doesn't lambast the team. He only really speaks to praise them, appreciating Ince's driving runs and Murphy's probing little passes and runs. McManaman occasionally comes in for a bit of stick from him, but he's a New Man. In fact, by far the most abusive and unconstructive supporter in our near vicinity, nowadays, is one Roy Boulter, who has developed an irrational and unhelpful dislike of poor Leonhardsen. Nothing is going right for Leo. He's being played out of position and, try as he might, he just looks like a park player at the moment, huffing and puffing and lacking any kind of creative or imaginative thrust. When, as he inevitably does, Leo takes an extra touch, then another one which allows Edworthy – no mug! – to get back and snuffle out an opportunity which might have gone in had he hit it first time, Roy jumps out of his seat and directs oaths and profanities in his direction. You can see Leo's head drop. He knows he's doing himself no justice at all.

Owen scores. Palace get an equaliser 15 minutes from the end which is either incredibly lucky or quite brilliant, Bent lobbing Friedel from the touchline. David Thompson comes on and harasses, runs, dribbles, tackles and generally takes on Palace by himself. In the last minute he wins the ball, slants a lovely, narrow-footed pass out to McManaman on the right then runs 40 yards to slide home the swinging cross-shot Macca plays behind the Palace defence. 2–1. It's a terrific goal, made tame by the fact that we're scrapping for a last-minute winner against Crystal bloody Palace. We're not playing well. Roll on next season.

19 APRIL 1998

Coventry, away

Kick-off is four o'clock. Coventry is two hours away. So it makes perfect sense that Jimmy Flowers' coach should be leaving at 9.30 a.m. We stop at The Rocket to pick up Jeff, Mono, Davey, Gram and Garner then sail down to Coventry. The talk is still of the trouble after the Man United game, which has become exaggerated by folklore and the usual add-ons from people who weren't there. Fellas who work in Manchester say that the *Evening News* has been full of disclaimers from the police who'd been lobbying for a morning kick-off. When Sky put the game back to 5 p.m., they feared the worst, but were still taken by surprise by the scale of the disturbances. Jimmy patrols his coach, making sure that everyone's drinking, and selling tickets for his Testimonial – cunningly disguised as an end-of-season party. They're £2 each. It's always a riotous night. I take ten off him, for distribution among the usual suspects.

We're pulling up outside Highfield Road and knocking at the nearest pub by midday. A marvellous sight greets us. The landlord, a skinny bloke of about 35, is a dead ringer for Rod Stewart. This is no accident, though. This is someone who, having survived the playground taunts of primary school about his enormous hooter, has decided to turn this fabulous nose of his to his advantage. Noting that Rod Stewart, too, has a gigantic, bulbous snipe – and that it doesn't seem to have harmed *his* participation in the Love Game – the bloke from the pub in Coventry has decided to become Rod Stewart.

He's cut his hair in a proto-mullett barnet, streaked it with dirty, straw-blond strands and wears a pair of tight plastic jeans and a flowing white blouse. By God, sir! This man IS Rod Stewart!

We file into the pub, take it all in, order drinks and run to the jukebox. It is, of course, stacked with classics by Rod, The Faces and Python Lee Jackson. Mono and Garner are still by the bar. As money is poured avidly into the jukey, they beat us to it with a caterwauling chorus:

'Ah-wake up Maggie I think I got something to say to yooooo . . .!!'

The whole pub takes it up. The licensee stands back and beams. He loves it. He bows, then struts around the pub floor, miming to the juke box. What a start to the day!

We get split off into different tables. We're still mumbling about Man. United. Garner reckons the last 'friendly' occasion between Liverpool and United was the 1977 Cup Final, when history has it that United's fans applauded Liverpool off the pitch to wish them luck in the European Cup Final the following Wednesday. I was at that game. I don't recall anything like that happening. Garner's insistent. He didn't see it himself, but it's chronicled in this book, *The Red Army Years*.

'Well they would say that, wouldn't they? Maybe a few of them gave us a little hand when we did the lap of despair, but don't you remember before the game? There was murder. And inside the ground.'

The old debate rages. My argument is that United came back up from the Second Division, where they'd been taking 15,000 away to places like Oxford, thinking they could just carry on where they left off – invading town centres and taking over whole grounds. Obviously they found out that you can't do that in Leeds or Tottenham or Birmingham in quite the same way you can in, say, Watford. That was 1975. There was no love lost between Man. U and a whole host of other teams from that season onwards. George Best was gone. So was

Denis Law, Bobby Charlton and all the greats. Any residual goodwill, any reserves of grudging respect those maestros had left in the tank were well and truly drained by the time they came back up in '75. This was the new Man. U, and they were hateful. Brash and arrogant, with nothing whatsoever in the world to be brash and arrogant about, they were on course to become the most despised collective in the land. We call over Jimmy Flowers and Lenny Woods to see if they recall this outburst of humanity at the Friendly Cup Final of 1977, but they don't remember it either.

The time flies by. As the pub fills up, the supporters seem polarised. Towards the back, where the pool tables are, there's a coachload from Gloucester and others from various parts of Britain and Ireland. They're easy to tell apart. They're all wearing the yellow away shirt. They all have at least ten earrings, the boys as well as the girls. And they're singing *Scouser Tommy*. They all love that one. At the other side of the pub sit the Scousers and the likes of me and Danny, who, coming from Birkenhead – Over The Water – are neither fish nor fowl. Until we win the League and the European Cup again, we're left with little choice but to blame these harmless geezers with earrings for ruining our great club. You've got to blame someone, haven't you?

We shuffle out at 3.45 and down the hill to Coventry's ground. It's raining, it's dull, it's Sunday. In a flash of foresight I see a dull, rainy, Sunday game and stop dead in my tracks. I ask Danny and Davey if they fancy coming back to the pub and watching the game from there. I'm only half serious, but if either one of them had shown the tiniest bit of interest . . .

If you're late to your seat at any Liverpool away game, you'll find a bunk-in sitting in your place. We've done all right this season. There was only really Leicester when we missed kick-off completely and it was only kids in the seats. There was room for everyone. This time, Danny's still queuing for pies when the game kicks off and there's a bleary-eyed rogue straddled across our two seats when we get inside. He moves slightly to the left to allow the two of us to cram our arses onto one seat. He shuffles himself from side to side to make sure that both of his buttocks have ample room. Every five minutes or so he does a weird semi-yawn, flapping his elbows, pushing me out and making more and more room for himself. Michael Owen comes to our rescue, with a quite fantastic goal, dragging the ball out of the air with his right foot and smashing it home with his left. 1–0 to us. Everyone jumps up, hugging each other in disbelief and that's it. Danny nips back into his seat, while I straddle my own. The Slumper's out. If he'd've been a bit more humble about robbing someone else's place we would have cheerfully made room for him. But he's pissed. He's leaning everywhere, like Duncan Ferguson jockeying for a corner-kick. He's making a boring afternoon at Highfield Road uncomfortable as well as uninspiring. He's still standing up when everyone else sits down again. He shuffles down the row and parks himself on the steps. The second half can only be better.

Can we hold onto our lead? Can we force Manchester United to finish third place in a one-horse race? Not us, mate – although the circumstances of Coventry's equaliser once again brings up the issue of the suitability of referees to do a professional job in this new, extra-pressurised, professional environment of Premier League Football. To the crowd behind the Nicholls Street goal and in the M&B stand, it's as clear as tapwater that Huckerby takes the ball out of play before coming back into the Liverpool box and being tripped by Babb. It's obvious. Everyone sees it. Except the ref. The ref does not see it. Instead, he gives a penalty which Dublin slots with ease, and our flickering hopes of the Champions League are extinguished. To rub salt into the wound Jamie Redknapp, who's been starting to play like an international quality midfielder week in and week out, limps off with 20 minutes to go.

We stop off at Coventry's central police station to collect one of our miscreants who has been arrested for drinking alcohol outside the ground. Shame on him! Waiting outside the nick, engine running, we witness a sight for sore eyes. Trailing up the road, the first of them 500 yards ahead of the rearguard, come the bedraggled diehards who've come by train. Sully's there, smiling as always, and behind him pads the gargantuan figure of Wilcox, wet through, glowering at Lenny through the window. Lenny went down with them on the train but has jumped on the coach to save the walk back to the station in the rain. The sight of them all sums up, in a way, what it is to support an enormous club like Liverpool. It's like a time-capsule. You know that, whoever Liverpool are playing, wherever it is in the world, ten years from now or 20 years ago – there will always be a motley crew making their long and winding way back after the game. They'll be arguing with each other, complaining, taking the piss – but most of all, they'll be sticking together.

We crawl home through ten-mile-an-hour motorway traffic. Mono and the Halewood bunch aim a volley of songs at Jimmy for living in Formby. Jimmy tinkles a few verses back about Halewood's proximity to Manchester. A lad who's been asleep from the moment he got on the coach suddenly wakes and rubs his eyes:

'D'you think that's the League gone, then?' he says.

Danny, who toddled off to the dangerously brimful portaloo ages ago, has not returned. I crane around to see him leaning over the gorgeous Fiona, sipping daintily from a bottle of red wine. Fiona, a regular on Flowers tours, seems entranced by him. I always thought she was married or engaged to one of Jimmy's mates, but apparently not. Could the season have a magical end to it yet? She asks Danny if he's coming to The Albert when the coach finally docks at Anfield. They seem to disappear across the road but, when I flag down a taxi, there's Danny shuffling in next to me.

25 APRIL 1998

Chelsea, extremely far away

It's Jegsy's fault. He spotted these flight-only deals to Los Angeles for £195, all taxes included. He convinced me that, not only would Liverpool not win the League but Chelsea would twat us and we'd finish up fifth in the table. His argument is this: why spend £100 on a trip to London to see our enfeebled team surrender meekly when, for a little bit more, you can have a week of fun in the sun – and catch Madness, live.

I sort of know Suggs out of Madness. He produced The Farm's first album *Spartacus* and he phones occasionally with bulletins. He's a Chelsea supporter, Suggs, dating back to the '70s when he and his mate Chalky used to spray their names outside The Shed. A few weeks ago he told me he wouldn't be going to the Chelsea v. Liverpool game because an American promoter had stumped up a fortune to fly the band to California for a two-week tour. By telling Jegsy Dodd this, I was effectively sealing my fate. I was going to California to see Madness.

Very splendid they were, too. It took some adjusting to reconcile all these non-smoking, non-drinking, clean-living Californian kids with a bunch of the most debauched hedonists in the history of popular music. What did they have in common? What did these callow body-builders with their annoying goatee beards and their billowing Modern Rock Pest shorts get out of a group of aged Cockney Rude Boys? What did they make of lines like:

> *I bought it in Muswell Hill*
> *From a bloke from Brazil*

It didn't seem to matter to them. From the first strains of *One*

Step Beyond to the jaunty skank of *Madness* itself, the crowd, a jubilant, eddying mob of punks, mohicans, mods and Modern Rock Pests, danced like only students can. They loved it.

At 7.00 a.m. on the Saturday morning, while hundreds of soccer-crazy Englishmen sat in a bar in Santa Monica waiting for the match to start, Jegsy and I snoozed on like children. The jetlag, and our forlorn attempts to drink as much as Madness, had caught up. Suggs and Chas Smash stayed up through the night for the Chelsea v. Liverpool game, while the lightweights from Liverpool collapsed in a heap.

Something similar happened at Stamford Bridge. Jegsy's friend Paul Spencer, a Liverpool ex-pat now living in Orange County, California, described the performance against Chelsea as the worst from any Liverpool side he'd ever seen. Chelsea won 4–1, but the common consensus from Paul and from the Madness contingent was that it could've been double figures for Chelsea. Liverpool were rank. So at least we've achieved something, this season, that we hadn't done before. We've given three of the worst-ever displays from a Liverpool side in one season. Strasbourg, Everton and now Chelsea. I am now officially baffled. I don't know why we're so bad. Even news that Everton are back in the bottom three and heading for relegation courtesy of a 3–1 home spanking by awful Sheffield Wednesday seems irrelevant.

1 MAY 1998

Birkenhead Park

Mayday, mayday. All amateur footballers beware. Anybody seeking to play this game at half-pace, uncaring whether they win or, indeed, 'just for fun' is advised that K. Sampson of this parish is now fully recovered from his nightmare rib injuries and will start a game for the first time in . . . a long time. Expect red face, poor control and refusal to accept share of blame if results go wrong.

I'm back! Since I last played, the Friday match has been transformed. Puffa, Jimmy and co., disillusioned by their regular beatings by the Wirral Beauts, have stopped coming. But just as their appearances have stopped, Adam Kennedy has come to the rescue. Adam, one of the kids we've played against over the years, is in a group called Lazy who've started gigging around Liverpool and Chester and already have three record companies after them. They also have a big following among youngsters who are hip to the latest sounds. They know where they're coming from. You know what I'm saying, man? So, for the past four or five weeks, Lazy and their road-crew and their fans have been turning up, 12 of them, to take on the fabled Old Men of Birkenhead Park. Myself and Blackie, maimed by the enormous weight of a Roy Boulter calf falling on him, have been forced to watch as the Old Men teach Lazy a footballing lesson every week. Last week we won 10–0, though all the other games have been closer.

I haven't looked forward to a game so much in ages. Disappointingly, I'm stuck in goal for the first 20 minutes on grounds of being a 'newcomer'. We go into a 2–0 lead and I have to resort to fluffing a simple header so I can get out and play. Treeman takes over in goal and we don't concede again until ten minutes from the end.

In between, a fierce contest is fought. Literally. Liam trades punches with one of their boys over by the corner flag while Charlie is being chopped down in the box by two wild tackles. They only half-dispute the penalty. Up steps the scrawny new boy, Sampson. There's no doubt in his mind. He angles·his body to the left and cuts the ball inside the right-hand post. 3–1 to the old boys. If there's any such thing as a good penalty, then that was a good penalty. Lazy give it everything, but a little bit of luck runs our way. Roy scores from a double rebound off his knee and his, frankly, enormous lower leg before Peter Hooton wraps it up with a goal out of the Kinkladze manual, jinking inside one lunging tackle, pulling back outside another and clipping over the keeper with his left foot. It ends up 8–3 to the Old Gits, one of whom, Colin 'Chopadopalis' Hill, is 46.

2 MAY 1998

West Ham, home

I'm in Dooley's, mopping up a sea of tinned tomato juice and egg and sauce, listening to DD's theories on why Liverpool are crap. It's the first time I've been in here for ages – Birkenhead's award-winning Breakfast Bar has been closed for refitting and expansion, so it's a bright, sparkling, not-at-all-greasy spoon where I'm scoffing my breakfast this morning.

Dave Dooley, too, thinks Liverpool's surrender at Chelsea last week is the worst display he's ever seen from a Liverpool side. These performances are bewildering, bemusing and totally unacceptable from any Liverpool team. When they play like that, it utterly takes the piss out of the supporters. It makes you know, know for sure, that the players don't give one fuck about you anymore. They don't. They can write what the fuck they want in their newspaper columns, they can tell you that, of course they care – but we're not listening anymore. Nobody cares what they have to say. They're nothing. Very well paid, but next to Ian Callaghan and Joey Jones, nothing. Nowhere in our hearts and nowhere in our memories. Not long ago, Liverpool would put in one, two at most nightmare performances like that each season. You can name them. That midweek game at Villa. That was one. But we do it once a month, now. If Roy Evans decided to get rid of six or seven of them and start again, he wouldn't find much cause for complaint after a showing like that. What is going on? The Dool offers more toast, but what I want is one of his impeccably sourced rumours that Matt Elliott, Chris Perry and Rio Ferdinand are all coming in the summer. He offers Carl Serrant instead, which will do for starters.

If ever we needed a good showing, just to prove to ourselves that we're still a team, then it's today against West Ham. With McManaman finally having to give in to his ankle injury and Redknapp still out, the scope is there for experimentation. Matteo and Rob Jones are injured, too, though Jason McAteer has made a miraculously quick recovery and is ready to start his first game since snapping his ankle against Blackburn. Roy Evans can afford to be quite creative, here, without sacrificing what solidity we still have in defence. He could play Friedel; Kvarme–Carragher–Babb–Bjornebye; McAteer–Murphy–Ince–Berger, and Owen and Riedle up front. So it's a somewhat confused Nice Scotsman and myself who are left scratching our heads as the teamsheet's read out over the tannoy. This is the team.

Friedel; Kvarme–Harkness–Babb–Bjornebye; McAteer–Carragher–Ince–Leonhardsen, and Owen and Riedle up front.

Nice Scotsman, who is right about all things footballular, believes Jamie Carragher is a future England international, but is stunned by the lack of imagination in the team. I, too, would love to see us go out and field our most gifted, most technical team. Just once. Give Berger a game in that left midfield berth. He's a left-sided player. That's why we bought him. Give Murphy a start. Take the game by the scruff of its neck – there's absolutely fuck all to lose! But no. This is the team and the match is about to start. I crane backwards to Nice Scotsman:

'This lot'll probably go out and tank West Ham 5–0, now.'

Which we do. It's 4–0 at half-time. No one is more relieved than Oyvind Leonhardsen, who celebrates his 45th-minute goal as though it's the Derby winner that's sent Everton down to Division One. At half time we leg it down for the scores. In particular, we want to know how Everton's relegation rivals Bolton and Tottenham are doing. Three dressed-up Asian boys are over by the TV, all labelled-up with Armani and Tommy Hilfiger clobber. We ask them the scores:

'Blackburn are losing!' they beam. Blackburn's is possibly the most insignificant result in the whole of the Premiership this afternoon. It has no bearing on anything at all, other than who's going to finish ninth. What about the others, we ask?

'Flowers has been sent off – and he wasn't even playing!!'

We carry on immediately where we left off in the second half. Riedle rattles the West Ham crossbar with a hurricane drive and Owen continues to turn his old pal Rio Ferdinand inside out. West Ham bring on Samassi Abou, which is worth it just to hear the whole ground shouting '*Abooooooooo*' every time he touches the ball. It starts to get carnival. The West Ham fans start up a Beatles medley, while the Liverpool supporters boo our every touch. Owen, McAteer and Paul Ince carry the game. Ince scores with a bobble shot on the hour to make it 5–0. Really, though, we were rubbish.

It's Jimmy's end-of-season party tonight, up at the Mere Lane Social Club. Michael Owen is reported to be attending. After waiting for the results we head down to The Albert. Danny's in there, hovering by Fiona and her friend but not chatting to them. I call him over:

'Come on, Danny. She's too good to be true. Beautiful. Funny . . . I take it she knows the 1974 Cup winning team AND the 1965 one. Why don't you, you know, invite her on a guided tour of the ground or something? Go and visit the L.F.C. Museum together?'

Danny winces.

'Don't think so, lad. Wouldn't get a clear run on goal with a fraulein like that. It'd be man-to-man marking.'

I shake his hand and clink glasses with him. Jimmy's by the door, chuckling at the news that Bolton's 5–2 win has plunged Everton into the relegation positions. I try to put it to him that we're a sad and pathetic bunch, drawing solace from a dire season of feeble under-achievement by Man. United's failure to win anything and Everton's possible relegation. He chews on this:

'Yeah, but it's great though, isn't it!?'

He tells me he needs £25 as soon as possible to secure my place on the pre-season tour to Dublin, where we compete with Lazio, Leeds and whoever the champs of Ireland turn out to be. We head on up to the party, me with a pocketful of pound coins after unexpectedly recouping the ticket money I laid out at Coventry.

Tommy Cross is in there. Tommy is an Evertonian who has a Liverpool season-ticket. He also has a Fun Implant in his left nipple. This is a failsafe, laser-guided indicator which takes Tommy wherever a laugh is to be found. Switch on the Winter Olympics and there he is, winking at the camera. Turn over to the Grand Prix and he's up on the podium, squirting champagne over Michael Schumacher. I make a mental note to stick to Tommy Cross like a leech this evening. He's entertaining the company with a story about a boxing night in Manchester which ended with the promoter taking his guests to a swingers club in Swinton. After watching a succession of strangers brutally make love to his wife from behind a two-way mirror, one of the promoters' pals got upset when someone slapped her backside. Tommy, to much guffawing, describes the naked brawl which ensued, a cross between *Up Pompeii* and *Raging Bull*.

In all the hilarity we fail to notice a slight figure who slipped into the club and is standing at the bar. Good lord! It's Michael Owen. A buzz of recognition ricochets around the club and, within seconds, he's mobbed. This is no Boyzone-style mobbing with shrieking, pre-pubescent girls standing off that final yard so that they can get a good picture. These mobsters are heavily pubescent. They have hair sprouting from their noses, their ears – anywhere but their heads. Some of Liverpool's most famous fans are reduced to a gasping pulp by the presence of young Michael, and Jamie Carragher who has now appeared at his side to rescue him. Colonel Hogan and Jonesy, two of Liverpool's finest, wrestle him free of the crowd:

'Give him a chance!' shouts Jonesy. 'Let him breathe!'

They manage to smuggle him out of the bar and reception area and into the main club. It's like Jesus on the banks of Galilee. The entire reception room empties as grown men follow in Michael's footsteps. It's futile trying to get in there. They're already backed out through the swingdoors and spilling back into the bar. Danny comes back with Bard from Norway. They just pull a face and laugh. We can hear Owen making some sort of speech, which is drowned out by singing.

He reappears at the bar. Mono, wriggling along the floor like Sir Hiss in *Robin Hood*, squirms up the side of the bar and appears next to Owen. Janus Stark, *Smash* comic's amazing rubber-boned man, could not have wriggled up to Owen with more elasticity:

'Hey Michael! Know that song we all sing about you? I made that up!'

Owen's starting to look panic-stricken. Jimmy Flowers bulldozes through the crowd, putting a protective arm round his star guest and steering him towards an emergency exit:

'Hey Michael! Know that song they all sing about you? I wrote that!'

Jimmy always says 'wrote' about football songs as though hours are spent in a garret with a pigeon feather and a pot of Quink, crafting that perfect ditty. Maybe he can get in touch with the Brits or the Mercury Awards and see if they'll introduce a new category next year. Best Football Chant.

'. . . and for Best Football Chant, 1997–8, please give it up for . . . Jimmy Flowers for Michael Owen Scores the Goals . . . but wait!! We have someone on the stage! Is that Jarvis Cocker with his kecks down? No. No! It's Steven Monaghan of Halewood claiming HE wrote the song. And now here's John Garner. He's lying down on the stage and he's refusing to move. He's gutted. He's saying it's a rigged vote . . . Bolton fans are showering the stage with inflatable fishes . . . West Ham voters are booooooooing . . . it's all gone horribly wrong . . .'

As Owen and Carragher head for the side stairs to escape the frenzy of bald, fanatical men, Danny and Bard suggest the party's over. We should hop a cab into town while we can still get one. I look around for Tommy Cross, Mr Fun, to make sure I can touch his sleeve and become blessed. I see him slumped in the corner. He's fast asleep.

I'm bladdered and starting to talk in a Dingle accent. It's definitely time to go home. Danny and Bard direct the taxi to The Blob Shop, positively the last place on earth I want to be right now. I look around frantically, and then I spot them. My salvation. Right opposite. Cash machines. I mutter something about getting some more lolly out and, once I'm sure they've gone inside the bar, run like the slightly clumsy, inebriated wind for the last train from Central.

3 MAY 1998

Watching Arsenal v. Everton, home

Arsenal pulverise Everton 4–0. This means Everton have to win their last game of the season to stay up, while hoping that

Bolton drop points at Chelsea. It's not funny. It really isn't.

P.S. – Arsenal also won League today.

4 MAY 1998

A strange charity game (neutral ground)

I could not be more nervous. Many things in my life have given me devastating outbreaks of nerves. Penalties in European Cup finals. Children born by Caesarean section. Driving tests (five). Walking down the Seven Sisters after despatching Tottenham from the FA Cup. But I've never been as nervous as this.

What's happened is as follows. Roy Boulter writes for *Brookside*. He sometimes plays for their football team – usually in non-competitive charity games. Today, the Brookside team are taking part in the Hoylake Charities Fair, playing a six-a-side fixture against a Liverpool Music team. The Music team comprises members of the pop group Space and a useful No. 9 called Ian Rush. He's allowed to play No. 9, even in six-a-side games.

On the morning of the game I get a phone call from Roy. Ian Rush can't play. Newcastle are in the FA Cup final. Even though it's a harmless, docile exhibition match, he can't take a risk so close to such a crucial match. Rushie is now going to act as the Music team's coach. Seeing as I live quite close to the pitch where today's match is taking place, maybe I'd like to stand in for Rushie.

Would I?! Would I!!

So, 150 minutes before kick-off, I'm here, milling around the stalls at the Hoylake Charities Fair, trying to take my mind off the game. I'm shitting myself. There's another thing, too.

Because I couldn't keep still, because I had to leave the house and just *get here*, I've come out with just my training-shoes for footwear. When I set off it was a brisk, slightly windy but very bright day. We haven't had rain for ages. But now, with the stiffening breeze, rain clouds are moving in. In another 20 minutes there could be showers.

Ian Rush is one of the first to turn up. What a lovely, unaffected man. He just stands there, chatting to adults and kids alike, signing autographs. But then, he can afford to be relaxed, can't he. He doesn't have to play today. He doesn't have to go out there and face that crowd. There must be 60 there already, and there's still another hour to go.

It is now drizzling persistently. I'm going to make a complete twat of myself in these trainies. I'm going to go sliding everywhere, everyone will laugh at me and my two nippers, Joe and Anna, who I have brought along to indoctrinate them into the passion and the beauty and the glory of Association Football will hang their heads in shame. They'll never want to go to a football match with me, anywhere.

The game is being played at Kingsmead School, Hoylake, organisers of the Charities Fair which, yearly, sends off a cheque to the Romanian Orphans Appeal, among other causes. I nab a passing teacher, fittingly called Mr Hope.

'Erm . . . any size eight boots anywhere on the premises?' I grimace, pointing to my now soaking training-shoes. He kindly agrees to go and have a look for me. When Mr Hope returns, I can't believe my eyes. He's carrying a pair of Adidas Predator! Now Adidas Predator don't come cheaply. They are, by common consent, the Best Boot in the World. The only reason that all players don't wear them is that other companies pay them to wear less good football boots. They cost £120. So the Predator is a dream boot, in every sense. I couldn't be more delighted. Suddenly the nerves have vanished. I'm going to make my debut in front of Ian Rush in a proper kit, on a pitch with nets, wearing a pair of Adidas fucking Predator. Nothing can beat this. Can it?

The game is surprisingly physical. Rushie is wise not to play. Brookside show their mettle right from the kick-off. Tinhead, Mike Dixon and Roy Boulter charge into their tackles to win the ball from winsome Space, while the new odd-job-man bloke, who's huge, sticks his arse into me whenever I try to go past him. We've got a proper ref today, though, and from one of these arse-checks, just as I'm going through to score, we get a penalty. 1–0 to us.

I'm not letting myself down, here. On one occasion I slot, I have to say it, a sublime angled ball right through the middle of their defence. I was too busy turning to the touchline to see if Ian Rush noticed the pass to see our main striker blast the ball over. Brookside come back strongly, though, and go in 3–1 up at half time (Tinhead; Boulter 2). Roy, who isn't the most dazzling talent in our Friday Spectaculars, has performed like Gerd Muller. Twice he's turned our central defensive duo and slammed the ball home like a Golden Boot winner. He spoils it by running back to the halfway line wagging his finger – something our manager picks up on.

'Why you letting that fat lad take the mickey out of you?' shouts Rush. 'He's laughing at you. Didn't you see him running around with his finger in the air . . .'

Second half (each half is 15 minutes) sees our bunch of tour-raddled, rock 'n' roll wasters move it up a gear, which is enough to rattle Brookside. With a couple of minutes to go it's 3–3, and I'm quite happy with that. I've miscontrolled a few balls out over the touchline trying to bring down overhit passes, but I've done some good runs and I left the big fella on his backside when I dragged the ball back and turned him in one move. A goal would've been nice in front of Liverpool's Greatest Ever Goalscorer . . . in front of my kids, too, of course – in front of my kids.

But what's this? Brookside who, a minute ago seemed

knackered, are sprinting down our left flank. Mike Dixon has sent Tinhead through. He turns in on himself, leaving the defender in his wake, steadies himself . . .

Roy Boulter is unmarked on the goal-line. If Tinhead spots him, that's game over. Tinhead looks up and sees Roy. The same adolescent squeals which have accompanied Tinhead's every touch now shriek from the touchline, 200 lusty maidens demanding that he shoots. Tinhead looks at Roy again, puts his head down and goes for glory. He beats the keeper and . . . oh! He's hit the post! But wait . . .

In excruciating slow motion, Roy Boulter bumbles towards the ball, which is rolling away, for a goal kick. Boulter intercepts the ball and, with a 270-degree turn which would have been difficult for a slimmer man, he scoops it into the net.

4–3 to them. That should've been it, but our manager won't have it.

'Just get forward, all of you. Go on, Kevin!! Run at them!!'

He said it! He said my name! Ian Rush knows who I am . . .

As though fuel-injected with turbocharged adrenalin, I run at Mike Dixon, chasing hard to close him down. A look of panic actually flashes across his face. He goes to pass the ball to Roy, but I prod out my right as far as it'll go, pulling my groin but winning the ball. The keeper's slightly off his line. There must be three seconds left. I take the ball forward a pace, nudging it slightly to the left, too, to give myself a better lie. I lean my body slightly to the right and curl the ball with my left, past the flailing goalkeeper and into the net. Forget the Adidas bloody Predator! That was all me, that was . . .

I can't hear a single thing. Not the congratulations of my team-mates, nor the referee's whistle. I want to go running over to the touchline, jump up and down and roll around on the turf, sharing my joy with Ian Rush. But that'd be silly. It's only a knockabout charity game. I should just shake hands with everyone, thank the ref and go and get changed. But I don't. Instead, I troop away in the other direction to the rest of them and burst into tears.

Later, when I'm dressed and back out in the thick of the fair, Anna and Joe come running towards me and jump all over me. They must be so proud of their old man.

'Well, then? Did you see my goal?'

'Nah,' says Joe. 'We were throwing sponges at the clown's face. It was cool!'

I return the Predators to Mr Hope and bundle the children into the car. Maybe they'll grow up to spend their time and their money on something better than football. I hope they invent that something soon.

6 MAY 1998

Arsenal, home

So here I am, walking up this hill again, the steady incline from Scotland Road up to Walton Breck Road, Anfield. In a few hours' time I'll be walking back again, walking the other way, my whole mood, my outlook on life affected by what's gone on out there on the pitch. The season's as good as over. It doesn't seem real that a whole season, a season of nothingness, has passed by so quickly. But for Arsenal, our guests tonight, it's been more than real.

I jog self-consciously across the dual carriageway opposite The Valley and, mindful that there's a packed double-decker bus idling its way up the hill, with a couple of coachloads of Ellesmere Port Reds behind, I attempt to clear the central reservation railing in one bound. Uh-oh. While most of my body, my arms and one of my legs make it over with ease, the ankle of my trailing right leg clips the top of the fence, bending me double in mid-air and sending me crashing to the floor on the other side. I can hear the cheers and mocking laughter from the coaches. They can see my fuming red ears. I hobble into The Valley.

Mick Potter and ace cartoonist brother John are already there. Peter Hooton soon joins us. We're waiting for the arrival of Señor Gag, who has become the besotted father of baby Alyssa in the past 24 hours. We intend to indulge ourselves, and him, in the time-revered pagan ritual of wetting the baby's head. Gag turns in at about 7 o'clock, time enough for two quick pints, but we all want to be inside the ground to applaud Arsenal, so it's a thirtysomething demi-stumble along Walton Breck Road to make the 7.45 kick-off.

Inside the Upper Centenary, I'm faced with a dilemma. After Tottenham away you'd think that the Big Toilet Lesson would've been well and truly learned word perfect. But this is a Big Occasion. Probably our last of the season. The new English Champions are about to run out onto Anfield's hallowed turf with the Liverpool team providing a guard of honour. You've got to be there for things like that. You've got to be there. So I ignore common sense, history's lesson and my aching bladder with one parry thrust of neat sentimentality and bound up the steps in time to see the Arsenal team – which comprises TWO of the regulars who actually won the League for them – jog out, slightly embarrassed, to a tumultuous welcome from both sets of fans. The Kop is decked out with all the old flags, souvenirs from the great journeys through Europe. No other team in the country has flags like these – so many of them, thousands of them, too. Those supporters deserve a better platform and a better reward for their unique and loyal patronage. Those flags should be gracing a European Cup final, not some well-done-Arsenal backslapping session. I'm yellow with envy.

The game's slow to fall into any kind of rhythm. Wenger has cunningly fielded a team of substitutes and Liverpool are wondering what the catch is. He's a master of football psychology, Wenger. Unlike Ferguson, who tries too hard, is easy to read and makes embarrassing remarks ('They'll soon find out what it's like at the top. Arsenal will start dropping points. Between now and the end of the season Arsenal will drop points – that's a fact.'), Wenger has an intuitive understanding of the real role of psychology in sport – which is to say nothing. If there is such a thing as this fabled Liverpool Way, it was to boringly, stoically concentrate on the game in hand, win it then look to the next one. Don't make predictions. Don't get too far ahead of yourself. Don't worry about what the opposition are doing. And don't do or say anything which could blow up in your face further down the line.

This game against Arsenal is a game Liverpool will always win, whether we're playing against Adams, Bergkamp, Overmars, Petit and Vieira, or whether we're up against this very impressive-looking 'reserve' line-up, which includes Platt, Bould, Hughes, Wreh, Boa Morte, Dixon, Parlour, Grimandi – no mug! – some geezer called Wright and Manninger, a goalkeeper who has yet to concede a goal in the Premiership. Wenger can't lose. If we thrash his team he can say so what? We're still on Cloud Nine and, anyway, look at the team I put out. If they win he can point to the strength in depth he's built up at Highbury, the will to win, no matter how unimportant the game. So I take it all back. I always thought Arsene Wenger too remote, too studious and, in general, too disapproving of the English game to be able to succeed in the Premiership. In the months since Ferguson pronounced that Arsenal 'will drop points' they've won every single game. *Every* game, one at a time. They've been brilliant. And so has their manager.

Our crowd, ignoring our own don't-crow-too-soon credo, are revelling in the prospect that Everton may be relegated on

Sunday. Among all the old European flags flies a new, red and yellow banner reading:

AGENT JOHNSON: MISSION ACCOMPLISHED

A cartoon Grim Reaper hovers to the right of the banner with a trickling scythe. This gives everyone a chuckle and will, in the perverse and superstitious way that football works, provide Everton with the incentive they need to stay up.

We click into gear after about 15 minutes, putting together some of the best moves we've seen all season. Everyone's swarming forward, interchanging neat passes and making clever runs. Owen, as usual, looks unstoppable. My bladder churns with a throbbing, pressurised agony. I'm determined to stay in my seat until half time, though. I hate these people who are up and down all through the game, buying Coca-cola and Kit-Kats and hats with many tentacles. Ince scores. '1–0, to the Liverpool', sing the Arsenal Party Platoon. Ince goes forward and bags number two, and the game's over. The Arsenal fans assume end-of-season knees-up mode, cheering Liverpool, singing anti-Man. United songs but, criminally, taking up their stupid:

'Champione, champione, olé, olé, olé!!'

One thing which is beholden of Arsenal's fans, now, as Champions, is the necessity for Good Songs. On tonight's evidence, they're witty enough but they ain't got any anthems. The Vieira one's a cracker, but apart from that there's nothing too inspiring. They sing 'We are the Champions' by Queen. They actually sing that.

Just before half time Michael Owen executes an outrageous scissor-kick volley. 3–0 and everyone's up on their feet, hugging each other – Arsenal fans included. I take the opportunity to dart out and down to the toilets. During the never-ending torrent that pours forth, I hear that unique stampeding of a football crowd's feet from above. Must be half time. I leg it to the servery and, knowing that Boulter will be down in a minute and that we'll be staying out for a few drinks

272

with Gag, I order four of Liverpool's gigantic meat and potato pies to soak up any more midriff pressure. I pay and shuffle over to one of the TV monitors. The game's still going on. Michael Owen, in fact, is running in and . . . MISSING a penalty! That's what the rumbling from up there was. Roy's watch made it just on half time when he scored our third but what the heck? No one cares. We're winning 3–0 and I've got four pies.

I get stuck in. The first one goes down with shameful haste and I start into the second. The three Asian boys from Blackburn – or Preston as it transpires – sit down all around me and stare in horror at my plate. Two-and-a-half huge pies and red sauce all over them.

'Shnerr yott orr fuh mee . . .' I protest, willing Roy to come down and devour the pie surplus of several poor countries in three greedy, hungry mouthfuls. The ref blows for half time on the telly. Good. Roy should be here in a jiffy. I polish off pie two and look around for him. No sign. Fuck it. I glance up at the Preston boys and, head down, eyeline averted, tuck into a third pie. This one's hard work. I'm halfway through it when Billy Bunter lands at my side and, with an enthusiastic cry of 'Yaroooh!', demolishes all that is left on the plate.

We natter with the Preston lads about why we're not Fab any more and agree to disagree. The oldest of them wants Gerald Houlier in as manager. I'm saying that Roy Evans, having been through everything he's been through, has now served the most real of apprenticeships. He now knows what it's all about. Everything. I think he'll act on his experience this summer and build a Liverpool who'll win everything in sight for the next five years. Everyone on the table wants to believe it. No one quite does. We'll see.

We carry on tearing Arsenal apart. This is more than Arsene Wenger's pride can take. He sends on Anelka and Patrick Vieira, a mystifying combination of superb vision, supernatural ability and shocking violence. Anyone who hasn't twigged this yet, do the following. Next time you get the chance to see Arsenal live, watch Vieira – just him, let your eye follow him round the pitch – for a good 15 or 20 minutes. You'll be outraged. He's the sneakiest, nastiest fouler in the game. He rakes, elbows, trips and rabbit-punches. And yet, on the ball, he is a god.

We see both sides of him tonight, leaving his foot in for challenge after challenge, then breaking, when the whim takes him, with contemptuous, cantering ease, shrugging off markers, right through the heart of Liverpool's midfield. Carragher and Ince are becoming very wound up by his presence, and the increasingly niggling taps and shoves of Boa Morte. Carragher takes matters into his own hands and whacks Boa Morte with one challenge and, fortunately for both players, completely misses Wreh with a venomous sliding tackle. It's getting nasty.

Liverpool break forward. Ince is in space on the angle of the box when Wreh runs back and cuts him down. Ince is vexed. He jumps up, doing that mad John Wayne walk, shoulders and chest compressed, arms carrying imaginary cannon-balls, eyeballs manically white. Vieira, Cock of the Premiership, runs over and, as he passes Ince, cracks him on the ankle. Ince turns round, irate, only now to see Ian Wright, who has sprinted back from the halfway line to join in the fracas. Wright says something to Ince who hurls the ball at him, hitting him in the face. Wright grins at him. They've succeeded in winding up Liverpool's volatile skipper.

Owen muffs the free-kick and Arsenal push out of defence. Vieira slides the ball to Wright, who tries to back into Ince and hold the ball up. Carragher comes hurtling in from one side while Ince attacks from the other. Neither of them has fair play on their mind. These are the new Liverpool midfield aggro boys, out to show that they've more in common with Bone Thugs 'n' Harmony than the Spice Boys. Wright is left writhing on the floor. Ince, immediately, looks gutted. Wright is his old pal and it looks as though he's extinguished any lingering hopes he had of making the World Cup finals. The stretcher's called for, and Wright's off. A sad end to the evening. Leonhardsen scores a cracker to make it 4–0, Danny Murphy comes on to display his full range of probing, prompting, incisive, attacking-midfield play but the Ian Wright incident – for which he has to accept a small portion of the blame himself – has taken the edge off things. I like Ian Wright.

A very weird scenario now unfolds. Arsenal, the Champions, trot straight down the tunnel with barely a nod to their revelling fans. Liverpool, on the other hand, another season of enormous disappointment almost over, take to the turf for a Lap of Disgrace. This is the moment we know absolutely that Steve McManaman is leaving us. He can't face the hypocrisy of running round in his red jersey, applauding the fans and making clench-fisted salutes. Looking back now, he did all that at Barnsley. That was his farewell. Now, though, he loiters at the back of the class with Robbie Fowler, both of them wearing dark training jackets, over-concentrating on whatever they're saying to each other in the way you do when you know people are watching your every move. They give out an occasional half-hearted clap to the crowd. I'd love to know what they're saying to each other. As Robbie Fowler reaches The Kop he gets a terrific and ever-building volley of applause, which gives way to a full-throttle roar as everyone chants his name. He seems chuffed. He claps back. McManaman makes no eye-contact with the crowd. Again, we'll see what happens in the summer, but for me this shows unquestionably that the lad is for the leaving of Liverpool. So it goes.

The talk in The Albert after the game is of the Evertonians' threat to march up to Anfield on Sunday and lay siege to this place, Sam Dodd's and The Sandon. If true, this seems a futile gesture. All the pubs around the ground revert to pensioners' and locals' bingo palaces on non-match days. They'll be wrecking an empty pub while, a hundred miles away, The Red Shite conga round the streets of Derby. John Garner comes in, grinning massively:

'D'you see me banner?'

'Which one was it?'

He looks offended and unfurls the huge red and yellow flag: 'AGENT JOHNSON: MISSION ACCOMPLISHED'

Might have known it was his. He takes his applause with embarrassed modesty, knowing that his banner will now make history with some of the classics over the years. The big Joey Jones one in 1977. Atkinson's Long Leather. Liverpool's Annual Bender. And my own, personal favourite – Lyons Is Shit from the 1975 vintage.

We take Gag down to The Marlborough, where Hooton entertains everyone by reminding them of my prediction that Arsene Wenger could never make a go of it in England. I know what I'm on about, me. I really do.

10 MAY 1998

Derby, away (with half an eye on Goodison and Stamford Bridge)

A tedious morning is spent waiting for Jegsy to wake up. With last night being Saturday, he'll have been doing the taxis until at least 3.00 a.m., possibly later, so I can't really phone him before 11.00. On the other hand, today is Party Day. The day that Everton finally go down.

Let's be frank about this. With nothing left to play for ourselves, we badly want to see Everton suffer the ultimate embarrassment. This season has not been about us winning things. It's almost pathetic that we're reduced to revelling in the misery of others, but that's just the way it is. And it's great. Man. United have won absolutely fuck all. Monaco knocked them out of Europe. Monaco! Barnsley knocked them out of the FA Cup. Barnsley! And *Ipswich*, mighty Ipswich, put them out of the League Cup, whatever it's called now. Today, our *schadenfreude* will be complete. Howard Kendall will send his team out for the biggest Warm Down of all – the one that sends Ever-ton To One.

The city has been unbearable in the humid heat and anticipation of the last few days. Evertonians we know and like have been almost pitiful in their 'don't hurt me' humility. Proud figures like John Potter, Tony Sage, Gary Hart and Colin Hill have all, slump-shouldered, whey-faced and defeated, slipped in and out of our company, quiet, distracted and dreading the next sentence. It's hard to cut them while they're so low down, but you only have to think back to the triumphalism that follows Everton's Derby performances, the spiteful, vengeful, petty meanness of their support, their gleeful taunting in the streets around Goodison. They're getting what they deserve. Misery.

At a minute past eleven I rouse Jegsy from his pit. He's still knackered. He tells me to call for him at 12.30. I circle the area in the car, listening to Liverpool's fine new music alternative, Crash FM. In the space of an hour we hear Finlay Quaye, Primal Scream, Massive Attack, Saint Etienne, Garbage, Mansun, Augustus Pablo, Gomez – they just play stuff that they like and the time flies by. I guffaw at nervous Evertonians with their snap bags and One To One shirts on, shuffling towards the train station. I kill the last few minutes reading an interview with Jaap Stam who says that, although Liverpool came in with a huge financial offer for him after he'd already agreed his move to United, he never even considered changing his mind. He had no interest in joining Liverpool.

He wanted to go to a club where he'll win things. Next to it is an Exclusive: Ravanelli is coming to Liverpool . . .

We're off, the sun is shining and it's going to be a wonderful day. We skirt over the formalities and get straight down to discussing sex. I'm happy to be able to advise Jegsy not to feel too sleazy about the 16-year-old he's seeing. In no time at all we've reached Burton-on-Trent and The Kestrel public house, where Jimmy's coach has scheduled its stop. Everyone's in there. The first faces we see are Mono and Philly, debating whether to sit down for a Sunday roast. Colonel Hogan and Jonesy are by the bar. I tell them Jegsy's written a brand-new poem to celebrate today, called Gone To One. He doesn't want to read it out before the match in case it's tempting fate. Jonesy gets up on a stool.

'Quiet please, everyone! I give you Jegsy Dodd!'

So he has to get up. Head almost touching the timbered roof of the pub he recites:

Close all the curtains
Fly the flags at half mast
Put the ball away quietly
The chance has now passed
You can drown all your sorrows
But make that your last

BECAUSE EVERTON HAVE FINALLY GONE DOWN

Lock all the doors
To keep out the Reds
Cancel the papers
Hide under your beds
Turn off the telly
The newsflash just said

THAT EVERTON HAVE FINALLY GONE DOWN

Unchain those melodies
That you hold so dear
Don't leave the house
'Til the coast is clear
Cry as loud as you like
Because no one can hear

NOW THAT EVERTON HAVE FINALLY GONE DOWN.

People are cottoning onto the chorus, and each new verse gets a more drunken take-up.

Every gesture and signing has been token
Every possible excuse has been spoken
Promises, promises, cynically broken

AND EVERTON HAVE FINALLY GONE DOWN

As your memories fade
Of European nights
Sit back in your chair
Dim all the lights
Let the Priest in the room
To serve the last rites

NOW THAT EVERTON HAVE FINALLY GONE DOWN

Take a sad trip
Down Memory Lane
You all said
It never could happen again
Time has come now
For the Finger of Blame

BECAUSE EVERTON HAVE FINALLY GONE DOWN

The pub's on its feet. Jegsy gets a prolonged cheer. The party's started. Four or five different relegation anthems are being pounded out at the same time, from the old standard set to *American Pie* to new, direct hits. People are up and dancing, punching the air and beating out a rhythm with their beer glasses. The Kestrel's Sunday lunch trade has been decimated – but its bar takings must be astronomical.

There are leaflets going around, with a travel guide for Everton's '98–9 season, with directions how to get to places like Grimsby, Stockport and Crewe. The best bit, though, is the Everton team crest which has been amended to read:

'Nil Satis Nisi Shite.'

We're all being far too smug. They're bound to stay up. But drat it, this is great while it lasts! Deep down, I think a lot of us are partying hard now because we know there'll be nothing to sing about by 6 o'clock. Everton will stay up. Next season, though – next season they're going to see a transformation. Teams like Leicester, Derby, Coventry – little teams, basically – are going to have a superiority complex over Everton. They're going to look at them as a team they should be beating. And Liverpool might just think that way, too. That's if Everton stay up, of course, but even if they do they're in for Hard Times.

Just as we set off from Burton, the heavens open. It pours down all the way to Derby. None of us has been to Pride Park before and we now have the rum spectacle of Jeff's car following me, a man who was once capable of mistaking John Scales for John Barnes if I left my glasses at home. Today I have forgotten my glasses – or I think they might be in the boot. I'm driving with my eyes screwed up to attain 3:20 vision. It's a quarter-to-four and we can see the new stadium just over the gridlocked flyover – so it's a case of parking wherever we can and legging it to the ground. I try a sharp left which leaves me facing a five-foot-high tunnel, then reverse and park in what I thought was a hospital, which turns out to be British Rail Transport Police's HQ. Jeff and co, mindful of Leicester, give me up for a bad job and nose off into Derby.

We park up next to the train station and begin the jog to Pride Park.

It's miles away. The nearer we get, the further away it moves. The whole, spaceship-sized monstrosity is a mirage, luring you closer then whipping itself away behind some building site. A man in a yellow jacket tells us the turnstiles will be closing in three minutes. We're still in the middle of the vast foundations of a will-be McDonalds or Pizza Hut, with Pride Park another ten minutes away. It's freezing. I've got a short-sleeved Comme de Garcons shirt on and it's starting to pour down again. Maybe today is just destined to be a shit day.

This inkling, which has been nagging away, the feeling that Nil Satis are going to squirm out of it again, is turned into horrible reality the moment we get to our seats, at 4.11. Mono is four rows behind.

'Everton are 1–0 up,' he murmurs, looking like his dog's been run over. His face is the same colour Tony Sage's was when I saw him on Monday. Grey. I try to concentrate on the Liverpool match, but it's one of those days when everything about football irritates you. Men in football shirts, earrings clanking, are standing up and turning round, faces so impassioned, they love Liverpool so much, urging everyone else to sing like they are. They're scooping their arms upwards, telling us all to stand up. They're drunk.

Meanwhile, the Derby crowd are worse. They try a:

'Stand up – if you hate Man. U',

but, holding firm for the whole season, we don't join in. We still don't join in, we still haven't got a song for Paul Ince and we still haven't won the League for years. These are the things which haven't changed since Crewe. The Derby then think it's great fun to sing stupid, infantile songs at the away fans. They think it's all a huge jape. You can hear them after the game, pints in hand, sideburns ruffled from the exertion, gelled heads slick with rain:

'So we sings or "You're Supposed To Be Away" and then

we all goes sssshhhhhhh! and the Skysers give it who the fucken 'ell are you and we all just jumps up and gives it aaaaaaaggh!'

I don't know why men like this bother me so much. But they do. I really hate them. As if reading my mind, Jegsy jumps up and shouts:

'Will all people wearing football shirts please leave the stadium NOW!!'

He gets a muted ripple of applause from all around. Half time comes. There's a couple of spare seats by Philly and Mono, so we head up there for the second half. It's desperately dull. All eyes are glued to the pitch while all minds are glued to events at Stamford Bridge and Goodison. Out on the pitch, the Liverpool team are taking the piss out of Michael Owen. Rather than work the ball through midfield, rather than try anything brave or creative, they're banging the ball long from defence, expecting him to scamper after any old shit they throw his way. On a couple of occasions he makes a chance out of nothing, but the more he's sent scurrying after long, thoughtless, wayward wellies, the more angry he gets. After chasing one dreadful ball from Bjornebye, chasing it 50 yards and nearly keeping it in, Owen plays the ball off the Derby defender for a throw. The linesman gives it the other way. Owen explodes, shouting at the linesman and kicking the ball back into the crowd. Wise Glenn Hoddle would see this as evidence that Michael Owen is not as clean-cut as many would like to believe. I see it as evidence that he's got more fire in his belly, even for meaningless drudgery like this afternoon's pale production – more guts and desire than anyone could've dared to hope. He's been the one shining light in this miserable season. He's great.

Derby score from a corner. Their fans go wild. They celebrate the goal as though it's won them the Champions League. The crowd in the front row of the stand down to our right run up and down the walkway, hugging each other, jumping up and down, kissing girls and mauling stewards. One lad, in a yellow sweatshirt and a baseball hat, celebrates so hard that he trips over and twists his ankle. I watch him limp back to his seat in much pain and, two minutes later, I watch him hobble out of the ground.

On 75 minutes the worst possible news. Chelsea have scored against Bolton. A moment of crashing realisation helps salvage a last minuscule scrap of satisfaction from the dying, ailing season for me, and it's this. I've never left the match early. I've always considered it a mark of disrespect to the team to turn your back on them while they're still playing. But now, suddenly, I see their carefree, clueless, gutless attempts to take the game to Derby. I see that walk back to the station. I see the never-ending traffic jams of Bolton, Leicester, Newcastle, Barnsley – so many places – and I think:

'Fuck you. I'm off.'

We're going to get back to the car and get home without any further pain. No party in Derby – but no more grief, either. Hitting the A500 I turn to the silent Jegsy.

'It's not the same, is it?'

'No. And it's going to get worse.'

'It's not just that the team's no good. The whole thing. It's . . . painful.'

'Just wait till Chelsea win the Cup Winners' Cup and England win the World Cup . . . you won't even be able to get a ticket for Southampton at home.'

Maybe we're just grumpy old men. Maybe, like people who were into Ocean Colour Scene in 1991, you don't want to share them with your little brother and all his mates in parkas. Would we feel any different if Liverpool had beaten Derby well this afternoon, and won the League in the process? Course we bloody would. But we'd have won it at another sterile, corporate-sponsored new stadium in another industrial estate away from the town centre. It wouldn't be like winning it at Wolves in 1976. Those days are gone, gone, gone.

What the likes of Mr Dodd and myself have to ask ourselves is whether we want to carry on mourning, moaning and dragging our heels or whether we can embrace the new face of New Football. Can we just accept that we've been part of something fantastic, but now it's time to put the memories in the scrapbook and get with the new reality? Can we sit next to guys and gals in football shirts with radios stuck to their ears, all part of one big, happy, football family? And aren't we just feeling shit because Everton stayed up?

We get home and face the music. Straight to The Millhouse, where Micky Musker and Markoosh are drained, ecstatic, and very, very drunk. I tell Micky I'm sorry they didn't go down. Why hang on like that, only to go through it all again next year? He smiles patiently and claps me on the shoulder:

'At least you're not one of these twats who says he's not bothered. Says he wants us to stay up. I can't handle them at all . . .'

I AM, though! Come back and feel bad! I AM one of those bastards . . . but Musker's gone, off to the bar for more pints and more jubilation. I can't believe that the Evertonians have ended the season happier than us. The bloke next to me at the Goodison Derby was right. Those *were* the points which kept them up. It's time to slope off home.

MONDAY 11 MAY 1998

My house

Postman brings the following. One mailshot from Portland Direct Holidays. One reminder about a council tax bill that's already been paid. One renewal form for Liverpool F.C. season-ticket. Whoopee! Can't wait until next season.